M000284989

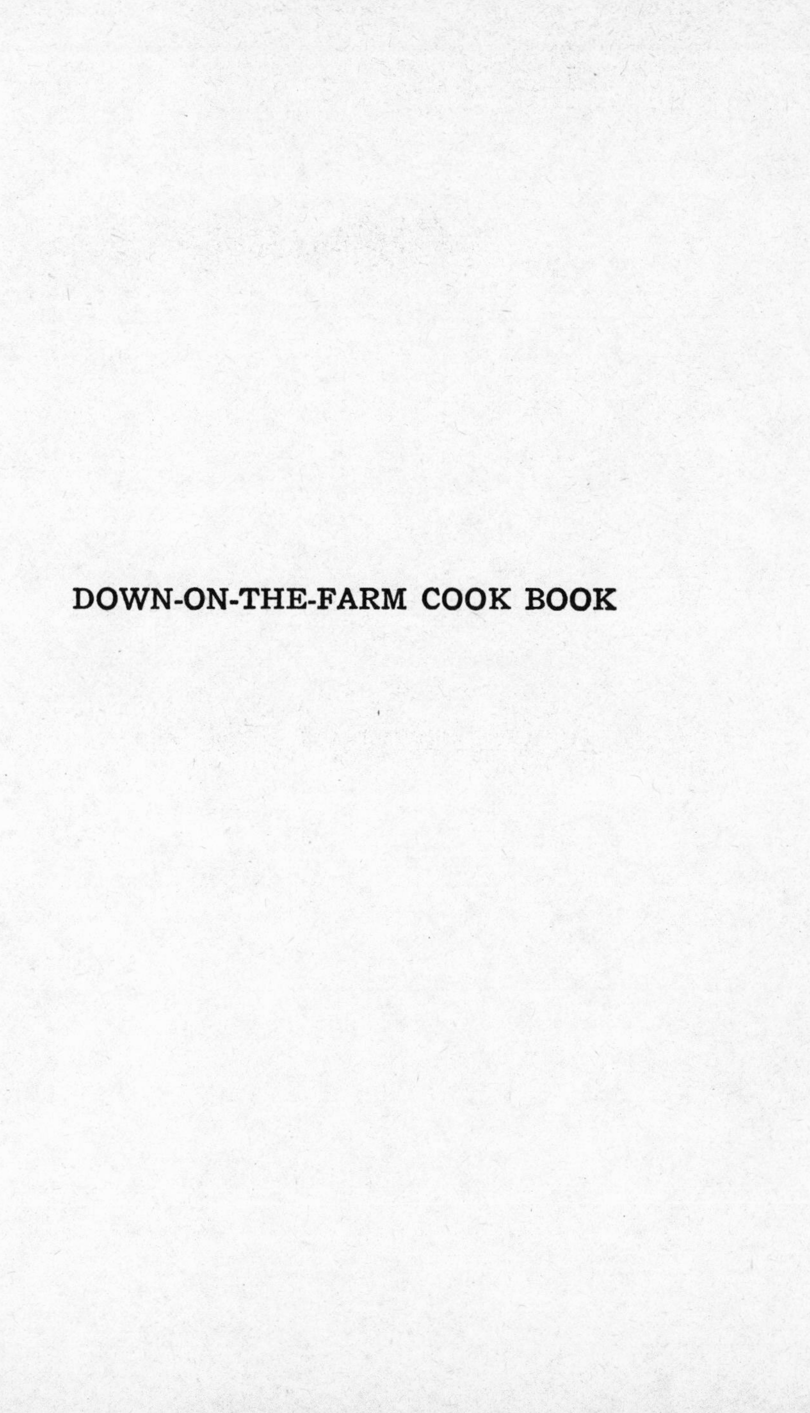

DOWN-ON-THE-FARM COOK BOOK

BOOKS BY HELEN WORTH

Down-on-the-Farm Cook Book
Shrimp Cookery
Cooking Without Recipes
Hostess Without Help
Damnyankee in a Southern Kitchen

Down-on-the-Farm Cook Book

Helen Worth

GRAMERCY PUBLISHING COMPANY
NEW YORK

This 1981 edition is published by Gramercy Publishing Company,
distributed by Crown Publishers, Inc.,
by arrangement with the author

h g f e d c b a

Manufactured in the United States of America

Library of Congress Cataloging in Publication Data

Worth, Helen Levison, 1913–
Down-on-the-farm cook book.

Includes index.
1. Cookery, American. I. title.
TX715.W93 1981 641.5 81-6742
ISBN: 0-517-357305 AACR2

To Monroe

CONTENTS

[*NOTE: A star (*) on the following pages indicates a receipt or directions to be found in this book. For exact page number, the reader should consult the Index.*]

PREFACE

This book began with a question. "How would you like to write a farm cook book?" queried advertising genius Maxwell Sackheim. He knew I had aspirations as a writer and had been teaching cooking since 1940. Also, he frequently had dined happily at my table.

More than a year followed my acquiescence. The book, my first, was reprinted four times—a not insignificant record, considering that cook books in the 1940s were not purchased with the avidity that they are today. I am also proud that a first edition is housed in Cornell University's Herndon Collection of rare books.

A year of intensive research preceded the writing and involved hours of immersion in back issues of rural newspapers—each state boasts several. I read everything I could lay my hands on that dealt with farm living, such as Della T. Lute's *The Country Kitchen,* Louise Andrews Kent's Appleyard series of farm sagas, Robert P. Tristram Coffin's *Saltwater Farming.*

My study was aided and abetted by a lavish batch of Ladies Aid cook books. One was a special treasure—an Indiana grandmother's nineteenth-century "receipt" book, penned in her spidery Spencerian hand. I painstakingly translated her receipts, calling for "2 cents worth of cloves, 5 cents worth of sugar," into workable modern-day recipes. Chocolate Sauce for a Dip is a standout example of such a translation.

Recipe testing followed recipe collecting, rewarding me with a kitchen full of delicious aromas: beef and bones and earthy vegetables simmering in a stockpot, the spicy smell of gingerbread and cinnamoned cookies, the fragrance of sweet, buttery buns.

As for authenticity, I even included some of my family's favorite old recipes. Those titled "Crooked Elm Farm" are mine. One, the sumptuous cheesecake, caused a guest to exclaim, "This could start a back-to-the-farm movement!"

The recipes titled "Osceola Farm" are my mother's. Her Strawberry Shortcake—not quite a biscuit, not quite a cake—is unlike any other. Gram Stone's Coffee Cake is a tribute to my adored grandmother's marvelous way with raised doughs. Aunt Sleide (slīde), a gabby lady who roams the pages, is purely imaginary. She arrived unbidden one day, demanding that I write her words down.

For assistance, belated tribute must be paid to Sylvia Ullman, who tested several of the recipes, and who, along with Olive Redfield, was a student in the first cooking class I ever taught. They still are my friends, and through the years, Olive, who proofread the manuscript with me, also instructed me in much more than proofreader's marks.

I find that each book I write contains seeds of the next. In addition to anecdotes, *The Down-on-the-Farm Cook Book* offers basic information, a procedure that flowered fully in my *Cooking Without Recipes*. There, for the first time, Brown-Quick, the precooking aid I originated, is mentioned. Its use would add savor to the dishes in this book, too.

I could not think to remove the book's Dedication, penned to the estimable Monroe Worth, who is responsible for my professional name. Now, an elegant sufficiency of years later, I am married to novelist Arthur Gladstone. Arthur, of the acute palate, urges you to open these pages promptly, thereby adding a cornucopia of simple, and simply delicious fare, to your repertoire.

July, 1981 HELEN WORTH

DOWN-ON-THE-FARM COOK BOOK

Aunt Sleide says: "There isn't much call for appetizers on a farm. Our appetites come from digging and planting, cultivating and harvesting. For the chores on a farm begin at sunup. And even when the sun isn't shining, there's work to be done. But the food we raise with the help of the Lord is sweet and fresh. And pretty near all of us know how to turn it into mouth-watering dishes that're brimful of nourishment and bursting with goodness."

1

SOUPS

To make soup stock, use 1 quart water for each pound of lean meat and bone. If a strong, dark soup is desired, use ⅓ pound bone for each pound of meat, and brown the meat and bone in fat. For a pale, clear, gelatinous soup, use ⅔ pound bone for each ⅔ pound meat and do not brown them. If part veal and part beef are used, the soup will be lighter than if made with all beef.

More flavor is extracted from the meat if it is cubed or ground before cooking. For extra flavor, soak the meat and bone for ½ hour in the water in which it is to be cooked.

Simmer soup in a partly covered container over a very low flame. There should be no movement or bubbling of the liquid. Soup has a better appearance if it is skimmed, but a good part of the food value is removed in the skimming process. To clarify any soup, use the method in **Jellied Chicken Soup.***

When the soup has finished cooking, strain it, let it cool, and place it in the refrigerator or other cold place. Soup has a better flavor the day after it is cooked. To use the soup, remove the hard cake of fat which has formed on top (the fat may be used for frying, etc.), simmer it until it is very hot, and serve it in warmed soup plates. If serving it jellied, beat it lightly with a fork and place the portions in well-chilled soup plates. A slice of lemon may

---

* A star (*) indicates a receipt or directions to be found in this book. For exact page number, the reader should consult the Index.

be stuck in the jellied soup or floated in hot soup. A sprinkling of finely cut herbs makes a nice contrast in color and in flavor and may be used with either hot or cold soups.

If the soup must be served immediately after cooking, remove as much of the fat as possible by skimming. A lettuce leaf may be thrown into the soup and removed after it has absorbed as much grease as it will hold, or the surface of the soup may be blotted with absorbent paper. The two latter procedures are wasteful, so it is best to use them only in an emergency.

Add vegetables to soup the last hour of cooking, as they may impart a strong flavor to the stock if cooked in it for a longer period of time. Any desired vegetables may be used.

The meat which was cooked in the soup may be served with it, or it may be served separately and dressed with a spicy sauce such as tomato ketchup flavored with horseradish. Hash may be made from the meat.

To make chicken stock, cook chicken as for **Huntington County Creamed Chicken Casserole.***

To thicken (bind) soup, use about 1 tablespoon flour for each cup of soup. Blend the flour with 1 tablespoon fat which has been removed from the soup, and proceed as for **Cream Sauce.***

Crisp additions to soup such as toasted croutons or salted popcorn make the soup more interesting. Dress cream soup up by topping each portion with a float of paprika.

Be sure to serve hot soup steaming, and cold soup icy.

BARLEY

Add **barley** to a quantity of boiling liquid and cook for about 1¼ hours, or until tender. Or soak for 1 hour and cook in boiling liquid for 45 minutes. One-quarter cup raw barley equals about ¾ cup cooked barley.

WICHITA COUNTY VEGETABLE SOUP

Grind or cube 3 **pounds shin or neck of beef.** Place in a kettle with **1 cracked knuckle bone or 1 cracked shank bone.** Add **3 quarts cold water** and soak 1 hour. Partly cover the kettle with a lid and bring the water to a boil slowly. Simmer 1 to 2 hours, or until the meat is almost tender. Ground meat will require less time to cook tender. Add **½ to ¾ cup tomatoes** (canned, cooked, or fresh tomatoes may be used), and **2 to 3 cups prepared vegetables**—cabbage, parsnips, celery, corn, onion, leek, turnip, carrots, potatoes, etc. Simmer about 1 hour more, or until meat and vegetables are tender. Season to taste with about **¾ teaspoon salt** and **¼ teaspoon pepper.** Makes 6 to 8 cups soup.

SUGAR ORCHARD FARM OXTAIL SOUP

Cube **1½ pounds neck or shoulder of beef.** Soak in **2½ quarts cold water** ½ to 1 hour. Brown **1 disjointed oxtail** in **2 tablespoons fat.** Add to the other meat and add the fat remaining in the pan. Partly cover the kettle with a lid and simmer 3 to 4 hours, or until the meat is almost tender. Add **1 large sliced onion, 1 tablespoon parsley, 3 carrots,** and **¼ cup celery,** and simmer about 1 hour more, or until the meat and vegetables are tender. Season to taste with about **½ teaspoon salt** and **¼ teaspoon pepper.** Makes about 10 cups soup.

A MAN'S SOUP

Cube or grind the meat from **5 to 6 pounds neck or leg of beef.** Soak meat and bone in **5 to 6 quarts water** ½ to 1 hour. Bring slowly to the boiling point and simmer until the meat is very tender, 3 to 4 hours. Ground meat will require less time. The last half-hour of cooking, add **1 cup dried lima beans** and the water in which they were cooked and **1 large onion.** Remove the bones from the soup and skim off the fat. Add **1 large carrot** and **1 large turnip,** diced, **3 branches celery,** sliced, and **2 potatoes,** diced. Cook ½ hour. Add **2 cups cabbage,** chopped, **2 cups tomatoes** (canned, cooked, or fresh), and **2 cups cooked** or **canned corn kernels.** Cook 15 minutes more, or until the meat and vegetables are tender. Remove the onion and as much fat as possible. Season to taste with about **¾ teaspoon salt** and **¼ teaspoon pepper.** Serve piping hot. Makes about 12 cups soup.

SCOTCH BROTH

Cube **3 pounds lamb** or **mutton.** Neck or shoulder may be used. Cover with **1½ quarts cold water.** Let soak ½ to 1 hour. Bring slowly to the boiling point. Add **½ cup barley** which has been soaked in cold water for 1 hour. Simmer until the meat is very tender, 1½ to 2 hours. Meanwhile, in a separate pot, cover the bones which have been removed from the meat with cold water. Bring to the boiling point and simmer 1½ to 2 hours with **1 bay leaf** and **2 whole cloves.** Strain and add to the meat and barley. Cube **2 medium carrots.** Dice **4 stalks celery** and **1 small onion.** Cook the vegetables in **2 tablespoons fat** for 5 minutes. Add to the soup and continue simmering until meat and vegetables are tender. Bind if a thicker soup is liked. Season to taste with about **1 teaspoon salt** and **⅛ teaspoon pepper.** Serve piping hot. Makes about 10 cups soup.

Aunt Sleide says: "Uncle claims that if it isn't thick enough to cut with a knife, it isn't good soup."

GOLDEN LEAF PLANTATION GUMBO

Prepare **3 pounds leg** or **neck of beef** as for **Wichita County Vegetable Soup*** and simmer 2 hours. When the meat is almost tender, add **1 large onion,** chopped, **1 button garlic,** chopped fine, and **4 tablespoons parsley,** cut fine. Continue cooking until the meat is very tender, about 1 hour. Strain and skim the stock. Cook **1 pound sliced okra** (fresh or canned), **1 cup celery,** sliced, and **1 small onion,** diced, in **2 tablespoons fat** for 5 minutes. Add to the stock. Add **2½ cups tomatoes,** (stewed, fresh, or canned), **3 carrots,** cubed, and **2 cups cabbage,** shredded. Simmer 30 to 45 minutes more. Add about **1 teaspoon salt** and **¼ teaspoon pepper** to taste. Add **1 cup rice** which has been cooked separately, and any remaining water in which it was cooked. If available, add **½ pound fresh shrimp** or **crabmeat** the last 15 minutes of cooking. Makes about 10 cups soup.

TOMATO BISQUE

Place in a saucepan **2½ cups tomatoes.** Stewed, fresh, or canned tomatoes may be used. Add **1 cup water** and simmer ½ hour. Strain, and discard the pulp. Make **2 cups thin Cream Sauce.*** Just before serving, pour the tomato liquid into the cream sauce, stirring it in. If the mixture curdles, beat it with a rotary beater for a minute or two. Season to taste with about **½ teaspoon salt** and **⅛ teaspoon pepper.** Stir over a low fire until piping hot. Serve with squares of buttered and toasted bread. Serves 4 to 6.

OKMULGEE COUNTY CORN CHOWDER

Chop **1 small onion** fine and cook in **2 tablespoons fat** for 5 minutes. Blend in **2 tablespoons flour.** Add **1 quart liquid** (juice drained from the corn plus enough milk to make 1 quart) slowly, stirring constantly. When the boiling point is reached, add **2 cups corn kernels,** cooked or canned, **1 teaspoon salt,** and **⅛ teaspoon pepper.** Cook 15 minutes. Beat **2 eggs** slightly. Beat in a portion of the hot soup. Return to the main mixture and cook 1 to 2 minutes more. Decorate the tureen with **1 tablespoon chives** or **parsley,** cut fine. Serves 4 to 6.

OLD FARM VEGETABLE CHOWDER

Prepare, and cut small the following vegetables: **2 medium onions, 2 branches celery, 1 sprig parsley, 2**

medium potatoes, 2 medium carrots, and **2 medium tomatoes.** Cover with **2 quarts boiling water.** Add **1 teaspoon salt** and **⅛ teaspoon pepper.** Cook slowly until the vegetables disintegrate, about 1 hour. Dice **3 slices bacon** and fry crisp. Add bacon and bacon fat to the vegetables. Roll **4 milk** or **soda crackers** fine, and add. Cook slowly 15 minutes. Season to taste and serve piping hot. Makes about 8 cups soup.

BAKED BEAN SOUP

Combine **2½ cups baked beans** (a No. 2 can may be used) and their sauce, **2 tablespoons chili sauce, 4 tablespoons onion,** chopped, **4 tablespoons celery,** chopped, **⅛ teaspoon dry mustard,** and **2½ cups stock.** Simmer for 30 minutes. Press through a strainer, using both liquid and solid matter. Add **1 tablespoon chili sauce.** Season to taste with about **½ teaspoon salt** and **⅛ teaspoon pepper** and serve piping hot. **Four strips of bacon,** diced and cooked, may be used to top the portions. Serves 4 to 6.

OSCEOLA FARM SPLIT PEA SOUP

Rinse and pick over **2 cups split peas.** Soak in cold water overnight. Increase the liquid to 3 quarts. Water in which smoked ham, beef, or tongue were cooked, and remaining bones and scraps may be used. Partly cover the kettle and simmer 3 hours. Add **1 small onion,** cut fine, **1 cup celery,** chopped, and **2 medium carrots** and simmer 1 hour more. Press the soup through a strainer, using both liquid and solid matter. Bind it and season to taste with about **½ teaspoon salt** and **⅛ teaspoon pepper.** If the ham or tongue water was salty, no salt will be required. Makes about 6 cups soup.

LENTIL SOUP

Cook as for **Split Pea Soup,** above, using **2 cups lentils,** plain water, and **1 pound smoked sausage.** Do not strain the soup. Press through a strainer **1 cup tomatoes** and add just before serving. Serve piping hot.

ANN ARUNDEL COUNTY TURKEY SOUP

Remove the stuffing and cut a **turkey carcass** into pieces. Place in a pot with any leftover turkey meat. Cover with cold water. Bring to the boiling point slowly and simmer covered for 1 hour. Add **1 cup celery,** sliced, **½ cup turnips,** diced, **1 medium onion,** and **1 cup tomatoes,** stewed, fresh, or canned. Simmer for 1 hour more or until the vegetables are tender. Strain. Remove fat. Season to taste with about **½ teaspoon salt** and **⅛ teaspoon pepper.** Leftover turkey gravy may be added, or, if the soup is too weak, dissolve 1 to 2 bouillon cubes in 1 cup of the liquid which has been brought to the boiling point, and add to the main mixture.

JELLIED CHICKEN SOUP

Prepare chicken stock as for **Huntington County Creamed Chicken Casserole.*** Strain and chill it. If you wish to clarify the broth, remove the fat and put the stock on to heat. Stir in **1 egg white** which has been beaten, and the **crushed shell.** Bring to a boil and strain. The process may be repeated, using another egg if the soup is not clear enough. Chill the broth again. If it had not been stiff enough when chilled before, soak in cold broth or water for 5 minutes **½ to 1 tablespoon unflavored gelatin** for each pint of liquid. Dissolve in boiling stock. Season to taste. Cool and chill until firm. Spoon portions into plates and beat each portion with a fork. Garnish with a slice of sweet pickle or other garnish.

CHICKEN SOUP WITH NOODLES OR RICE

Prepare broth as above. It does not have to be clarified. Heat to the boiling point and add slowly to each 2½ cups stock **½ to ¾ cup noodles.** Cook them in the broth until tender, 15 to 25 minutes. The noodles may be cooked separately, if desired. Chopped or shredded vegetables may be cooked in the soup and bits of cooked chicken added when it is served. Cooked rice rather than noodles may be added to the soup. **One cup cooked rice** to each quart stock is a good amount to use. For a rich soup, beat **1 egg** slightly for each person to be served and pour the boiling soup over the egg slowly, stirring it in. Or beat 1 egg in each plate.

SETTING HEN FARM CREAM OF CHICKEN SOUP

Bring **3 cups chicken stock** to the boiling point. Add **1 small carrot,** shredded, **½ small onion,** diced fine, **1 stalk celery,** sliced, and **1 cup green peas.** Cook slowly until the vegetables are tender, 8 to 15 minutes. Add **½ cup top milk.** Bind with **3 tablespoons soup fat** and **3 tablespoons flour.** Add about **½ teaspoon salt** to taste. Serves 4.

CREAM OF LIMA BEAN SOUP

Wash, pick over and soak **1 cup lima beans** in cold water overnight. Cook as for **Dried Vegetables.*** Melt **3 tablespoons fat.** Slice and brown **1 medium onion** in the fat, being careful not to let it burn. Press beans and onion through a strainer, using both liquid and solid matter. Add **1 cup top milk.** Thicken and season to taste with about **½ teaspoon salt** and **⅛ teaspoon pepper.** Serves 4 to 6.

DOLORES COUNTY POTATO SOUP

Slice and cook **2 medium onions** in **2 tablespoons fat** for 5 minutes. Add **2 cups raw potato,** diced, and **2 branches celery,** sliced. Cover with cold water and cook until the potatoes are very soft, about 40 minutes. Add more water, if necessary, while the vegetables are cooking. Press through a strainer, using both liquid and solid matter. Melt **1 tablespoon fat.** Blend in **1 tablespoon flour.** Add **4 cups milk** slowly, stirring constantly until the boiling point is reached. Add the potato mixture and heat. Add about **1 teaspoon salt, 1/4 teaspoon pepper,** and **1/2 teaspoon paprika** to taste. Serve piping hot. Sprinkle each portion with 2 tablespoons grated cheese, if desired. Makes about 6 cups soup.

OLD FARM EGG DUMPLINGS FOR SOUP

Beat **3 egg whites** stiff but not dry with **1/8 teaspoon salt.** Beat **3 yolks** and fold in the whites. Fold in **1/8 teaspoon salt** and **2 tablespoons parsley** or other herb, cut fine. Spread on top of soup which is being cooked in a wide-topped pot. Cook for about 3 minutes or until fairly firm. Then slash back and forth with a knife.

2

MEAT

Meat is best when it is cooked at low or moderate temperatures. The fat from the meat should be utilized whenever possible. For instance, trim portions of it off and fry it out until there is enough liquid fat for browning the meat. Wipe meat carefully with a damp cloth or paper towel to cleanse it.

COOKING IN WATER

When cooking meat in water, do not allow the water to become hotter than simmering. At a simmering temperature, there is no movement or bubbling of the water. If the meat is allowed to cool in the water in which it is cooked, the meat will be juicier and the flavor will be improved. This is only feasible, of course, if the meat is not to be served immediately.

It is better to add salt and pepper to the liquid which is cooking with the meat than to add it directly to the meat itself. The water is saved to use for soups and gravies or to use in other meat dishes.

BROILING

To broil the more tender cuts of meat such as steaks and chops, grease the broiler pan lightly with a piece of fat trimmed from the meat and place the meat 3½ to 4 inches away from the flame. Preheat the broiler to hot, 400° F. Broil the meat to the desired stage, turning it once. Be careful not to insert a fork in the meat when turning it as any puncture will allow the good meat juices to escape.

It is almost impossible to give exact broiling time because it varies so greatly with the amount of fat and bone the meat contains, with personal preference, etc. In general, a steak cut 1½ to 2 inches thick will require about 25 to 30 minutes to cook medium.

ROASTING

When roasting meat, place the meat on a rack in a baking pan. It is better if the pan does not have high sides. It is not necessary to preheat the oven. Roast uncovered in a moderate, 350° F. oven, until tender. Do not add water at any time. Onions or potatoes or both may be placed around the meat while it is roasting.

The only way to be perfectly sure that the meat is roasted to the desired stage is to use a roast-meat thermometer. Insert a skewer or a sharp knife in the fleshiest part of the meat. Remove it and place the thermometer in the incision, being sure that the bulb reaches to the center of the meat. Check the temperature on the thermometer immediately upon opening the oven door as the inrush of cold air will make the mercury drop.

It is not necessary to salt large roasts as the seasoning does not penetrate more than ½ inch and because of the danger of having over-salty drippings.

If meat dishes call for vegetables which are not liked, other vegetables may be substituted.

BEEF

JIM BOARDMAN'S BARBECUED STEAK

Mix together **½ teaspoon black pepper**, **½ teaspoon paprika**, **1 teaspoon chili powder**, and **1 teaspoon salt**. Add **¼ cup vinegar** and **¼ cup ketchup**. Add **3 tablespoons butter** and cook until thick. Brush **1 pound sirloin steak** with the sauce and broil.

Aunt Sleide says: "Jim Boardman could ride a horse almost before he could walk, and from the first time he heard about cowboys, he knew that was what he wanted to be. But when Jim was thirteen, he took sick. After that, he couldn't ride any more. For a long while, he couldn't even walk, and during that time he got interested in books. Now Jim's the best lawyer in the state. Every year he gives a barbecue and rodeo party for his friends. They're wonderful parties, and I enjoy them fine. But the minute I get home, I sit me down and cry like a baby."

SKY VALLEY LODGE ROAST BEEF

Put **ribs of beef** in roasting pan. Insert meat thermometer if using one. Place around the roast **1 medium onion** for each person to be served. Roast the meat uncovered in a moderate, 350° F. oven, allowing 20 to 25 minutes per pound if the beef is liked rare; 25 to 35 minutes per pound, if it is liked medium; and 35 to 45 minutes per pound if it is liked well done. Do not add water. It is not necessary to baste the meat. Add as many **medium potatoes** as needed the last 1 to 1½ hours of cooking, placing them around the roast. Larger than medium potatoes may be halved or quartered or they may be put in with the meat sooner so they will be tender and crisp when the meat is done. Serve the onions and potatoes around the roast. Don't worry if the onions look burned; they taste better that way.

SUFFOLK COUNTY BEEF AND KIDNEY PIE

Plunge **2 small beef kidneys** into boiling water. Remove the skins. If the kidneys are old, soak them in salted water (1 teaspoon salt to each quart water) 2 to 3 hours. Cut in 1-inch pieces. Cut **1 pound chuck beef** in pieces 1 to 2 inches square. Dredge the meat with **flour.** Fry out a portion of fat which has been cut from the meat and brown the meat in it. Turn the meat into a greased baking dish. Add **1 medium onion** which has been sliced, and **4 medium potatoes** which have been peeled and cubed. Add **3 cups liquid** (stock, gravy, vegetable water, or a combination of these) to the pan in which the meat was browned and rinse it well. Add to the meat. Cover the dish and bake in a moderate, 350° F. oven until the meat is tender, 45 to 60 minutes. Make **Gravy*** with the drippings. Return the gravy to the baking dish. Roll the dough for **Riz Biscuits,*** about ½ inch thick. Gash several times to allow the steam to escape. Cover the baking dish with the dough, pressing it to the sides. Bake in a hot, 425° F. oven 12 to 15 minutes or until the crust is nicely browned. Serves 4.

OLD FARM BEEF ROLLS

Have **round steak** cut ⅓ inch thick. Then cut in pieces 2 inches by 4 inches. Place on each piece a small piece of **celery,** a thick slice of **carrot,** a small piece of **salt pork** or a thin slice of **bacon.** Roll each piece up, and tie with string. Brown in **2 tablespoons salt pork or bacon drippings.** Pour enough **liquid** (gravy, stock, vegetable water, or a combination of these) in the pan to reach to ¼ inch. Cover and simmer for 2 hours or until tender. Remove strings. Make **Gravy.*** Allow 2 rolls to a serving.

BEEF TONGUE WITH TOMATO SAUCE

Place **1 fresh beef tongue** on a rack in a kettle with **1 onion, 1 carrot, 2 sprigs parsley,** and **2 branches celery.** Cover the tongue with boiling water, partly cover the kettle with a lid, and simmer the tongue for 2 hours. Remove the tongue, skin it and remove the roots. Place the tongue on a rack in a roasting pan and add **Osceola Farm Tomato Sauce.*** Cover and bake in a slow, 300° F. oven until tender, about 2 hours. The water in which the tongue was cooked may be used for dried pea or bean soups.

CALVES' TONGUES

Cook calves' tongues as for **Beef Tongue with Tomato Sauce,** above, simmering for 1 hour, or until tender. Remove skin and roots and serve without additional cooking. Part of the water in which the tongues were cooked may be used to make **Gravy.*** Use the remainder of the water for dried pea or bean soups. **One-half cup chopped sweet pickle** may be added to the gravy. Two calves' tongues serve 6.

NEW ENGLAND BOILED DINNER

Place **3½ to 4 pounds corned beef** on a rack in a kettle. Cover with boiling water, partly cover the kettle with a lid and simmer until tender, 3 to 5 hours. When half cooked, add 1 pound thinly sliced salt pork, if desired. Skim off the fat and scum. When the meat has finished cooking, remove it, keep it warm, and let the meat water come to a boil. Add **6 to 8 potatoes** which have been peeled and halved. After 10 minutes, add **3 young turnips** which have been peeled and left whole, **4 to 6 whole carrots,** and **1 small quartered cabbage.** Boil for 20 minutes or until all the vegetables are tender. Place the meat on a large platter and surround it with the vegetables. Place the sliced salt pork, if used, around the vegetables. Serves 6.

Carrots or turnips, or both, may be omitted. Beets or thinly sliced rutabaga may be added. In fact, any combination of vegetables may be used, but cabbage and potatoes are a must. If the vegetables are old, allow more time for cooking them. Save the water to use for making dried pea or bean soups.

BEEF SHANK WITH CORN MEAL DUMPLINGS

Brown a **3-pound piece of beef shank** in fat fried out from the meat. Place the meat on a rack in a kettle, add boiling water to cover, and the pan drippings. Partly cover the kettle with a lid and simmer the meat 1 hour. Add **2 medium onions** which have been peeled and stuck with **4 whole cloves, 2 carrots,** and **½ bay leaf.** Simmer for 1 hour more, or until very tender. Twenty minutes before serving, skim off the excess fat. Drop **Corn Meal Dumplings*** on the meat. Cover the pot tightly and steam for 15 minutes. Remove shanks and dumplings, strain the liquid, and make **Gravy.*** Serves 8.

CORNED BEEF HASH

Remove skin, fat and gristle from cooked **corned beef.** Chop the meat fine but do not grind it. Chop an equal amount of **cooked potatoes.** Mix together lightly and moisten with just enough **top milk** to hold the ingredients together. Season with about **¼ teaspoon salt** and **⅛ teaspoon pepper.** Melt **2 or more tablespoons butter** in a heavy skillet and spread the hash over the bottom of the pan. Let cook very slowly, 30 to 45 minutes, or until the bottom is well browned. Fold over and place on a platter.

The traditional accompaniment is **poached eggs.** To make them, fill a skillet to a depth of 1 to 2 inches with water. Bring to a boil. Add ½ teaspoon salt for each cup of water. Break eggs into a saucer one at a time and slip them into the boiling water. Cover the pan and turn off the heat. Let the eggs remain in the hot water 3 to 5 minutes or until of the desired firmness. Remove from the water with a slotted spoon.

CUMBERLAND COUNTY RED FLANNEL HASH

Cook **6 medium beets** and **4 medium potatoes.** Peel, chop and mix with **1 cup cooked chopped beef,** about **½ teaspoon salt,** and **⅛ teaspoon pepper.** Add **2 tablespoons cream.** Fry quickly in **3 tablespoons bacon drippings or other fat.** Serves 4.

This has to be tasted to be believed. It really is red and it really is good.

LIVER LOAF

Beef, calf, lamb or pork liver may be used.

Cover **1 pound liver** with boiling water. Let stand 10 minutes. Drain. Run through a food chopper with **1 medium onion.** Mix with **2 eggs, ½ teaspoon salt, ⅛ teaspoon pepper, 1 tablespoon chopped parsley, 1 tablespoon chopped celery leaves, 1 tablespoon chopped green pepper,** and **1 cup cooked rice.** Pour **1½ cups milk** over **½ cup bread or cracker crumbs.** Add to the rest of the ingredients and mix lightly but well. Grease a loaf pan, 9 x 5 x 3 inches. Turn the mixture into the pan and shape it into a loaf, being careful not to use too heavy a hand. Top with **2 strips bacon.** Bake in a moderate, 350° F. oven about 1 hour. Serve hot or cold. This makes good sandwiches. Serves 4 to 6.

BAKED LIVER WITH VEGETABLES

Heat **2 tablespoons fat** in a skillet. Dredge a **1-pound slice of liver** (beef, lamb, calf, or pork) with **¼ cup flour.** Brown the meat in the fat. Place it in a greased baking dish. Add any liquid from the pan, **1 medium onion,** diced, **¾ cup celery,** chopped, including the leaves, **8 small carrots,** quartered, **½ teaspoon salt,** and **⅛ teaspoon pepper.** Add **2 cups tomatoes.** Cover and bake in a slow, 300° F. oven 1½ to 2 hours. Slice across the grain. Serves 4.

ONE-EYE MEAT LOAF

Hard-cook **3 eggs.*** Grind twice **1½ pounds chuck beef** and **½ pound shoulder pork.** Run through the grinder **1 large onion, 1 medium green pepper,** and **1 slice stale bread** which has been soaked in **1 cup sour milk.** Add **1 raw egg, 1 teaspoon salt, ¼ teaspoon pepper,** and the sour milk to the mixture. Mix well but lightly. Place half the mixture in a loaf pan, 9 x 5 x 3 inches. Place the peeled hard-cooked eggs on the meat lengthwise. Cover with the remainder of the meat. Top with **2 strips bacon.** Bake in a moderate, 350° F. oven 45 to 75 minutes or until the meat is completely cooked. The loaf may be shaped in a large skillet with the required number of peeled potatoes placed around it. Serves 6 to 8.

Aunt Sleide says: "This is called One-Eye Meat Loaf because the egg looks like an eye when the meat is cut. But not according to Uncle. He says it got its name because it's so good that during grace folks've got one eye on the Lord and the other on the loaf."

COMPANY MEAT BALLS

Grind twice **2½ pounds shoulder veal, ½ pound shoulder pork,** and **1 medium onion.** Mix lightly but well with **4 beaten eggs, 1 cup top milk, 6 slices toast,** crumbled, **½ teaspoon salt, ½ teaspoon nutmeg** and **¼ teaspoon pepper.** Shape lightly into balls the size of an egg, roll in flour and brown in **3 tablespoons lard.** Place in a greased baking dish and bake in a moderate, 350°F. oven 1 to 1¼ hours. Place on a platter and sprinkle with **¼ cup chopped parsley.** Serve with pan gravy. Serves 8 to 10.

MEAT PIE

Prepare as for **Elk Horn Ranch Irish Stew*** with any vegetables. Omit dumplings, adding instead a crust, as in **Sky Valley Lodge Sparerib Pie.***

BREAD AND BUTTER POT ROAST

Cook for 5 minutes **½ cup sliced onions** and **½ cup diced celery** in **3 tablespoons beef fat** which has been fried out. Remove the vegetables. Brown a **4-pound beef chuck roast** in the fat, using a medium flame. Place the meat on a rack in a roasting pan. Cover with the vegetables and add **1 cup tomatoes.** Bake uncovered in a moderate, 350° F. oven 2½ to 3 hours or until tender. Make **Gravy.*** Serves 6 to 8.

RED CHIMNEY FARM ROUND STEAK WITH SAUERKRAUT

Partially fry ¼ **pound sliced bacon.** Place on **1½-pound round steak.** Cover with **1 pound sauerkraut.** Roll the steak and tie firmly. Place on a rack in a baking dish. Bake uncovered in a moderate, 350° F. oven 1 to 2 hours or until tender. Serves 6.

ELK HORN RANCH IRISH STEW

Cut **1½ pounds chuck beef** into 1- to 2-inch cubes. Dredge with **flour.** Fry out fat from the meat and simmer **1 large diced onion** in the fat for 5 minutes. Push the onion to one side and brown the meat in the fat. Add enough **stock, gravy, vegetable water, or a combination of these** to cover the meat. Partly cover the pan with a lid, and simmer until the meat is almost tender, about 45 minutes. Add **8 medium potatoes** which have been peeled and cubed and continue cooking until the meat is tender. Make **Gravy*** with the liquid in the kettle, return it and add **Dumplings for Stew.*** Cover the pan tightly, and cook until the dumplings are done. Serves 6.

Carrots or celery or both may be added with the potatoes, if desired.

OXTAIL STEW

Cut **1 oxtail** at the joints and dredge with **flour.** Cook **2 sliced onions** for 5 minutes in fat fried out from the meat. Add the oxtail and brown it. Place meat and onion in a kettle. Cover with boiling water, partly cover the kettle with a lid and simmer for 1 hour. Add **1 cup tomatoes, 1 cup quartered carrots, ¾ cup diced and peeled turnips,** and **½ cup diced celery.** Season with about **½ teaspoon salt** and **¼ teaspoon pepper.** Cover and bake in a moderate, 350° F. oven 2½ to 3 hours or until the meat and vegetables are tender. Make **Gravy.*** Serves 4 to 6.

SUGAR ORCHARD FARM SWISS STEAK

Mix ½ teaspoon salt and ¼ teaspoon pepper with ½ cup flour. Pound it into a 2-pound chuck steak which has been sliced 2 inches thick. Use a steak hammer, potato masher or the edge of a heavy plate to pound in the flour. Brown the steak in fried-out fat. Add 1 onion, peeled and sliced, ½ diced green pepper, and 1 cup tomato juice. Partly cover the kettle with a lid and simmer for 2 hours, or until tender. Serves 4 or 5.

VEAL

ROAST VEAL

Roast as for Sky Valley Lodge Roast Beef,* allowing 25 to 40 minutes per pound.

BERTHA LEWIS' RECEIPT FOR BREADED VEAL STEAKS AND POTATOES

Have veal cut from the round ½ inch thick, then cut it into individual serving pieces. To coat 1 to 2 pounds veal, beat 1 egg lightly. Beat in 1 tablespoon water. Dip the veal in cracker or bread crumbs which have been seasoned with ½ teaspoon salt and ⅛ teaspoon pepper. Dip the meat in the egg. Then dip in crumbs again. If any egg or crumbs are left when all the meat has been coated, dip it again to use the remainder. If the meat is allowed to stand in the refrigerator or other cold place for at least ½ hour, the coating will adhere better when the meat is fried. Melt fat in a skillet to a depth of 2½ inches and heat it. Put in the veal. Cook over a moderate flame until one side is nicely browned. Turn and brown the other side. Reduce the flame and cook until tender, 20 to 30 minutes. Drain off the excess fat, leaving the crumbs in the pan. Place in the skillet, for each person to be served, 1 large potato which has been boiled, peeled, and halved. Stir the potatoes until they are well coated with crumbs and fat. Serve around the veal.

Aunt Sleide says: "Bertha Lewis attracts friends like a magnet. Her husband Carl says that if he didn't know better, he'd think their farmhouse was permanent headquarters for King Solomon's family reunion!"

LAMB

SHOULDER LAMB CHOPS WITH APPLES

Sprinkle **4 shoulder lamb chops** with **salt, pepper** and very little **ginger.** Fry out a portion of the lamb fat in a skillet and brown the chops in it. When brown on both sides, cover with **3 medium apples** which have been cored and sliced into rings. Sprinkle the apples with **2 tablespoons brown sugar.** Dot with **2 tablespoons butter.** Cover the skillet, and bake in a moderate, 350° F. oven until the chops and apples are tender, 40 to 60 minutes. Serves 4.

SKY VALLEY LODGE LAMB ROAST WITH TURNIPS

Peel **8 medium turnips.** Hollow out the centers. Soak **6 slices stale bread** in **2 cups cream.** Stuff the turnips with the bread. Place them in the bottom of a roasting pan. Sprinkle a **5-pound leg of lamb** with **1 teaspoon ginger.** (Do not have the fell removed from the lamb.) Cut **4 or 5 sprigs of mint** over the lamb. Place the lamb on top of the turnips, fat side up. Pour over any cream that has not been absorbed by the bread. Roast, uncovered, in a moderate, 300° F. oven 30 to 35 minutes per pound. Make **Gravy.*** Serves 6.

LAMB SHANKS WITH BARLEY

Place **4 lamb shanks** in a kettle. Cover with boiling water and add **1 onion, 3 branches celery, 1 bay leaf** and **1 carrot.** Partly cover the kettle with a lid and simmer 1 hour. Remove the meat and place in a roasting pan. Strain the broth. Add water if necessary to make 1 quart liquid. Add ½ **teaspoon salt** and bring the liquid to the boiling point. Add ½ **cup pearl barley** slowly so the water does not stop boiling. Cook 1 to 1½ hours or until the barley is tender. Add more boiling water if necessary. Meanwhile, finish cooking the lamb shanks in a roasting pan, adding **1 cup tomato juice.** Roast uncovered in a moderate, 350° F. oven until tender, basting frequently. Drain the barley, mix with the pan gravy, and serve around the meat. Serves 4.

LAMB SHOULDER WITH CHERRY PRESERVES

Place in a pan a **5- to 6-pound lamb shoulder** which has been boned and rolled. Bake in a moderate, 350° F. oven 1½ hours. Skim the excess fat from the liquid in the pan. Tie in a cheesecloth ½ **bay leaf, 3 whole allspice,** and **3 whole cloves.** Mix together **1½ cups hot water,** ½ **cup cherry preserves,** ¼ **cup vinegar,** and ½ **teaspoon salt.** Add to the lamb. Place the spices in the pan. Bake it about 2½ to 3 hours more or until the meat is tender, basting frequently. Remove the spices and make **Gravy.*** Serves 8 to 10.

COMANCHE COUNTY LAMB STEW

Brown **4 pounds lamb neck** (cut in serving pieces) in fried-out fat from the meat. Add **3 cups hot water.** Hot vegetable water may be used for part or all of the liquid. Season with ½ **teaspoon salt** and ¼ **teaspoon pepper.** Cover and simmer 1½ hours. Add **8 small white onions, 3 large carrots** quartered, **1 small head cabbage** quartered, **1 pound shelled peas, 3 sprigs parsley** cut fine, **10 medium potatoes** quartered, and **1 small green pepper** diced. (The potatoes may be omitted and dumplings substituted. Make **Dumplings for Stew.*** Drop them in after the gravy has been made. Cover closely and cook for 12 minutes.) Cook the stew 30 minutes more, or until the vegetables and lamb are tender. Make **Gravy.*** Serves 8.

PORK

It is dangerous to health to eat pork that is not well done, so be sure that it is thoroughly cooked before serving it. No pink should show when the pork is cut.

PORK ROAST

Pork should be roasted on a rack in an open pan. It is not necessary to add water to the pan at any time. **One medium onion** for each person to be served may be placed around the roast. For best results, roast in a moderate, 350° F. oven. A fresh ham requires 30 to 35 minutes per pound; a whole loin, 15 to 20 minutes; a center loin, 35 to 40 minutes; and loin ends, 45 to 50 minutes per pound. A whole shoulder takes 30 to 35 minutes; a boned and rolled shoulder, 40 to 45 minutes; and a pork butt, 45 to 50 minutes per pound.

ROAST SUCKLING PIG

Draw, scrape, clean, and wash well a **suckling pig.** Dry inside and out. The pig, dressed, should weigh about 12 pounds. Rub the inside of the pig with **1 tablespoon salt.** Fill lightly with **Onion Stuffing**: Cook **8 cups diced onions** in a quantity of boiling salted water for 10 minutes. Drain. Add **12 cups soft bread crumbs, 4 beaten eggs, 1 pound melted butter, 1 teaspoon salt, ½ teaspoon paprika,** and **1 teaspoon sage, marjoram, thyme,** or **poultry seasoning.** Mix well. Add more seasoning to taste. Sew the pig up, put a block of wood or a potato in its mouth to keep it open, and skewer the legs into position by pulling the forelegs forward and the hind legs backward. Rub the pig with **oil or butter.** Dredge it with **flour.** Cover the ears with pieces of well-greased paper and secure it with paper clips. Place the pig on a rack in an open pan. Roast in a moderate, 350° F. oven 30 to 40 minutes per pound, or until tender and completely cooked. The last half-hour of cooking, remove the paper from the pig's ears, so they may brown. Before serving it forth, place the pig on a heated platter. Remove the wood from its mouth and insert a **shiny red apple.** Place **cranberries** in the eyes and give the pig a necklace of **small green leaves.**

OLD FARM HEADCHEESE

Clean a **hog's head** by quartering the head and removing the ears, brains, eyes, snout, and skin. Remove the fattest parts to use for lard. Scrub hair from the hog's ears and nose. Soak the lean and bony parts in cold water overnight to remove the blood. The hog's tongue, heart, feet and other meat scraps may be used. Remove the hoofs from the feet. Cover the meat with boiling water. Bring to a boil again and simmer in a partly covered kettle until the meat falls from the bones. Drain and reserve the liquid. Strip the meat from the bones and chop fine. To each **25 pounds of chopped meat** add **1 gallon of the liquid in which it was cooked, ½ to ¾ pound salt, 1 ounce black pepper, ¼ ounce red pepper,** and **crushed dried sage** or any other herbs or spices. Mix well. Place in a kettle and add more liquid to cover the meat if necessary. Cook for 20 to 30 minutes or until reduced enough to form jelly. Turn into pans 2 to 3 inches deep and chill until firm. When cold, slice and serve with vinegar or fry in batter, as for **Jasper County Batter-Fried Chicken,*** frying for 5 minutes. Vinegar may be added to a portion of the pan drippings to make gravy if the headcheese is fried in batter.

PIGS' FEET AND HOCKS PICKLED

Clean feet and hocks carefully by scraping and singeing them. Place **4 good-sized pigs' feet and hocks** in a kettle. Add boiling water to cover. Partly cover the kettle with a lid and simmer until the meat falls from the bones, about

6 hours. Lift out with a skimmer and place in a jar or bowl, first removing the largest bones. Set the liquid aside to cool. Place on the fire **1 quart strong vinegar, 4 bay leaves, 1 tablespoon whole cloves, 1 teaspoon salt, ½ teaspoon pepper, ½ onion,** sliced, and **1 tablespoon broken cinnamon stick.** Let cook slowly for 45 minutes. Strain. Remove the fat from the liquid in which the feet were cooked and add 1 quart of the liquid to the vinegar. (Less may be added if the vinegar was not strong originally.) Add more seasoning if necessary. Pour over the meat and stir thoroughly. Let stand in a refrigerator or other cold place for at least 5 days. Serve cold. Serves about 6.

PIGS' KNUCKLES STEWED WITH SAUERKRAUT

Wash **8 pigs' knuckles** in cold water. Repeat twice. Drain and place in a kettle with **6 cups sauerkraut.** Add boiling water to cover. Partly cover the kettle with a lid and simmer until the knuckles are very tender, about 2 hours. Season with about **½ teaspoon salt.** Serves 6 to 8.

ELK HORN RANCH PORK CHOPS BAKED WITH CABBAGE

Shred and cook **1 small head of cabbage.** Drain and mix with **1 cup cream.** Grease a baking dish. Put in half the cabbage. Place on top of the cabbage **4 or 5 double pork chops** which have been browned in fat. Cover the chops with the remainder of the cabbage. Top with **Buttered Bread Crumbs.*** Bake in a moderate, 350° F. oven 1 to 1¼ hours, or until the chops are tender and completely cooked. Serves 4 or 5.

BREADED PORK CHOPS

Follow the recipe for **Bertha Lewis' Receipt for Breaded Veal Steaks and Potatoes.*** Be sure that the pork is cooked until it is well done.

YAKIMA COUNTY PORK CHOPS WITH CORN

Grease a baking dish. Mix together **2½ cups cooked corn kernels, 1 cup diced celery, 2 tablespoons green pepper,** diced, **1 cup soft bread crumbs** and **⅓ cup tomato ketchup.** Cover the bottom of a baking dish with the mixture. Brown **5 thick pork chops** in **2 tablespoons fat.** Place the chops on top of the corn mixture and pour over any fat in the skillet. Cover and bake in a moderate, 350° F. oven 1 to 1¼ hours or until the meat is tender and completely cooked. Serves 4 or 5.

TWO HILLS PLANTATION PORK CHOPS

Cut or have pockets cut in **6 double rib pork chops** by slicing from the outer edge toward the bone. Rub the pockets very lightly with **salt.** Peel, core and quarter **2 apples.** Stuff each pocket with apple. Skewer the edges of the chops together (toothpicks may be used). Brown the chops on both sides in **2 tablespoons fat.** Place any remaining apple quarters in the pan. Cover the pan and bake in a moderate, 350° F. oven 1 to 1¼ hours or until the meat is tender and completely cooked. Serves 5 or 6.

PORK CHOPS WITH SWEET POTATOES

Lightly stuff the pockets in **double pork chops** with mashed leftover sweet potatoes. Cook as above.

OPEN GATE FARM PORK AND POTATOES

Brown **4 thick pork chops,** then place in a greased baking dish. Cover the chops with **2 medium onions** sliced thin. Peel and slice **5 medium potatoes** and lay them neatly over the onions. Dot with **3 tablespoons butter** and add **1½ cups milk.** Bake in a moderate, 350° F. oven 1 to 1½ hours, or until the pork is tender and completely cooked. Serves 4.

SALT PORK WITH MILK GRAVY

Slice **1 pound salt pork** very thin and freshen by soaking in cold milk to cover for 2 hours. To eliminate soaking time, pour boiling water, to cover, over the salt pork. Let stand for 5 minutes. Then slice thin. Drain, dredge with **flour** and fry until crisp. Remove from the pan and drain off all but **2 tablespoons grease.** Make gravy by blending in **2 tablespoons flour.** Stir in gradually **1 cup scalded milk** and stir constantly until the gravy reaches the boiling point. Add **¼ teaspoon pepper** and salt, if necessary. Serve boiled or mashed potatoes with the pork and gravy. Serves 4.

BATTER-FRIED SALT PORK

Freshen **salt pork** as above. Drain and dry the slices. Dip in batter and fry as for **Jasper County Batter-Fried Chicken.*** Serve with mashed potatoes.

PORK SHOULDER ROAST STUFFED WITH SAUERKRAUT

Have a **pork shoulder** boned. Rub the cavity lightly with **salt.** Stuff loosely with **sauerkraut.** Skewer or sew up the opening. Place on a rack in a roasting pan and roast uncovered in a moderate, 350° F. oven about 45 minutes to the pound. Do not add water at any time. Allow ⅓ pound meat per person.

PORK SAUSAGE

Run **12 pounds lean pork scraps** through the food grinder twice. Mix thoroughly with **5 tablespoons salt, 6 teaspoons pepper,** and crushed dried **herbs**—2 tablespoons sage and 2 tablespoons summer savory or others.

BAKED TURNIPS WITH SAUSAGE

Scrub **1 large turnip per person.** Core with an apple corer, being careful not to cut through the turnip. Stuff the cavity with **pork sausage.** Bake as for **Baked Turnips.***

CHET SCHAEFFER'S HICKORY-SMOKED SAUSAGE WITH SAUERKRAUT

Cover **2 pounds smoked sausage** with boiling water. Bring the water back to boiling and simmer 10 to 20 minutes or until the meat is completely cooked. Drain and add the meat to **Big Bay Farm Sauerkraut.*** Serves 8.

Aunt Sleide says: "Chet Schaeffer is the local politician and his sausage is as smooth as his tongue."

BAKED SAUSAGES, SWEET POTATOES AND APPLES

Boil **4 medium sweet potatoes** until tender, 30 to 45 minutes. Peel and cut into halves lengthwise. Cover the bottom of a greased casserole with the potatoes. Fry until golden brown **1 pound pork sausage** which has been shaped into patties. Place over the potatoes. Peel, core and slice **3 large apples** into rings 1 inch thick. Place over the sausage. Sprinkle with **¼ cup brown sugar** which has been packed firmly in the cup. Add **¼ cup drippings** from the pan the sausage was fried in and **¼ cup boiling water.** Cover and bake in a moderate, 350° F. oven 40 to 60 minutes or until the apples are tender and the sausage is completely cooked. Serves 4.

DU PAGE COUNTY BARBECUED SPARE RIBS

Cut **4 pounds spareribs** into sections of 2 bones each. Place in a roaster and cover with **3 medium onions** which have been sliced. Mix **1 cup tomato ketchup** with **¾ cup water, ½ teaspoon salt, ¼ cup vinegar, 2 tablespoons sugar,** and **1 teaspoon dry mustard** and pour over the ribs.

Bake in a slow, 300° F. oven for 2 hours, or until the meat is crisp and completely cooked. Baste frequently. Serves 4.

SKY VALLEY LODGE SPARERIB PIE

Have spareribs chopped into pieces convenient for serving. Allow **1 pound spareribs for each serving.** Sprinkle with **salt** and **pepper,** and dredge with **flour.** Place the ribs in a baking dish, add water to a depth of ¾ inch. Bake in a moderate, 350° F. oven until tender, 1 to 2 hours, basting frequently. Be sure that the meat is completely cooked. Spread over the spareribs the dough for **Riz Biscuits,*** which has been rolled about ½ inch thick. Gash several times and press it to the sides of the baking dish. Bake in a hot, 425° F. oven until the crust is nicely browned, 12 to 15 minutes.

SPARERIBS AND SAUERKRAUT

Allow **1 pound spareribs for each portion.** Have cut in pieces convenient for serving. Brown in **bacon fat.** Season with **salt** and **pepper.** Place a layer in the bottom of a baking pan, add a layer of **raw sauerkraut,** using 2 cups sauerkraut for each pound of spareribs. Continue alternating layers, ending with spareribs. Add boiling water to cover. Cover and bake in a very moderate, 325° F. oven for 2 hours, or until the spareribs are tender and completely cooked.

CREAMED PORK TENDERLOIN

Cut or have pork tenderloin cut in 3-inch slices. Stand on end and flatten with a cleaver. Melt **2 tablespoons fat** in a fry-pan and cook **8 pork tenderloins** over a low fire until they are tender and completely cooked, 20 to 30 minutes. Remove them and add to the pan **1 cup cream** which has been mixed to a smooth paste with **1 tablespoon corn starch.** Stir over a low fire until slightly thickened, and until there is no taste of raw starch, about 10 minutes.

Return the meat to the pan, season with about **½ teaspoon salt** and **⅛ teaspoon pepper** and simmer for 5 minutes. Serve with mashed potatoes.

Aunt Sleide says: "My great-nephew Paul Sleide wanted to know why he always likes what I cook, and I told him it's because I always cook what he likes!"

BACON

To fry bacon, place strips of it in a cold skillet and cook over a low to medium flame, turning the bacon frequently to cook it evenly. Fry to the desired stage, being careful not to let it get too brown. Remove from the pan and drain on unglazed paper. Strain the fat, keep in a cool place, and use as needed.

For small pieces of bacon, dice it and fry slowly in a cold pan, turning when necessary. Drain. Or cook strips of bacon, then crumble them.

PRE-COOKED HAMS

Remove the skin from a pre-cooked ham, score the fat, add any of the finishes in the following recipes (brown sugar, cloves, honey, etc.), and bake uncovered on a rack in an open baking pan in a moderate, 350° F. oven. Baste occasionally and bake about 15 to 20 minutes per pound, or until a meat thermometer registers 150° F. A half ham may be treated the same way.

BOILED HAM WITH HONEY

Wash the ham thoroughly and scrub it well with a stiff brush. Place it rind side up on a rack in a large kettle or a ham boiler. Add water to cover, partly cover the container with a lid, and simmer the ham 25 to 30 minutes per pound, or until tender. Add more water as needed to keep the ham well covered. For extra flavor, simmer the ham with **1 onion, 1 carrot, 1 teaspoon whole cloves, 1 bay leaf, 3 branches celery,** and **2 sprigs parsley.** A roast-meat thermometer may be used to determine exactly when the ham has finished cooking. The bulb of the thermometer should reach the center of the fleshiest part of the meat. Before inserting the thermometer, make a small incision through the ham rind with a steel skewer or a sharp knife. Cut short gashes around the opening with a scissors, then insert the thermometer. The ham has finished cooking when the thermometer registers 170° F. Allow the ham to cool in the broth, if possible. Remove it and pull off the rind. Place the ham fat side up on a rack in a baking pan. Score the fat with a sharp knife, pad it with **1 cup dry bread crumbs** and stick a **clove** in each square or diamond of fat. Pour **3 cups honey** over the ham. Place in a hot, 500° F. oven and bake until nicely glazed and beautifully browned, 10 to 15 minutes. Baste once or twice. Use the water in which the ham was cooked for making any dried pea or bean soup.

HAVEN FARM BOILED HAM IN CIDER

Cook the ham as above, using cider instead of water. Omit the vegetables, adding to the water **1 cup raisins, 1 teaspoon whole cloves** and **1 bay leaf.** When the ham has finished cooking, let it cool in the cider. Remove the ham, pull off the rind and score the fat. Spread the fat with **prepared mustard,** then pat **brown sugar** over it. Stick a clove in each square of fat and bake in a hot, 500° F. oven as above. Strain the liquid in which the ham was cooked, remove as much fat as possible and use instead of cider in **Raisin Cider Sauce.*** Discard the raisins which were cooked with the ham and use additional raisins in the sauce.

Extravagant, but oh my!

BAKED MAMMY HAM

Wash the ham thoroughly and scrub it well with a stiff brush. Place it in a large pan, add cold water to cover, and soak it overnight. Wipe the ham dry and place on a rack in an open baking pan. Do not add water. Bake uncovered in a slow, 260° F. oven 25 to 30 minutes per pound, or until tender. If baking a half ham, allow 40 to 45 minutes per pound for the shank end or 45 to 55 minutes per pound for the butt end. If using a meat thermometer, insert it as directed for **Boiled Ham with Honey.*** The ham has finished baking when the thermometer registers 170° F. At the end of the baking period remove the ham, remove the rind, and score the fat. Mix **3 cups brown sugar** with **2 teaspoons cloves** and **1 teaspoon allspice.** Add enough **vinegar** to make a paste. Spread over the fat and bake in a hot, 500° F. oven 10 to 15 minutes or until the fat is brown and crusty.

FRIED HAM WITH MILK GRAVY

Trim the rind and the lean edge from a **center slice of ham** which has been cut ½ inch thick. Fry out the fat in a skillet. Remove it and fry the ham slice in the melted fat over a low flame. It will take about 30 minutes to cook it completely. Remove the ham and add ½ **cup milk** to the skillet. Cook it until it is hot, but do not let it boil. Thicken if desired, as for **Gravy.*** Serves 2 or 3.

BELKNAP COUNTY BAKED HAM SLICES WITH CRANBERRIES

Stick **cloves** generously into the fat of **2 center ham slices** which have been cut 1 inch thick. Place one slice of ham in a baking dish. Wash and pick over **2 cups cranberries** and mix with **1 cup honey** and **1 teaspoon lemon juice.** Cover the ham in the baking dish with the mixture. Top with the second slice. Bake in a slow, 300° F. oven 1 to 1½ hours, basting frequently. Serves 6.

HAM SLICE WITH GINGER PEARS

Place in a saucepan **2 cups water, 1 cup sugar, 2 teaspoons grated lemon rind, juice of 2 lemons** (about 6 tablespoons), **½ cup preserved ginger,** chopped, and **⅛ teaspoon salt.** Boil 5 minutes, stirring until the sugar is dissolved. Peel, halve and core **6 pears.** Drop into the syrup and cook gently for 5 minutes. Spread a **2- to 3-pound center slice of ham** with **¼ cup brown sugar.** Place the ham in a baking pan. Add the syrup and bake in a slow, 300° F. oven for 45 minutes. Arrange the pear halves around the ham and bake until the ham is tender, about 20 minutes longer. Serves 6.

OPEN GATE FARM BAKED HAM AND POTATOES

Place a **2-pound center slice of ham** in the bottom of a greased baking dish. Peel **6 large potatoes** and slice them thin. Cover the ham with the potatoes. Dot with **4 tablespoons butter** and add **2 cups milk.** Bake in a moderate, 350° F. oven 1 to 1½ hours, or until the potatoes and ham are tender. Serves 6.

BLACK HAWK COUNTY BOILED DINNER

Bring to a boil enough water to cover a **1½- to 2½-pound cottage ham.** Place the ham in the water and simmer 2 to 3 hours or until tender. Remove the ham and keep it warm. Bring the water to a boil again and add **1 to 2 peeled, halved potatoes** for each person to be served. Let boil 10 minutes. Add **1 medium head of cabbage,** quartered, and boil 10 to 15 minutes longer or until the potatoes and cabbage are tender. Serve the vegetables around the ham. Serves 4 to 6.

A corresponding cut of fresh ham may be substituted for cottage ham.

LANGLADE COUNTY HAM LOAF

Grind **¾ pound smoked ham, ¾ pound lean pork, ½ small green pepper,** and **¼ medium-sized onion.** Mix with **⅛ teaspoon pepper, ¼ teaspoon salt,** and **2 eggs.** Add **¾ cup bread crumbs** which have been soaked in **¾ cup milk.** Mix well, shape lightly into a loaf and place in a pan. Peel and core **1 apple** and slice into rings. Cover the top of the loaf with the apple rings. Sprinkle the apples with **2 tablespoons brown sugar** and dot with **1 tablespoon butter.** Bake in a moderate, 350° F. oven, 60 to 75 minutes or until the meat is completely cooked. Serves 4.

HAM BALLS IN SOUR SAUCE

Grind **1 pound ham, 1½ pounds lean pork,** and **½ small green pepper.** Add **2 eggs** and **1½ cups bread crumbs** which have been soaked in **1 cup milk.** Mix well and make small balls, handling lightly. Place in a baking dish. Mix **1¼ cups brown sugar** packed firmly in the cup with **½ cup vinegar, ½ cup water, 1 teaspoon dry mustard,** and **½ teaspoon cloves.** Add to the meat and bake in a moderate, 350° F. oven 1 to 1½ hours or until the meat is completely cooked. Turn the balls over after they have cooked ½ hour. Serves 6.

GAME

RABBIT

If preparing wild rabbit, protect the hands with gloves because of the danger of rabbit fever. Be perfectly sure that the rabbit is thoroughly cooked before serving it. Joint wild or domestic rabbit, bread it and fry as for **Bertha Lewis' Receipt for Breaded Veal Steaks and Potatoes,*** making **Gravy*** from the pan drippings, or fry as for **Fried Chicken Maryland.*** Rabbit may be made into a pie, as for **All-Chicken Pie,*** or served stewed. Cook 1 to 1½ hours, depending upon the maturity of the rabbit.

PHEASANT

Young pheasant may be grilled. Split it down the back, truss it open, brush it all over with melted butter and either grill it outdoors or broil it. If the last big wing feather is pointed, the bird is young enough to grill.

On an old pheasant, the last big wing feather is rounded. In this case, it should be simmered gently for a while in salted water to cover. Remove from the water when partly done, dot with butter and grill or broil.

To roast pheasant, tie a piece of fat bacon on its breast and roast it in a moderate, 350° F. oven 1 to 1½ hours, or until tender. Baste frequently.

WILD DUCK

Clean canvasback, red-head, or other ducks of similar size, and split them down the back. Rub lightly with salt and pepper. Brush with melted butter and roast in a hot, 450° to 500° F. oven 12 to 15 minutes, depending upon the size. The duck should be served rare but not raw. When cooked to the correct stage, the meat will be red but not purple when cut, and blood will not follow the knife. Allow 18 to 25 minutes if the duck is liked medium, or 35 to 45 minutes if it is preferred well done.

If the game flavor is not liked, place the duck on a rack in a kettle, add boiling water to cover, then add **1 onion** and **2 branches celery** to the water. Partly cover the kettle with a lid and simmer the duck 10 to 15 minutes before roasting.

Wild Rice* is good served with wild duck.

If cooking mallards, allow a little more time than for cooking other ducks.

ROAST QUAIL

Clean, pluck, singe and draw quail. Wipe them inside with a cloth wrung out in hot water. Roast in a moderate,

350° F. oven 8 to 15 minutes, basting with butter. Serve with currant jelly.

Quail may be broiled as for **Perfection Broiled Chicken.*** Allow approximately 15 to 30 minutes, depending on the size.

SQUIRREL

Prepare squirrel as for **Rabbit.***

POSSUM AND SWEET POTATOES

Skin possum, remove the musk glands from small of its back and beneath its front legs, slit down the breast and draw it. Scald it in boiling water and scrape it clean. Rub the inside with **salt.** Stick an **onion** all over with **cloves** and place it and a **bay leaf** inside the possum. Roast in a moderate, 350° F. oven, 20 to 35 minutes per pound, turning and basting as for chicken. Boil until almost tender **1 medium sweet potato** for each person to be served. Peel the potatoes and place them around the possum the last half-hour of roasting.

VENISON OR MOOSE

Steaks, loin cutlets, and chops are cut 1½ inch thick, brushed with melted butter or oil and broiled or grilled. See the directions for **Broiling.*** Increase the length of broiling time. Put on the platter and top each piece with a pat of butter. Roast leg of venison on a rack in an open pan, placing bacon strips all over the top. Roast in a moderate, 350° F. oven 25 to 30 minutes per pound.

To be perfectly sure that venison or moose will be tender, braise it. Brown steaks or roasts in a small amount of fat. Add a small amount of liquid, cover the vessel, and simmer on top of the stove or in a moderate, 350° F. oven until tender.

Currant jelly is a good accompaniment to venison or moose.

MEAT AND VEGETABLE SAUCES

GRAVY

To make gravy, pour the drippings out of the pan after meat is cooked and allow the fat to rise to the top. Skim off the fat. Measure the liquid, strain it if necessary, and for each cup of liquid blend **1½ to 2 tablespoons flour** with an equal quantity of **skimmed fat.** Add the liquid gradually, stirring constantly. Cook until thickened. Smooth out any lumps with an egg beater. Season to taste with **salt** and **pepper.** Add chopped herbs or cooked mushrooms if desired. Serve piping hot.

CREAM SAUCE OR WHITE SAUCE

	Tablespoons		Tablespoons		Cup		Teaspoon	
Thin	1	Fat	1	Flour	1	Liquid	¼	Salt
Medium	2	"	2	"	1	"	¼	"
Thick	2	"	2	"	½	"	¼	"

Melt butter or other fat. Blend in the flour. Add the warm liquid gradually, stirring constantly, until the sauce comes to a boil. Milk, cream, stock, vegetable water, gravy, or a combination of these may be used to make up the cup of liquid. Makes 1 cup sauce.

A thin sauce is used for soup or gravy.

A medium sauce is used for creamed meat or vegetables.

A thick sauce is used for croquettes, souffles, or cooked mayonnaise.

A quick substitute for stock is **2 bouillon cubes** dissolved in **1 cup water.**

CELERY SAUCE

Pour over **1 cup diced celery** just enough boiling salted water to cover. Boil until the celery is tender. Drain, reserving the liquid. Make **medium Cream Sauce,*** using the celery water as part of the liquid. Add **1 teaspoon onion juice** and the cooked celery.

EGG SAUCE

Make **1 cup medium Cream Sauce.*** Add **1 hard-cooked egg*** which has been chopped fine.

CROOKED ELM FARM GIBLET SAUCE

Cut the green gall-bladder out of the liver of a fowl, being careful not to break the sac. Remove the fat from the gizzard, cut through the lean and discard the inside sac. Slit the heart open and remove blood vessels and clots. Wash the giblet and heart in cold water and place them in a kettle with the neck. The feet may be used if desired. To prepare them, cut off the nails and pour boiling water over the feet. Let stand in the water for a few minutes or until the thin outer skin may be pulled off. Remove and discard the skin, add the feet to the kettle, and add cold water to cover. Add onion, celery, parsley, carrot, any or all, in any amount or proportion. Partly cover the kettle with a lid and simmer until the giblet is tender, 1 to 1½ hours. Strain the broth. Add an equal amount of milk or cream and make **medium Cream Sauce.*** Chop and add the giblet, heart, and neck meat.

HORSERADISH SAUCE

Wash and scrape horseradish root. Cut out any discolored portions. Grate the root and mix **½ cup grated horseradish** with **¼ teaspoon pepper, ¼ teaspoon salt,**

¼ teaspoon sugar and **vinegar** to cover it (about 5 tablespoons). Add more seasoning to taste. Seal tightly and keep cool. Use on corned beef, salt pork, baked beans, etc.

MUSHROOM SAUCE

Cook **1 cup sliced mushrooms.** Add with their juice to **1 cup medium Cream Sauce.***

RAISIN CIDER SAUCE

Place in the top of a double boiler **1 cup cider, ¼ cup brown sugar** which has been packed firmly in the cup, **⅛ teaspoon salt,** and **½ cup seedless raisins.** Scald. Make a smooth paste with **1½ tablespoons cornstarch** and **2 or 3 tablespoons water.** Add to the cider mixture and stir until smooth. Add **8 whole cloves** and **1 stick cinnamon** which have been tied in cheesecloth. Cook covered over hot water for 15 to 20 minutes or until there is no taste of raw starch. Stir occasionally. Serve hot with ham. Makes 1½ cups.

OSCEOLA FARM TOMATO SAUCE

Cook for 15 minutes **2 cups tomatoes, 1 sprig parsley, 2 branches celery,** chopped, and **1 carrot,** diced. Strain. Melt **3 tablespoons fat.** Grate **½ small onion** and simmer in the fat for 5 minutes. Blend in **3 tablespoons flour.** Add the strained liquid gradually, stirring constantly. Cook the sauce until the boiling point is reached. Season with about **¼ teaspoon salt, ⅛ teaspoon pepper** and **¼ teaspoon sugar.**

CORN MEAL DUMPLINGS

Sift, then measure **½ cup flour.** Resift with **1 teaspoon baking powder, ½ teaspoon salt** and **½ cup corn meal.** Beat **1 egg.** Beat in **¼ cup milk.** Add to the dry ingredients gradually, stirring only until smooth. When the mixture can be dropped from a spoon without sticking to it, test it in boiling liquid. If the dumplings will not hold together, add more flour. Add only small amounts of flour at a time as too much of it will make the dumplings heavy.

These dumplings are planned to be used with stew, and should be cooked in the stew itself. Be sure to drop the dumplings directly onto pieces of meat or other solid matter. If there is too much liquid in the stew pan, remove some of it. Do not remove the cover of the pot while the dumplings are cooking. Steam for 15 minutes. If the dumplings are not to be served immediately, prick them to let the steam escape, or they will become soggy. Serves 6 to 8.

DUMPLINGS FOR STEW

Sift, then measure **1 cup flour.** Resift with **¼ teaspoon salt** and **1½ teaspoons baking powder.** Add **2 tablespoons melted shortening** to **½ cup milk.** Stir enough liquid into the dumplings to make a soft dough. Continue as above. Cook 12 minutes. Serves 6 to 8.

3

POULTRY

All poultry should be cooked at moderate heat. The cooking method is varied according to the age and fatness of the bird. Broil, fry, or open-pan roast young, tender, well-fatted birds. Braise lean young birds or full-grown birds too old for roasting but not old enough to be in the stewing class. Long, slow cooking in water or steam is the best method to use for very old birds.

Before cooking a bird, see that it is drawn properly and well groomed. Cut off the head and feet. Remove the pin feathers with a strawberry huller or a tweezers. Hold the bird over a flame to singe off the hair or down. Wash the bird thoroughly with a wet cloth and corn meal or use a little mild soap. Cut out the oil sac on top of the tail. Remove the windpipe and crop and cut the neck off short. Be sure that all the viscera on the inside of the bird are removed. Wash the bird with cold water and dry it thoroughly inside and out.

For each person to be served, allow ¾ to 1 pound dressed weight of turkey; about 1 pound dressed weight of chicken or guinea; and 1½ pounds dressed weight of fat duck or goose. Dressed weight is the weight of a bird which has been picked but not drawn and on which the head and feet still remain. The drawn weight of a bird is about one-fifth less than the dressed weight.

Poultry is extremely perishable. It should be kept cold when raw, and chilled quickly after cooking unless it is to be eaten at once.

ROASTED TURKEYS, DUCKS, GEESE, GUINEAS, AND CHICKENS

To prepare poultry for roasting, sprinkle the inside lightly with salt. Fill the body cavity loosely with stuffing, allowing room for it to expand. If the stuffing is hot when inserted, the cooking process will be speeded up somewhat. Use warm stuffing only if the bird is to be cooked immediately. To hold the stuffing in at the tail, slip the heel of a loaf of bread or any large piece of crust into the opening.

Stuff the loose skin at the base of the neck. Fold the neck skin toward the back and fasten with a skewer, poultry pins, or a few stitches. Fold the wing tips back on the wings. Do not tie string across the breast. Rub a stuffed and trussed chicken, turkey, or guinea all over with butter or other fat. Any bird may be dusted lightly with flour. A lean bird is improved if several strips of salt pork or bacon are laid over it.

Place poultry on a rack in a shallow pan; do not cover and do not add any liquid.

Baste turkeys, chickens, and guineas with melted fat or pan drippings when turning.

Ducks and geese do not have to have any fat added, nor do they have to be basted. If they are very fat, prick the skin during roasting to let some of the fat out. Ducks, geese, and chickens are started breast down in the roasting pan and turned alternately from breast down to breast up. Start a turkey or guinea on one side of its breast, turn in order from one side to the other side, then turn breast up and repeat. A chicken may be started on the side of its breast and turned as for turkeys and guineas if its shape makes this method more practical. Turn birds weighing under 12 pounds every 30 to 45 minutes. Turn birds weighing 12 to 20 pounds every hour. Turn very large birds every 1½ to 2 hours. In order not to break the skin of a bird, turn it with cloth-protected hands rather than with a fork.

Roast until the flesh is slightly shrunken underneath the skin and the bird gives or bends slightly when picked up by the ends. The joints will wiggle easily when it has finished cooking, and the breast and thigh will not show pink juice when carefully speared with a skewer or ice pick.

The roasting times given below are average. Some birds may cook in less time and some in more.

TIMETABLE FOR ROASTING POULTRY*

Fowl	Pounds	Temperature °F.	Hours
Chicken	4–5	350	1½–2
Duck	5–6	350	2–2½
Goose	10–12	325	3–4
Guinea	2–2½	350	1½
Turkey	6–9	325	2½–3
"	10–13	300	3½–4½
"	14–17	275	5–6
"	18–23	250–275	6½–7½
"	24–30	250	8–9

* All weights given are for dressed birds.

Make **Gravy.*** Chop and add the **giblets** which have been simmered in salted water to cover or which have been cooked with the neck, heart, and feet as for **Crooked Elm Farm Giblet Sauce.***

STUFFINGS

Stuff poultry lightly, rather than packing the stuffing in. Soft crumbs are used in stuffings. To make them, use

2- to 3-day-old bread. Cut the loaves in half and pull the bread out with a fork, leaving the crust. With fingertips pull the pieces of bread apart until the crumbs are fine and even in size. The crumbs may be prepared in advance and kept covered in a cold place until ready for use.

Any extra stuffing may be baked outside the bird, or the receipt may be doubled and the remainder of the stuffing baked separately.

Eggs may be added to stuffing. They are beaten, then mixed with the stuffing. Use 1 egg for 2 to 6 cups crumbs. If the stuffing is to be baked outside the bird, add the eggs and moisten it with stock. Pile lightly into large, or individual greased baking dishes, and bake with the bird. The stuffing will be light, puffy, and beautifully browned on top.

It is not necessary to stuff a bird.

Any of the stuffings may be used for other birds, or other stuffings may be substituted.

CORN BREAD STUFFING FOR A 4- TO 5-POUND CHICKEN

Melt **6 tablespoons fat.** Cook in the fat for 5 minutes **¾ cup diced celery, ¼ cup chopped parsley,** and **1 small chopped onion.** Beat **1 egg.** Mix it with **4 cups soft corn bread crumbs.** Add the fat, the cooked vegetables, **¼ teaspoon thyme, ¾ teaspoon salt,** and **⅛ teaspoon pepper,** and mix well.

CELERY STUFFING FOR A 10- TO 12-POUND GOOSE

Cook for 5 minutes **1 cup chopped parsley, 1 cup chopped onion,** and **¼ cup diced green pepper** in **½ cup fat.** Add to **8 cups soft bread crumbs.** Add **4 cups diced celery** (leaves and branches), **1 teaspoon celery seed, ½ teaspoon savory seasoning,** about **1 teaspoon salt,** and **¼ teaspoon pepper.** Mix well but lightly.

SALT PORK STUFFING FOR TWO 2-POUND GUINEAS

Wash the loose salt from 1/4 **pound mild salt pork** which is fairly lean. Dice it and fry it until it is crisp. Remove the crisp pieces of fat and meat (cracklings), and add to **4 cups soft bread crumbs.** Cook **1 cup chopped celery, 1 cup chopped parsley,** and **1 small chopped onion** for 5 minutes in the pan drippings. Add to the crumb mixture. Season with about 1/8 **teaspoon salt** and 1/8 **teaspoon pepper.** Mix well but lightly.

WILD RICE STUFFING FOR A 3½-POUND DUCK

Cook **1 cup wild rice*** until nearly tender, 20 to 30 minutes. Cook for 5 minutes **3 tablespoons chopped onion** and **2 tablespoons chopped green pepper** in **3 tablespoons fat.** Add to the drained rice.

OYSTER STUFFING FOR A 10- TO 12-POUND TURKEY

Let **1½ pints oysters** slip through the fingers and remove any bits of shell. Heat the oysters in their liquid for a few minutes. Drain. Cook **2 tablespoons chopped parsley** and **1 tablespoon chopped onion** in **¾ cup fat** for 5 minutes. Add the vegetables, the fat, and the oysters to **8½ cups soft bread crumbs.** Add **½ teaspoon savory seasoning, ¼ teaspoon celery seed,** about **1½ teaspoons salt,** and **⅛ teaspoon cayenne pepper.**

SAUSAGE STUFFING FOR A 12- TO 15-POUND TURKEY

Cook **3 tablespoons chopped onion, 1½ cups diced celery,** and **3 tablespoons chopped parsley** in **6 tablespoons fat** for 5 minutes. Remove the vegetables and add **1 pound sausage meat.** Cook for 5 minutes. Add with the vegetables to **6 to 8 cups soft bread crumbs.** Season with **¼ to 1 teaspoon sage** or **1 to 2 teaspoons savory seasoning, 1 to 2 teaspoons salt,** and **¼ teaspoon pepper.**

DRIED CORN STUFFING FOR A 10- TO 12-POUND TURKEY

Cook **1 small chopped onion** and **4 tablespoons chopped green pepper** in **6 tablespoons fat** for 5 minutes. Add to **4 cups cracker crumbs** (25 to 30 crackers crumbled coarsely). Add **2½ cups cooked dried corn** or well-drained whole kernel canned corn. Beat **1 egg.** Beat in slowly **⅔ cup cream,** scalded. Add to the crumb mixture with **1 teaspoon celery salt, ½ teaspoon savory seasoning,** and about **½ teaspoon salt** and **⅛ teaspoon pepper.**

PERFECTION BROILED CHICKEN

Clean **2 plump young chickens** weighing 2½ pounds or less, dressed. Cut them in half by splitting down the back and the breastbone. Break the joints and remove the wing tips. Wipe the chickens as dry as possible. Brush them generously with **melted butter.** Sprinkle them with **salt** and **pepper.** Place skin side down on a rack in a pan. Heat the oven to moderate, 350° F. and place the chickens 3½ to 4 inches away from the flame. Cook 35 to 45 minutes, until tender and nicely browned, turning and basting frequently with melted butter. Pour the pan drippings over the cooked chickens. Serves 4.

BROILED SQUAB, GUINEA, DUCKLING

Broil as above.

JASPER COUNTY BATTER-FRIED CHICKEN

First dress and clean a **2½- to 3½-pound chicken.** Cut the chicken in pieces for serving. Sift, then measure **1 cup flour.** Mix with **½ teaspoon salt.** Beat **1 egg** well. Beat in **¾ cup milk.** Add to the dry ingredients gradually, stirring until smooth. Heat enough fat in a deep kettle to cover the chicken. The fat should be hot enough to brown an inch cube of bread in 40 seconds, 350° F. Fry the chicken at 300° to 325° F. (the temperature to which the fat will drop when the chicken is put in). Do not overcrowd the kettle. A quarter of a 2½-pound dressed chicken will take 10 to 15 minutes to fry. Drain the cooked chicken on heavy unglazed paper and keep it hot until it is ready to be served.

The chicken may be browned lightly in the fat, drained and baked in a very moderate, 325° F. oven 20 to 30 minutes or until tender.

If there is any batter remaining after the chicken has been fried, drop it into the hot fat and fry until it is crisp and brown. Serves 4.

FRIED CHICKEN MARYLAND

Clean **1 plump, young chicken** weighing between 2½ and 3½ pounds dressed. Cut it in pieces for serving. Dry each piece thoroughly, then roll in **½ cup flour** which has been seasoned with **¼ teaspoon salt** and **⅛ teaspoon pepper.** Dip into **1 egg** which has been beaten lightly with **2 tablespoons water.** Roll in a mixture made by combining **¾ cup flour** and **¾ cup corn meal.** Brown the pieces in **½ cup hot salt pork drippings.** Remove them to the baking pan and finish cooking in a very moderate, 325° F. oven until tender, about 1 hour. Make **Gravy*** from the pan drippings. Serves 4.

SETTING HEN FARM CHICKEN IN CREAM

Prepare and split **2 young chickens** as for **Perfection Broiled Chicken***, then quarter them. Dry the quarters and dip them in **1 cup flour** which has been seasoned with **½ teaspoon salt** and **⅛ teaspoon pepper.** Cook **1 small diced onion** and **2 sprigs of parsley** cut fine in **3 tablespoons fat** for 5 minutes. Remove the vegetables and brown the chicken in the fat. Place in a pan with the vegetables and add **cream** to the pan to a depth of ¼ inch. Cover the pan and roast the chicken in a very moderate, 325° F. oven 40 to 60 minutes, or until tender. Remove the liquid in the pan and make **Gravy.*** Meanwhile, place the chicken under the flame, skin side up, to become golden brown. Serves 4.

HUNTINGTON COUNTY CREAMED CHICKEN CASSEROLE

Clean and draw a **4- to 5-pound chicken.** Place it on a rack in a kettle. Add hot water to half fill the kettle. Add to the water the **neck, giblet,** and **heart** of the chicken, **1 sliced carrot, 1 medium onion, 2 branches celery, 1 sprig parsley, ½ teaspoon salt,** and **3 or 4 peppercorns.** Partly cover the kettle with a lid and simmer until the bird is tender, 3 to 4 hours, turning it occasionally so that it cooks evenly throughout. If possible, allow the chicken to stand in the broth to cool, breast down. Let cool in a cold place, as broth spoils rapidly. Remove the skin and pick the meat from the bones, cutting it into chunks. Prepare a cream sauce, using **5 tablespoons fat** skimmed from the broth. Cook **2 diced green peppers** in the fat for 5 minutes. Blend in **½ cup plus 2 tablespoons flour.** Add gradually, stirring constantly, **2 cups milk, 2 cups cream,** and **1 cup strained chicken broth,** all of which have been heated. Cook, stirring until the sauce reaches the boiling point. Grease a large casserole or a small roaster. Put in half the chicken. Add **3 hard-cooked eggs,** sliced, and **1 pint cooked mushrooms.** Add half the sauce, the remaining chicken, and the rest of the sauce. Top with **Buttered Bread Crumbs.*** The crumbs may be mixed with fat skimmed from the broth. Bake in a moderate, 350° F. oven 40 to 60 minutes or until the top is nicely browned. Serves 10 to 12.

TWO HILLS PLANTATION CHICKEN PILAU

Disjoint and cook a **4- to 5-pound chicken** as above, omitting the vegetables. When the chicken is tender, add **1 cup rice** which has been washed and picked over. Cook 30 to 40 minutes longer, or until the rice is tender and the mixture is thick. Serves 6 to 8.

BROWNED-IN-BUTTER CHICKEN

Cook **old chicken** as for **Huntington County Creamed Chicken Casserole.*** When tender, drain, disjoint, and fry slowly in **butter** until golden brown. Use the stock to make **Gravy.***

ALL-CHICKEN PIE

Disjoint a **4- to 5-pound chicken** and cook it as for **Huntington County Creamed Chicken Casserole.*** Skim off the fat if the stock is very greasy. Make a sauce by diluting **5 tablespoons flour** with **¼ cup strained stock.** Cook until thick. Blend in slowly **1¼ cup stock** and **1 cup cream,** stirring constantly to avoid lumps. Cook, stirring, until the sauce reaches the boiling point. Season to taste with about **½ teaspoon salt** and **¼ teaspoon pepper.** Place the chicken in a baking dish, discarding the breastbone and cutting the white meat into pieces suitable for serving. Use the two pieces of back in the center to support the crust. Add the sauce. Make one-half the recipe for **Old Farm Rich Shortcake,*** roll it ⅓ inch thick, and gash it 3 or 4 times. Lay the crust on the dish, pressing it against the sides. Bake in a hot, 425° F. oven 12 to 15 minutes, or until nicely browned. Serves 6.

CHICKEN POT PIE

Prepare as above, adding **6 small whole carrots, 8 small potatoes,** and **1 cup peas,** all of which have been cooked.

LADIES AID CHICKEN KING

Stew a **4- to 5-pound chicken** as for **Huntington County Creamed Chicken Casserole.*** Skim **2 tablespoons fat** from the broth. Dice **1 medium green pepper** and cook it in the fat for 5 minutes. Blend in **¼ cup flour.** Add gradually **2 cups cream** and **1 cup milk.** Stir constantly until the boiling point is reached. Add the chicken, which has been skinned and cut in chunks. Cream **4 tablespoons butter.** Add **3 egg yolks** one at a time and beat well. Beat a portion of the sauce into the eggs, and add, stirring constantly, to the main mixture. Add **1 cup peas,** cooked or canned, **1 small onion,** grated, **1½ tablespoon lemon juice, 1 cup cooked mushrooms, ½ cup diced pimiento,** cooked or canned, **½ teaspoon salt,** and **¼ teaspoon paprika.** Serve on waffles, biscuits, rice, etc. Serves 6 to 8.

CHICKEN FRICASSEE WITH DUMPLINGS

Cut a **4- to 5-pound fowl** into pieces for serving. Cook as for **Huntington County Creamed Chicken Casserole.*** Remove the fowl to a hot dish and keep it warm. Measure the broth. There should be 3 to 4 cups of it in the kettle. Make **Gravy,*** allowing **2 tablespoons skimmed fat** and **2 tablespoons flour** for each cup of strained broth. When the gravy boils, drop the dumplings in by spoonfuls. Cover the kettle tightly and cook for 15 minutes. When the dumplings have finished cooking, remove them to the dish in which the chicken is being kept warm. Beat **1 egg yolk.** Beat in, one at a time, several spoonfuls of the hot gravy. Return to the main mixture and cook for a few minutes over a low fire, stirring constantly. Be careful not to overcook the mixture or the egg will separate. Add to the chicken and dumplings. Serves 6.

Dumplings: Sift, then measure **¾ cup flour.** Resift with **2½ teaspoons baking powder** and **½ teaspoon salt.** Beat **1 egg** well. Beat in **⅓ cup milk.** Add to the dry ingredients gradually, only stirring until smooth. Continue as for **Corn Meal Dumplings.***

WILLOW FARM CHICKEN LOAF

Prepare a **4- to 5-pound chicken** as for **Huntington County Creamed Chicken Casserole,*** or use 3 to 4 cups leftover chicken. Make a sauce by blending **4 tablespoons fat** skimmed from the broth with **½ cup flour** and adding gradually **1 cup strained chicken broth** and **½ cup milk.** Stir constantly until the boiling point is reached. Cook **2 tablespoons diced onion** and **2 tablespoons diced green pepper** in **1 tablespoon fat** from the broth for 5 minutes. Add to the sauce. Add **3 cups soft bread crumbs** and the chopped, skinned chicken. Season with about **½ teaspoon salt.** Turn the mixture into a greased loaf pan, 9 x 5 x 3 inches, and bake in a moderate, 350° F. oven 30 to 45 minutes, or until the loaf is nicely browned. Serve with **Mushroom Sauce.*** Serves 6.

BAKED CHICKEN CROQUETTES

Prepare a **4- to 5-pound chicken** as for **Huntington County Creamed Chicken Casserole,*** or use leftover chicken. Make a thick sauce by blending **4 tablespoons fat** skimmed from the broth with **5 tablespoons flour** and adding gradually **1 cup milk** and **½ cup strained broth.** Stir constantly until the mixture reaches the boiling point. Let stand until cold. Add 3 to 4 cups chicken which has been skinned and ground or chopped fine, **1 teaspoon chopped onion, 1 tablespoon chopped parsley** or other herb, and **½ teaspoon salt.** Add enough **dry bread crumbs** to make a mixture stiff enough to bake. Mold into flat cakes. (If preferred, the mixture may be shaped into croquettes, breaded and fried in deep fat, hot enough to brown an inch cube of bread in 40 seconds, 350° F.) Dip in additional bread crumbs, then in **1 egg** beaten lightly with **1 tablespoon water,** then in crumbs again. Allow to stand in a cold place for an hour or more, to dry the coating. Place on a greased sheet and bake in a hot, 400° F. oven until brown on the bottom. Turn and brown the other side. Serves 6.

GRAND COUNTY CHICKEN CUSTARD

Make **medium Cream Sauce*** with **1½ cups top milk** and **½ cup strained chicken stock.** Beat **3 eggs** slightly and add to them a portion of the sauce, a tablespoon at a time, beating it in. Stir into the main mixture and add **2 tablespoons herbs,** cut fine, **1½ cups cooked, leftover chicken,** skinned and cut in dice, **¼ teaspoon salt,** and **⅛ teaspoon pepper.** Fill a greased casserole or greased individual custard cups ⅔ full. Set in a pan of hot water and bake in a very moderate, 325° F. oven 20 to 60 minutes, or until the tip of a paring knife thrust in the center will come out clean. Serves 4 to 6.

ST. LOUIS COUNTY BRUNSWICK STEW

Disjoint a **4-pound stewing chicken.** Dice **¼ pound bacon or salt pork.** Cook the chicken and the bacon or pork as for **Huntington County Creamed Chicken Casserole,*** omitting the vegetables. After 2 hours, add **2 cups corn,** green or canned, and **2 cups lima beans.** Continue cooking until the chicken is tender, 1 to 2 hours. Season to taste with about **½ teaspoon salt** and **¼ teaspoon pepper.** Thicken the stock as for **Gravy.*** Serves 6.

There are endless variations of Brunswick Stew. Half squirrel and half chicken may be used. Rabbit may be used. Two cups okra or 2 cups tomato, or half of each, may be added.

4

FISH

Fresh fish is firm and has bright, unsunken eyes. The body is not slimy and the fish has a fresh but characteristic odor. A fresh fish will sink in water.

Fish is sweetest in flavor immediately after it is caught, so it is wise to cook it as soon as possible after catching or buying it. Fish deteriorates rapidly. If it must be held over, pack it in ice, or keep it in the coldest part of the refrigerator. If kept in the refrigerator, be sure that it is covered tightly so the odor will not penetrate other foods. Fish should be served as soon as possible after it is cooked.

To clean a whole fish, place it on a large sheet of paper. Remove scales with a knife or fish scaler, starting at the tail and proceeding toward the head. To remove the fins, cut them off or pull them out. Cut through the skin on the abdomen and discard the entrails. Wipe the fish thoroughly inside and out with a cloth wrung out in cold water, removing any blood which adheres to the backbone.

Bone the fish if necessary. Use a sharp knife and make as clean a cut as possible. Begin at the tail, and run the knife under the flesh close to the backbone, following the entire length of the bone and removing half the flesh. Turn and bone the other side. Pick out any remaining bones with the fingers.

Fillets, steaks, or pan-dressed fish are fish which have been cleaned, skinned and boned, and are ready for cooking.

The skin may be removed from fat fish before frying,

if desired. Plunge the fish into boiling water and allow it to remain in the water for about ½ minute after the water resumes boiling. Remove from the water and skin the fish while hot.

Fish odor will not cling to the hands if they are chilled thoroughly in cold water before the fish is touched. When through handling the fish, wash the hands in hot water and salt. Rinse the salt off, then wash the hands with soap.

To remove the odor of fish from dishes, use hot water in which a strong solution of salt has been dissolved.

One-half pound chopped seafood equals approximately 1 cup. One-third pound boned fish makes approximately 1 serving. One-half pound fish with bone makes approximately 1 serving.

Fish is naturally tender, so it is not necessary to subject it to long cooking, but it should be served thoroughly cooked. If the thick part of the flesh along the center back separates into flakes easily when a fork is inserted, the fish has finished cooking.

Any fish is good when fried or broiled, but lean fish are best when boiled, steamed, or used in chowders. Fat fish are best when baked.

FAT FISH

Alewife
Barracuda
Bass (Black, Striped)
Blue Runner
Buffalo fish
Butterfish
Chub
Eel
Lake Trout
Mackerel (Boston, California, Spanish)
Pilchard (Sardine)
Pompano
Porgie (Scup)
Sea Herring
Salmon
Shad
Smelt
Sturgeon
Whitefish
Yellowtail

LEAN FISH

Bluefish
Blue Pike
Carp
Catfish
Cod
Crappie
Croaker (Hardhead)
Cusk
Flounder
Grouper
Haddock
Hake
Halibut (with fat trimmed out)
Kingfish
Mullet (Popeye)
Pike (Pickerel)
Red Drum (Redfish, Channel Bass)
Red Snapper
Sea Bass (Black fish)
Sheepshead (Gaspergou, River Drum)
Sole
Spot (Cape May Goodie)
Sucker
Sunfish
Yellow Pike
Swordfish
Weakfish (Gray Trout, Sea Trout)
White Bass
Whiting (Silver Hake)
Yellow Perch

All shellfish are lean.

Fish five-eighths of an inch thick are the best size for the amateur to cook, whether whole or cut in steaks or fillets.

Butter, lemon, crisp cucumbers, tiny red beets, parsley, and chives are soul-mates of fish and help to make the catch a thing of joy!

BOILED FISH

Fish is simmered in liquid to give it variety and extra flavor rather than to tenderize it. The fish is less likely to break if it is placed in an oiled wire basket, in an oiled perforated pan, or tied in cheesecloth before it is placed in the stock. It is better cooked in stock than in water. A well-flavored stock gives fish additional flavor and the stock may be used for making sauces, etc., for the fish.

FISH STOCK

Place in a kettle enough water to cover the fish. Add **3 tablespoons lemon juice or vinegar to each quart of water.** If available, add the discarded **head** and **bones** of the fish. (Be sure that they are perfectly clean, with no blood adhering to them.) Add **1 small onion,** chopped, **1 carrot,** sliced, **1 branch celery,** diced, **2 or 3 sprigs parsley,** and about **½ teaspoon salt for each quart of water.** More or less of each vegetable mentioned may be used, or other or additional vegetables or herbs may be substituted for those mentioned. Partly cover the kettle with a lid and simmer the stock for 20 minutes. Return the stock to the boiling point and add **2 pounds fillets or steaks, or 3 pounds whole fish.** Simmer the fish very gently approximately 8 to 12 minutes per pound, or until cooked. It may be necessary to place the kettle on an asbestos pad to keep the heat low enough only to poach the fish. Remove the fish to a warm platter. Boil the stock until it is reduced to a quantity anywhere from ½ to 1 cup. Strain and use as part of the sauce for the fish. The French term for the stock, Court-Bouillon, is in general use.

BAKED FISH

To bake, leave the skins of fat fish whole, but cut 3 or 4 deep gashes across lean fish to keep it from shrinking excessively. Fat fish require less care in baking than do lean fish. Remove the backbone from a cleaned, trimmed **4-pound fish,** but do not split it. The head and tail may be left on if desired. Dissolve **2 tablespoons salt** in each cup of cold water and allow the fish to stand in the solution for 5 minutes. Drain and brush the fish with melted fat or cooking oil. Place **2 strips bacon** in a greased baking pan. Stuff the fish lightly, tie it up with string to hold the stuffing in and lay the fish on the bacon. Place **2 strips bacon,** in addition, over the fish. Place the baking pan in the center of the oven. Bake in a very hot, 500° F. oven 10 minutes. Reduce the heat to hot, 400° F., and continue baking 8 to 10 minutes longer. Add 5 minutes cooking time for each additional pound of fish.

STUFFING FOR A 4-POUND FISH

Melt **6 tablespoons butter.** Cook **¼ cup diced onion** and **¾ cup finely diced celery** in the fat for 5 minutes. Add **¼ cup water** and cook gently until the vegetables are tender. Add **¾ teaspoon salt** and **¼ teaspoon pepper.** Mix **4 cups soft bread crumbs** with **2 teaspoons crushed, dried sage** (or other herb). Add to the other ingredients and mix well. Cook covered, 1 to 2 minutes.

BAKED SMALL FISH, FILLETS, OR STEAKS

Preheat the oven to very hot, 500° F. Mix **¼ teaspoon pepper** with **1 cup dry bread crumbs.** Cut the **fish** into serving pieces and dip them in a salt solution (2 tablespoons salt disolved in each cup of cold water). Drain the fish and cover with the peppered crumbs. Place on a well-greased baking pan. Sprinkle the fish with **cooking oil or melted butter** and with 2 tablespoons finely chopped onion, celery, or green pepper, if desired. Bake on the top rack of the oven 8 to 15 minutes, depending upon the thickness of the fish. Enough cream, milk, or stock may be poured in to cover just the bottom of the pan before the fish is baked, if desired. Baste with the liquid once or twice.

BROILING

Do not cut fish into serving pieces. Dip **2 pounds fish fillets or steaks or 3-pound whole fish** (split) in a salt solution. (2 tablespoons salt dissolved in each cup cold water.) Allow very thin fish to stand in the solution for about 1 minute. Fish ⅝ inch thick should stand 5 to 8 minutes. Preheat the broiler pan to very hot, 550° F. Oil it, brush the fish with melted **fat or oil,** and place it on the broiler pan. Broil the fish 2 inches away from the flame. If the skin has been left on the fish, place it skin side up. The skin will begin to bubble and become brown at the end of 5 minutes. Continue cooking until very dark brown bubbles cover the entire surface of the fish. Turn and cook the flesh side until brown, basting with **peppered butter** (¼ teaspoon pepper added to ¼ cup melted butter). Allow 6 to 12 minutes in all to broil the fish, being careful not to overcook it.

FRIED FISH

For frying, it is best to use steaks or fillets about ⅝ inch thick or small fish of equal thickness. For pan frying, heat **fat** slowly in a heavy skillet. Butter is the least satisfactory fat to use for frying fish because it smokes at relatively low temperatures. Vegetables fats smoke at an even higher temperature than do animal fats, so they are often preferred. Cut **fish** into pieces convenient for serving, dip the pieces in water, then roll them in the following mixture: Sift, then measure ½ **cup flour.** Resift with **1⅓ teaspoon salt** and ½ **cup fine yellow corn meal.** Place the fish in the pan as soon as the fat begins to smoke, and cook 3 minutes. Cover the pan, remove it from the fire, and allow the fish to cook in its own steam for about 2 minutes. Remove the cover, turn the fish carefully with a spatula, and cook uncovered over heat for 3 minutes more.

DEEP FAT FRYING

Prepare **fish** as above. Use a kettle which has a frying basket. Heat deep fat to 385° to 400° F. An inch cube of bread will brown in 20 to 25 seconds at this temperature. Place only 1 layer of fish in the frying basket at a time, and cook until it is an even golden brown, 4 to 8 minutes. Continue until all the fish has been fried. The fish may be fried without a basket. Do not overcrowd the kettle as the fish will rise to the surface when it has finished cooking. Fry only a few fish at a time, to prevent the temperature of the fat from becoming too low. **Osceola County Tomato Sauce*** is good with fried fish. The traditional accompaniment is potato chips.

YANKEE CHOWDER

Prepare **Fish Stock.*** Simmer 20 minutes, then bring it to the boiling point. Plunge **2-pound white-meated, lean, boned fish** into the boiling stock and allow it to remain in the stock for about ½ minute after boiling is resumed. Remove the fish and skin it while it is hot. Return the skin to the stock and boil rapidly until the stock is reduced to 1 cup. Strain it. Dice **⅔ cup fat salt pork.** Fry the pork in a heavy kettle. When the meat is golden brown, add **⅔ cup sliced onions** and cook for 5 minutes. Add **3 cups cubed or sliced potatoes** and the strained fish stock which has been seasoned with **1 teaspoon salt** and **¼ teaspoon pepper.** Cook until the potatoes are about half done, 8 to 10 minutes. Add the fish and cook until the potatoes are tender, about 15 to 30 minutes longer. Flake the fish coarsely and serve. Serves 4 to 6.

Chopped green peppers, diced celery, stewed tomatoes, etc., may be added with the potatoes, if desired.

MILK CHOWDER

When **Yankee Chowder,** above, has finished cooking, add **1 cup milk.** Heat, but do not boil. Crush a few **Boston chowder crackers** and add them to the chowder before serving. Serve with additional crackers.

WINDHAM COUNTY FISH PUDDING

Flake any leftover fish. Add **1 teaspoon lemon juice** to **1 cup flaked fish.** Make a thick **Cream Sauce*** with **3 tablespoons fat, 3 tablespoons flour, ½ cup Fish Stock,*** and **½ cup milk.** Beat **3 egg yolks** well. Beat the sauce in. Add

½ teaspoon salt. Mix with the fish. Fold in **3 egg whites** which have been beaten stiff but not dry. Turn into a baking dish. Set the dish in a pan of hot water and bake in a very moderate, 325° F. oven 45 to 60 minutes. If the pudding is to be turned out, grease the baking dish. Serve with **Osceola Farm Tomato Sauce or Stock Sauce for Fish.*** Serves 4 to 6.

TO FRESHEN SALT CODFISH

Freshen **boned salt fish** by cutting away any parts which seem inedible. Soak overnight in cold water to cover if the fish is to be boiled. If other methods are to be used and if the fish is very salty, soak for 24 hours, if necessary. Change the water 2 or 3 times, depending upon the saltiness of the fish. If too much salt has been soaked out, additional salt may be added to the fish during cooking. To freshen shredded codfish, place in a saucepan, cover with cold water, bring the water to the boiling point and drain. Repeat once or twice more, or until the fish is sufficiently freshened.

THURSTON COUNTY FRIED CODFISH BALLS

Freshen **1 pound salt codfish** as above. Cut in very small pieces with a scissors. Peel and quarter **2 pounds potatoes.** Cover fish and potatoes with boiling water and cook until the potatoes are tender, 15 to 30 minutes. Drain, then shake over a flame until dry. Add **2 tablespoons butter, ⅛ teaspoon pepper,** and **2 eggs** which have been beaten well. Mash and beat well. Fry spoonfuls in butter until nicely browned, or fry for 1 minute in deep fat which will brown an inch cube of bread in 1 minute, 360° to 370° F. Serves 4 to 6.

CODFISH WITH PARSNIPS

Peel and slice **2 pounds parsnips.** Freshen **2 cups salt codfish** as demonstrated two receipts above, then cut in pieces with a scissors. Place parsnips and fish in a kettle. Add boiling water to cover, and boil until the parsnips are tender, about 30 minutes. Drain, then shake over a flame until very dry. Add **2 tablespoons butter** and **1/8 teaspoon pepper.** Serve with **Egg Sauce,*** if desired. Serves 4 to 6.

CHESHIRE COUNTY DEVILED CRABMEAT

Rub the yolks of **4 hard-cooked eggs** to a paste. Make a **medium Cream Sauce,*** using 1/2 **cup milk** and 1/2 **cup cream.** Stir it into the egg yolks. Add **1 cup crabmeat,** cooked or canned, which has been picked over and flaked, about 1/2 **teaspoon salt,** and 1/8 **teaspoon pepper** to taste, and **1 tablespoon parsley or chives,** cut fine. Grease a casserole and cover bottom and sides with **bread crumbs.** Add half the crabmeat mixture. Cover with crumbs. Add the remainder of the crabmeat mixture and cover the top with buttered crumbs. About 1 cup crumbs will be needed in all. Bake in a moderate, 350° F. oven 30 to 40 minutes, or until the top is nicely browned. Serves 4.

FRIED FROGS' LEGS

Skin and clean **frogs' legs.** Bread as for **Bertha Lewis' Receipt for Breaded Veal Steaks and Potatoes,*** or dip in batter as for **Jasper County Batter-Fried Chicken.*** Pan fry or fry in deep fat until brown. Serve with **Salem County Lemon Butter*** or **Osceola Farm Tomato Sauce.***

NATRONA COUNTY OYSTER PIE

Pick over **1 pint oysters** by letting each one slip through the fingers and removing particles of shell. Melt **3 tablespoons butter.** Cook 1/2 **cup diced celery** and 1/2 **cup sliced mushrooms** in the butter 10 minutes. Blend **3 tablespoons flour** into the butter. Add **1 cup top milk** gradually, and stir constantly until the boiling point is reached. Add 1/2 **teaspoon salt,** 1/8 **teaspoon pepper,** and **1 teaspoon lemon juice.** Prepare the dough for **Riz Biscuits.*** Roll it 1/8 inch thick. Line the bottom and sides of a small greased casserole with it. Coat the dough with melted **butter.** Fill with the oyster mixture. Put a top crust on, gashing it 3 or 4 times. Press the edges of the dough firmly together, then press against the sides of the casserole. Bake in a hot, 450° F. oven 10 minutes. Reduce the heat to very moderate, 325° F., and bake 15 to 20 minutes longer, or until the crust is nicely browned. Serves 4.

MIZ JASON CHOATE'S RECEIPT FOR OYSTER SHORTCAKE

Cook **½ cup diced celery** in **4 tablespoons fat** for 5 minutes. Blend in **4 tablespoons flour.** Gradually stir in **1½ cups milk** and **½ cup cream.** Cook until the boiling point is reached, stirring constantly. Pick over **1 pint oysters** by letting each one slip through the fingers and removing particles of shell. Cook them gently in their own liquid until they are plump and the edges begin to curl. Strain and add the oysters to the sauce.

Bake **Old Farm Rich Shortcake*** in a pie tin. Split and place the bottom half on a very hot plate. Add half the oysters and sauce. Cover with the top half of the shortcake and pour the rest of the oysters and the sauce over it. Sprinkle with **1 to 2 tablespoons finely cut parsley or chives.** Serve immediately. Serves 4.

Aunt Sleide says: "Miz Jason Choate is one of the best cooks in the county, but it's all wasted on her husband, who never knows what he's eating. Nor does he ever compliment her on anything she's cooked. One day she got good and mad and told him that the only time he opened his mouth at a meal was in order to put food in it and that she'd just as soon eat with the chickens 'cause at least they sounded pleased when she fed them. Jason didn't answer her, but when he got up from the table, he said, 'Cluck-cluck, Miz Choate.' And ever since then it's been, 'Cluck-cluck, Miz Choate,' at the end of every meal."

FISH SAUCES

SALEM COUNTY LEMON BUTTER

After pan-frying fish, remove it and add to the pan **1 to 2 tablespoons butter** and **½ tablespoon lemon juice** for each pound of fish. Heat until it sizzles, then pour it over the fish. Cut **1 tablespoon chives or parsley** over the fish.

STOCK SAUCE FOR FISH

Reduce **fish stock*** to ½ cup. Combine with **½ cup milk or cream** and use in **medium Cream Sauce.*** Chopped chives, parsley, olives, etc., may be added to the sauce. Serve hot with fish.

MENDOCINO COUNTY FISH MAYONNAISE

Beat **2 egg yolks** until thick. Add **2 tablespoons oil** in four additions, beating constantly. Add **1 tablespoon lemon juice** and **¼ cup hot water** gradually, stirring them in. Add **1 teaspoon dry mustard, ¼ teaspoon sugar, ¼ teaspoon salt,** and **⅛ teaspoon pepper.** Cook over hot water, stirring constantly, until thickened. Add **1 teaspoon parsley,** or other herb, cut fine. Serve hot with fish cooked in stock.

TARTAR SAUCE

Add the following to **1 cup mayonnaise: 1 tablespoon onion,** minced fine, **1 tablespoon parsley,** cut fine, **2 tablespoons sweet or sour pickles,** diced, **2 tablespoons green pepper,** diced, **1 tablespoon lemon juice,** and **1 teaspoon grated horseradish.** Mix and serve with fish.

5

VEGETABLES, CHEESE, EGGS AND CEREALS

VEGETABLES

All vegetables should be washed thoroughly before they are cooked. Remove waste portions, then wash vegetables rapidly, rather than allowing them to soak in water. Leafy vegetables are best washed if placed in a pan of cold water, then lifted out. Pouring the water off would return the grit and sand to the vegetables. As many waters as necessary are used to free the vegetables from all dirt. A small brush will aid in cleaning other than leafy vegetables.

Vegetables are cooked as rapidly as possible. Large vegetables, such as cabbage, cauliflower, and onions, require a quantity of water when cooked whole, but most are best cooked in very little water. Add one to two teaspoons salt to each quart of water. Bring the water to a boil and add the vegetables slowly so the water does not stop boiling. Cover the container, and when the water is boiling rapidly again, reduce the heat and finish cooking in gently boiling water. The vegetables noted above are cooked uncovered throughout in rapidly boiling water. Leafy green vegetables, such as spinach, are another exception. They are cooked in just the water which clings to them and kept covered only until they have wilted. The spoon is the enemy of food value, so don't stir vegetables while they are cooking.

Vegetables should be boiled until they are just tender,

so that some of their crispness is retained. Older vegetables require longer cooking than young vegetables, so the time stated in the recipes should be used only as a guide to the correct cooking period. Soda should never be added to the water in which vegetables are cooked.

The water in which vegetables are cooked should be retained for use in soups, sauces, or gravies.

Additional salt to taste, pepper and melted fat may be added to the cooked vegetables. Herbs may be added. For ease in cutting herbs, use a scissors. Buttered crumbs are a good addition. Sauces may be added to cooked vegetables.

Canned vegetables may be substituted for cooked vegetables in made dishes. When serving canned vegetables plain, drain off the liquid in the can and boil it rapidly until it is reduced to half. Add the canned vegetables and cook only until heated. Serve them with the liquid. Season with salt and pepper to taste. Add butter, herbs, sauces, crumbs, etc.

DRIED VEGETABLES

Soak dried vegetables (lima, navy, kidney beans, etc.) in cold water overnight. Add more water to cover and simmer until tender, 1 to 2 hours.

If the vegetables are to be baked, prepare as above but cook only until the skins burst. Place a few on a spoon and blow on them. If the skins burst, they have been cooked sufficiently.

ASPARAGUS WITH SOUR SAUCE

Remove the tough woody portion from **2 pounds asparagus.** Scrape the scales off with a knife and tie the asparagus into 2 or 3 bunches. Stand upright with the tips up in boiling salted water which reaches halfway up the stalk. Boil for 10 to 15 minutes. Immerse the entire stalk and cook 5 or 10 minutes more or until tender. Drain and add **Sour Sauce.*** Serves 6.

SWIFTWATER FARM CREAMED ASPARAGUS

Prepare and cook **asparagus,** as above. Drain and cover with **medium Cream Sauce,*** which may be made with half vegetable water and half milk or cream.

A MESS OF BEANS

Place in a saucepan **½ pound salt pork** which has been cut in small cubes. Cover with cold water. Bring to a boil and simmer covered, 30 to 45 minutes. Add **1 pound snap beans** from which the ends and strings have been removed. Add more water to cover the beans and cook until the beans and meat are tender, 20 to 30 minutes. Drain. Serves 4.

WAX BEANS IN SOUR CREAM

Cut the ends from **1 pound wax beans,** but leave them whole. Place in a saucepan and add boiling water to cover. Boil until the beans are tender, 15 to 20 minutes. Drain, reserving the liquid in which they were cooked. Melt **1 tablespoon butter.** Blend in **1 tablespoon flour.** Stir in gradually the water in which the beans were boiled and cook, stirring constantly until the boiling point is reached. Add **2 tablespoons vinegar** and **about 2 teaspoons sugar, ½ teaspoon salt** and **¼ teaspoon pepper,** to taste. Add **1 cup sour cream** which has been warmed. Add the beans and let the mixture come to a boil. Beat **2 egg yolks.** Beat in a little of the hot liquid and stir into the main mixture. Serve warm or cold. Reheat over hot water if necessary. Serves 4 to 6.

FINNEY COUNTY BEETS IN SAUCE

Cook **5 large beets** 35 minutes to 2 hours. (Old beets take a long time to cook tender.) A quantity of boiling salted water will be required for old beets, boiling salted water to cover for young beets. Slip off the skins and dice the beets. Dice **3 strips bacon.** Fry until crisp. Add the diced beets and heat them. Blend **2 tablespoons vinegar** with **1 tablespoon flour.** Bring to a boil. Add **1 teaspoon sugar** and pour over the beets and bacon. Season to taste with about **1/4 teaspoon salt** and **1/8 teaspoon pepper.** Simmer for 5 minutes. Serves 4.

PICKLED BEETS ON GREENS

Cook **1 pound beets** as above. Peel, cube and keep warm. Melt **1 tablespoon fat.** Blend in **1 tablespoon flour.** Stir in gradually **1/4 cup cream.** Stir constantly and add **1/2 teaspoon salt, 1/8 teaspoon pepper,** and **2 tablespoons sugar.** Continue stirring and add **1/4 cup vinegar.** Stir until the boiling point is reached. Add the beets. Cook slowly until the beets are heated. Wash the **beet tops** and cook as for **Yuba County Sunny Spinach,*** until tender. Serve the beets on the greens. Serves 4.

CABBAGE CUSTARD

Shred **1 medium head of cabbage** and cook for 5 to 7 minutes or until just tender in very little boiling salted water. Drain well. Beat **2 eggs** slightly. Beat in **1 cup milk.** Add **1 tablespoon melted fat, 1 teaspoon sugar, 1/4 teaspoon salt,** and **1/8 teaspoon pepper.** Mix with the cabbage. Turn into a greased baking dish and dot the top with butter or other fat. Set the dish in a pan of hot water and bake in a very moderate, 325° F. oven 40 to 60 minutes or until the custard is firm.

PENNSYLVANIA DUTCH RED CABBAGE

Wash and shred fine **1 medium head of red cabbage.** Melt **2 tablespoons fat** in a spider. Dice and add **1 small onion.** Simmer the onion 5 minutes. Add the cabbage and **2 tart apples** which have been peeled, cored, and sliced thin.

Add **1/4 cup vinegar, 1/2 teaspoon salt,** and **1/8 teaspoon pepper.** Cover and simmer until the cabbage is tender, 20 to 40 minutes. Mix **1 tablespoon flour** with **1/4 cup brown sugar** which has been packed firmly in the cup. Stir into the cabbage and cook 5 minutes more or until the sauce has thickened slightly. Serves 4 to 6.

CARROTS AND ONIONS

Wash **carrots.** (It is necessary to scrape only old, blackened carrots.) Cut in quarters lengthwise. Place in a greased baking dish in alternate layers with an equal quantity of sliced **onions.** Season each layer with salt and pepper and dot with butter. Cover and bake in a moderate, 350° F. oven 40 to 60 minutes or until tender.

OLD FARM CARROTS WITH BACON

Dice **6 strips bacon** and cook until crisp. Remove the bacon and simmer in the fat for 5 minutes **2 medium onions** which have been diced. Return the bacon to the pan and add **12 carrots** cut in strips. Add **1/4 cup boiling water** and cook until the carrots are tender, 20 to 30 minutes. When they are tender, spoon out some of the liquid and mix it with **1 tablespoon flour, 1 teaspoon sugar, 1/4 teaspoon salt,** and **1/8 teaspoon pepper.** Stir into the main mixture and cook 5 minutes more. Add more salt and pepper if necessary. Serves 6 to 8.

SWEET CORN

Remove husks and silk from ears of corn. Place in boiling water to cover and cook until no juice comes out when a kernel is pricked, about 5 minutes. Drain and serve hot.

To remove whole kernels from the cob, thrust a skewer into the top of the ear. Stand the ear upright on a plate and with a sharp knife remove as much of the kernel as possible, being careful not to cut off any of the hull. Green corn may be stripped this way.

In made dishes where a creamy product is desired, or for creamed sweet corn, strip the corn by inserting a skewer, standing the ear of corn upright on a plate and with a sharp knife cutting off only the tips of the kernels. Scrape the ear with the sharp side of a table knife. Scrape again with the dull side of the knife to remove all the pulp. Green corn may be stripped this way.

One large ear of corn makes about ½ cup stripped corn.

AUTAUGA COUNTY BACON AND CORN FRY

Fry **8 strips of bacon.*** Drain off most of the fat and place in the pan **2 cups corn kernels** which have been cooked and stripped from the ears as above. Cook and stir until the corn crusts, about 5 minutes. Add **½ cup milk or cream, ¼ teaspoon salt,** and **⅛ teaspoon pepper** and let simmer 15 minutes. Serve with the bacon. Serves 4.

GOLDEN LEAF PLANTATION FRIED CORN

Simmer **2 cups cooked corn kernels** (see two recipes above), **4 tablespoons** diced **green pepper, 5 tablespoons diced onion,** and **4 tablespoons diced pimiento** for 5 minutes in **2 tablespoons fat.** Add **¼ cup cream, ¼ teaspoon salt,** and **⅛ teaspoon pepper** and simmer for 3 minutes more. Serves 4.

MAGNOLIA HOUSE CORN PUDDING

Beat **2 eggs** slightly. Beat in **2 cups rich milk.** Add **¼ cup sugar, ¼ cup dry bread crumbs, ½ teaspoon salt, ⅛ teaspoon pepper,** and **3 cups corn kernels** which have been cooked and stripped from the ear. Mix well and turn into a greased baking dish. Set in a pan of hot water and bake in a very moderate, 325° F. oven 40 to 60 minutes or until the tip of a paring knife inserted in the center will come out clean. Serves 4.

CORN SCRAMBLE

To **2 cups cooked corn kernels** add **2 tablespoons cream, ¼ teaspoon salt, 1 teaspoon sugar,** and **1 beaten egg.** Scramble over low heat in **2 tablespoons bacon or other fat** until nicely browned, stirring the mixture and scraping it up from the bottom as it cooks. Serves 2 or 3.

POLLY LYONS' RECEIPT FOR SUCCOTASH

Cook **1 pint lima beans, 1 pound string beans,** and **3 large peeled tomatoes** until tender in a small amount of boiling salted water. Ten minutes before serving, add the cut kernels* from **4 medium ears of corn** and continue cooking. Melt **2 tablespoons butter** in a separate pan. Blend in **2 tablespoons flour.** Add **½ cup warm sour cream** gradually and stir until it thickens. Add to the vegetables with **2 teaspoons sugar** and cook 5 minutes more. Season to taste with about **½ teaspoon salt,** and **⅛ teaspoon pepper.** Serves 8 to 10.

Aunt Sleide says: "Polly Lyons was raised by six aunts. They were all good cooks, but none of them could leave a receipt alone; they were always adding something. Polly's succotash even outdoes the aunts'."

FARMHOUSE SCALLOP

Peel an **eggplant** and cook it in boiling salted water to cover until tender, 15 to 20 minutes. Dice and place a layer in a greased baking dish. Cover with diced **onions,** put in a layer of **sliced tomatoes** and sprinkle with **bread crumbs.** Dot with **butter.** Repeat, seasoning each layer with **salt** and **pepper.** Top with bread crumbs. Dot with butter and bake in a moderate, 350° F. oven until the top is nicely browned and the vegetables are tender, 30 to 45 minutes. Serves 6.

MUSHROOMS

Wash mushrooms carefully in order not to break them. Scrape with a knife, if necessary, to remove stubborn dirt. Cut off stems just where they stop being tough. (The stems may be cooked in soups, sauces or gravies and then strained out.) Mushrooms may be sliced or cooked whole. Place **1 pound mushrooms** in the top of a double boiler with **2 tablespoons fat, ½ teaspoon salt,** and **⅛ teaspoon pepper** and cook over boiling water 20 minutes or until tender.

Mushrooms may be cooked over direct heat. Melt **2 tablespoons fat** in a pan, add mushrooms, season to taste with about **½ teaspoon salt** and **⅛ teaspoon pepper** and cook over a low flame, 5 to 10 minutes.

ELKO COUNTY CREAMED ONIONS

Peel **8 small onions** and cook in a quantity of boiling salted water until tender, about 30 minutes. Drain and add to **1 cup medium Cream Sauce.*** Serves 4.

ONIONS BAKED IN CREAM

Peel medium **onions.** Place a single layer in a greased baking dish. As many onions may be used as can be placed on the bottom of the dish. Allow one medium onion for each person to be served. Brush each onion with **melted fat** and sprinkle with **salt** and **pepper.** Add **1 tablespoon cream** for each onion. Bake in a moderate, 350° F. oven until tender, about 1 hour.

RIVER VIEW FARM CREAMED KOHLRABI

Wash **8 medium kohlrabi.** Peel, dice and cook in very little salted water until tender, 10 to 20 minutes. Prepare **1 cup medium Cream Sauce,*** using ½ cup cream and ½ cup water in which the kohlrabi was cooked. Add to the drained kohlrabi. Serves 4.

ALCORN COUNTY FRIED OKRA

Wash **1 pound okra.** Remove the stem ends and cut the okra into thin slices crosswise. Cook in very little boiling salted water 5 minutes. Drain. Melt **2 tablespoons bacon fat** in a spider. Add the okra and cook, stirring frequently, until tender and nicely browned, 8 to 10 minutes more. Season to taste with about **½ teaspoon salt, ⅛ teaspoon pepper,** and **¼ teaspoon sugar.** Serves 4.

Do not cook okra in an iron vessel, as the okra will blacken.

MIZ LIJE KRUEGER'S RECEIPT FOR PARSNIP PUFF

Remove leaves and stems from **1 pound small young parsnips.** Add boiling salted water to cover and cook until tender, 20 to 30 minutes. Drain, plunge into cold water and remove skins. Mash and beat in **2 tablespoons fat.** Melt an additional **2 tablespoons fat** in a separate pan. Blend in **2 tablespoons flour.** Stir in gradually **½ cup milk,** stirring constantly until the mixture reaches the boiling point. Beat **3 egg yolks** well. Beat in the hot sauce a little at a time. Add to the parsnips with **½ teaspoon salt** and **⅛ teaspoon pepper.** Beat **3 egg whites** stiff but not dry with **¼ teaspoon salt.** Fold into the parsnip mixture and turn into a casserole. Place in a pan of hot water and bake in a very moderate, 325° F. oven 45 to 60 minutes or until firm. Serves 4 to 6.

If the puff is to be turned out, grease the casserole.

Aunt Sleide says: "Cooking is a chore for Miz Krueger and the best you can say about her cooking is that it wouldn't kill anyone. Her daughter Ella is just the opposite, she's always hankering to cook something. If there weren't anything around, she could make a feast out of a bunch of rocks from the garden."

FRIED PARSNIPS

Cook **parsnips** as above. Leave whole and fry slowly in butter until nicely browned. One pound will serve 4.

OLD FARM PARSNIP STEW

Remove leaves and stems from small, young parsnips. Scrub with a vegetable brush and scrape to remove skins. Drop in cold water to prevent discoloration. Place in a kettle **¼ pound salt pork** which has been cut in small cubes. Cover with cold water, bring to a boil, then simmer, covered, until partially cooked, 30 to 45 minutes. Add **3 cups cubed parsnips** and **1½ cups potatoes** which have been peeled and cubed. Add boiling water to just cover. Cover and cook slowly until the ingredients are almost tender, about 20 minutes. Uncover and cook over a higher flame until the water evaporates and the meat and vegetables brown and become tender, about 10 minutes. Serves 4 to 6.

FLORENCE COUNTY SWEET POTATO PUFF

Cook sweet potatoes or yams in boiling salted water to cover until very tender, 20 to 35 minutes. They may be peeled before or after cooking. Leftover sweet potatoes may be used. Rice or mash the potatoes. Scald **1 cup milk.** Add **2 tablespoons shortening, 2 teaspoons sugar,** and **½ teaspoon salt.** Add **2 cups riced sweet potato** and mix thoroughly. Beat **2 egg yolks** well and add to the potatoes. Mix in **1 teaspoon allspice, ½ cup broken nuts,** and **½ cup raisins** and beat until light and fluffy. Beat **2 egg whites** stiff but not dry, and fold into the potato mixture. Turn into a casserole, set in a pan of hot water, and bake in a very moderate, 325° F. oven 45 to 60 minutes or until firm. Serves 6.

If the puff is to be turned out, grease the casserole.

SCALLOPED POTATOES

Wash and peel potatoes. Slice thin. Place a layer of **potato slices** in a greased casserole. Sprinkle with **salt, pepper,** and **flour.** Dot with **butter.** Continue until all the potatoes are used. Pour in **top milk,** just to where it may be seen through the top layer of potatoes. Bake in moderate, 350° F. oven, 60 to 75 minutes or until the potatoes are tender and the top is nicely browned. No proportions can be given because the seasoning is a matter of taste and as much butter may be used as liked. Sprinkle the potatoes fairly generously with flour or the sauce will be watery.

For a more exact method, cook and cube potatoes. Prepare **medium Cream Sauce.*** Mix the potatoes with the sauce in the proportion of 2 cups sauce for each cup of cooked potato. Turn into a greased baking dish and brown in a moderate, 350° F. oven. It will take 20 to 30 minutes.

CRUMB POTATOES

Peel and slice thin **6 medium potatoes.** Coat with **3 cups dry bread crumbs.** Melt **⅔ cup shortening.** Fry the potatoes in it until they are brown. If they are not tender, cover and steam them for a few minutes. Serves 4 to 6.

Aunt Sleide says: "Frank Gear just got married to a girl from the city. I saw him the other day and asked him if she was a good cook. 'Well, Aunt Sleide,' he said, 'the potatoes she serves are crisp on the inside!' "

LAURENS COUNTY FRIED YAMS

Peel and slice raw **yams.** (Jersey sweet potatoes may be used.) Heat a heavy spider. Place in it **1 tablespoon bacon or other fat** for each large potato. Brown the potatoes lightly on both sides. Cover and let cook until tender,

20 to 30 minutes. Remove the cover and cook for 5 minutes more if not browned sufficiently.

SWEET POTATOES BAKED IN MAPLE SYRUP

Boil **4 medium sweet potatoes** in salted water to cover until almost tender. Peel and cut in eighths. Melt **3 tablespoons butter** in a drip pan. Put the potatoes in and pour over them **¼ cup maple syrup.** Bake in a moderate, 350° F. oven, 30 to 45 minutes, basting frequently until glazed and tender. Add more maple syrup if necessary. Serves 4.

MASHED POTATOES

Peel **6 medium potatoes.** Drop into cold water to prevent discoloration. Cook in boiling salted water to cover until very tender. Drain off the water, cover the pan and shake the potatoes over a flame for a minute to dry them. Mash with a wire masher or an electric mixer to remove all lumps. Add **1 teaspoon salt** and **5 tablespoons butter** which has been melted in **½ cup cream.** (Do not let the cream get hotter than scalding.) Beat the potatoes thoroughly with a fork or mixer. Pile lightly into a hot dish. Dot with additional butter and serve piping hot. If using an oven dish, the potatoes may be placed in a hot, 400° F. oven until the butter topping melts. Serves 4.

Aunt Sleide says: "Brick Biscomb was from back country, but the minute she stepped out of church after marrying John Anthony, she started putting on airs. Her furniture was too fancy to sit on and you couldn't see her dresses for the trimmings. John didn't complain until the first thrashing dinner at their farm. Brick served the thrashers mashed potatoes. They were good mashed potatoes but there were maraschino cherries on top of them."

BUSY FARMER POTATOES

Place **3 cups peeled cubed potatoes** in the top of a double boiler. Add **1 cup top milk, ½ teaspoon salt,** and **⅛ tea-**

spoon pepper. Put over cold water and cook over a medium flame until the water boils. Reduce to simmer and continue cooking 30 to 40 minutes or until the potatoes are tender. Stir in **2 tablespoons butter** and serve. Serves 4.

HAVEN FARM FRIED RADISHES

Remove leaves and stems from **2 cups radishes** and slice thin. Melt **2 tablespoons fat** in a skillet. Fry the radishes in the fat until tender, turning frequently. It will take about 10 minutes. Serves 3 or 4.

CREAMED RADISHES

Prepare **2 cups radishes** as above and cook in boiling salted water to cover, being careful not to get them too tender. Drain and add **1 cup medium Cream Sauce.*** Serves 4.

OPEN GATE FARM PEAS

Place a layer of **pea pods** in the bottom of a heavy saucepan and cover with a thick layer (about 1 inch) of **shelled peas.** Dot with **butter,** and repeat until pods and shelled peas are all used, ending with a thick layer of pods. Add ¼ **cup water,** cover tightly with a lid and simmer until the peas are tender, 12 to 20 minutes. Remove pods and, just before serving, season each 3 pounds peas with ½ **teaspoon salt** and ⅛ **teaspoon pepper.** (Three pounds unshelled peas will serve 4.)

SWEET SOUR SUMMER SQUASH

Slice a **summer squash** into strips the size of a little finger. Melt **1 tablespoon shortening.** Add **1 onion** diced fine and simmer for 5 minutes. Add **2 tablespoons vinegar,** the squash, and very little boiling water. Boil until the squash is tender, 15 to 25 minutes. Season to taste with about ¼ **teaspoon salt** and ⅛ **teaspoon pepper.** Mix to a smooth paste **2 teaspoons flour** and ½ **cup sour cream.**

Stir into the squash and cook 5 minutes more. Parsley, dill, or both, may be cut over the squash, if desired. Serves 4.

FRIED SUMMER SQUASH

Prepare **squash** as above and cook in very little boiling salted water. Drain when almost tender and fry in **butter** until brown.

BAKED WINTER SQUASH WITH MOLASSES

Peel and remove the spongy portion and seeds from **squash** and cut in 2-inch pieces. Sprinkle each piece lightly with **salt.** Place flesh side down on a roasting pan and bake in a moderate, 350° F. oven for 20 minutes. Turn flesh side up, drizzle with **molasses** and cook about 30 minutes more or until tender. Serve with **butter.** Two pounds of squash serves 4 to 6.

BOILED WINTER SQUASH WITH BUTTER

Prepare **squash** as above and cook in very little boiling salted water until tender, 20 to 30 minutes. Serve with **salt, pepper,** and **butter.** Mash if desired and beat in the seasoning. It is best to use this method only if the squash is very dry.

STEAMED WINTER SQUASH

Prepare **squash** as above, sprinkle lightly with **salt** and place in a perforated steamer which has a tight-fitting cover. Steam for 40 minutes or until tender. Add more salt if necessary. Sprinkle with **pepper** and drench with **butter.**

BAKED ACORN SQUASH

Cut the **squash** in half, crosswise. Remove the seeds. Sprinkle with **salt.** Place a strip of **bacon** in each half. Bake in a moderate, 350° F. oven, 40 to 60 minutes or until tender. Serve hot in the shell with plenty of **butter.** One squash serves 2.

PUMPKIN

Prepare by the methods used for **Squash.** If preparing pumpkin or winter squash to be used for pie or other dishes, do not add butter, pepper, salt, or molasses.

GOLDEN LEAF PLANTATION FRIED PUMPKIN

Cook **pumpkin** as for **Winter Squash with Boiled Butter,*** using any of the methods, and mash it. Fry in **bacon fat** until brown. The pumpkin may be shaped into cakes, then fried. Serve with bacon for breakfast or lunch.

NOWATA COUNTY GREEN TOMATOES

Wash, core and slice **green tomatoes.** Season with **salt** and **pepper** and fry in **bacon fat** until soft but not falling apart. Season to taste. Allow **1** medium tomato for each person.

HERB GARDEN TOMATOES

Scoop the pulp from **tomatoes.** Sprinkle the cavities with **salt** and turn upside down to drain. Prepare herbs by cutting them with a scissors. Parsley, chives, thyme, sweet basil, summer savory—any or all may be combined in any amounts. Place a small lump of **butter** in each tomato. Stuff lightly with **1 tablespoon herbs** which have been sprinkled with **salt** and **pepper.** Top with **Buttered Bread Crumbs.*** Bake in a moderate, 350° F. oven 20 to 40 minutes or until the tomatoes are tender but not falling apart, and the top is nicely browned. Allow one medium tomato for each person.

BAKED TURNIPS

Scrub **1 large turnip** for each person. Bake in a hot, 400° F. oven 50 to 70 minutes until the turnips feel soft when pressed with a towel-protected hand. Gash the skins to allow the steam to escape and put a lump of **butter** in each gash.

TURNIPS IN CREAM

Wash, peel and cook **5 medium turnips** in boiling salted water to cover until almost tender, 15 to 30 minutes. Slice. Add **1 cup cream, 2 tablespoons butter, 2 teaspoons sugar, ½ teaspoon salt,** and **⅛ teaspoon pepper.** Simmer for 5 minutes. Mix part of the liquid to a smooth paste with **1 tablespoon cornstarch.** Add to the main mixture and cook gently about 20 minutes or until there is no taste of raw starch. Chopped parsley or chives may be sprinkled over the top. Serves 4.

OLD FARM TURNIPS

Dice **6 strips bacon** and cook until crisp. Set aside. Place in a saucepan **2 pounds peeled, diced turnips, 2 peeled, diced potatoes, 1 tablespoon bacon fat, ½ teaspoon salt, ⅛ teaspoon pepper,** and **½ teaspoon sugar.** Pour very little boiling water over and boil until the vegetables are tender, 20 to 35 minutes. Add **¼ cup cream** and mash. Mix with the bacon pieces. Serves 6 to 8.

WEBER COUNTY RUTABAGA PUFF

Peel and cook rutabagas in boiling salted water to cover until tender, 20 to 35 minutes. Drain and mash. To **3 cups mashed rutabagas,** add **½ teaspoon salt, ⅛ teaspoon pepper, ½ cup cream,** and **2 beaten eggs.** Turn into a greased casserole. Dot the top with **3 tablespoons butter.** Bake in a moderate, 350° F. oven about 45 minutes or until nicely browned. Serves 4 or 5.

SALSIFY CAKES (Oyster Plant)

Dissolve **1 tablespoon salt** in **3 cups water.** Scrape and slice **1 bunch salsify** (about 6 roots) and drop it into the prepared water at once to keep it from discoloring. Cover with boiling salted water, and boil until soft, 30 to 60 minutes. Drain and mash with **2 tablespoons butter, ½ teaspoon salt,** and **⅛ teaspoon pepper.** Shape into cakes. Roll the cakes in **flour** and fry them in **butter.** When all the cakes have been fried, remove them, add an additional **2 tablespoons butter,** to the pan, and let it brown over a slow fire. Add about **2 tablespoons chopped parsley** or other herb and pour over the cakes. Serves 4.

BIG BAY FARM SAUERKRAUT

Melt **2 tablespoons fat** in a kettle. Add **1 large onion** diced, and simmer 5 minutes. Add **4 cups sauerkraut.** Add boiling **water or stock** to cover. Simmer 30 to 40 minutes. Add **½ teaspoon celery seed or ½ teaspoon caraway seed.** Serves 8.

BAKED SAUERKRAUT

Melt **3 tablespoons shortening.** Place in a baking dish. Peel **2 tart apples,** core and cut in eighths. Place in the dish. Add **1 onion** chopped fine, **2 tablespoons brown sugar** and **1½ pounds sauerkraut.** Bake in a moderate, 350° F. oven 30 minutes. This is good with spareribs. Serves 4 to 6.

YUBA COUNTY SUNNY SPINACH

Cook **1 pound spinach** until tender in just the water which clings to it, cooking 15 to 20 minutes. Drain, reserving any liquid. Chop the spinach fine. Melt **1 tablespoon butter.** Simmer **½ small onion,** diced, in the butter for 5 minutes. Blend in **1 tablespoon flour.** Add enough **cream** to the spinach water to measure ½ cup. Add gradually and stir constantly until the mixture comes to a boil. Stir in the chopped spinach and the chopped whites of **2 hard-cooked eggs.** Season to taste with about **½ teaspoon salt** and 1/8 **teaspoon pepper.** Place in the serving dish and top with the sliced egg yolk. Serves 4.

SPINACH WITH BACON

Substitute **2 pounds spinach** for the carrots in **Old Farm Carrots with Bacon.*** Garnish with **4 hard-cooked eggs,** sliced. Serves 8.

SOUR SAUCE

Prepare **1/2 cup medium Cream Sauce*** (1/4 cup vegetable water and 1/4 cup milk or cream may be used). Add **1 cup hot Cooked Salad Dressing*** to the hot sauce. This may be used on asparagus, Brussels sprouts, broccoli, kohlrabi, or cauliflower.

BUTTERED BREAD CRUMBS

Melt **3 tablespoons butter** or other fat in a skillet. Add **1/2 cup bread crumbs** for each 3 tablespoons butter and stir until the crumbs are well coated.

CHEESE, EGGS, AND CEREALS

CHEESE

Any cheese which is hard enough to grate may be used in recipes calling for grated cheese. If a mild flavor is liked, a mild cheese should be used. Use a sharper-flavored cheese if a more pronounced flavor is desired.

Cheese will become tough and stringy if a high degree of heat is used for cooking it, so be careful to use a low flame.

BERKS COUNTY LIMA BEAN LOAF

Cook **2 cups dried lima beans.** Drain. Combine with **1/4 pound grated cheese, 2 tablespoons grated onion, 2 tablespoons diced green pepper, 4 tablespoons melted butter, 1/2 teaspoon salt,** and **1/8 teaspoon pepper.** Add **3/4 to 1 cup dry bread crumbs** to make a mixture firm enough to form a loaf. Place in a greased pan. Set in a pan of hot water and bake in a moderate, 350° F. oven 30 to 40 minutes. Serves 4.

GREEN MEADOWS RANCH BAKED BEANS

Cook **1 quart kidney, navy, or pea beans** until the skins burst. Scald **¾ pound salt pork** and scrape it. Cut off a ¼-inch slice. Place in the bottom of a bean pot or casserole. Place the beans in the pot. Bury **1 small peeled onion** in the beans. Cut through the rind of the remainder of the salt pork every inch, making cuts 1 inch deep. Bury this in the beans, leaving the rind exposed. Mix together **½ teaspoon salt, ¼ cup brown sugar** which has been packed firmly in the cup, **½ cup molasses, ½ teaspoon dry mustard,** and **¼ cup ketchup.** Bring to a boil **1 cup juice from pickled fruit or 1 cup water.** Mix with the molasses mixture. Add to the beans. Add enough additional boiling water to cover the beans. Cover the dish and bake in a slow, 250° F. oven 6 to 8 hours, adding more water from time to time if necessary. Uncover the pot the last hour of cooking to brown the salt pork. Serves at least 8.

BAKED LIMA BEANS

Cook **1 pound dried lima beans** until almost tender. Peel **2 cups tomatoes,** or use stewed or canned tomatoes which have been strained. Season with **½ teaspoon salt, ⅛ teaspoon pepper,** and **¼ teaspoon sugar.** Add to the beans. Place in a greased baking dish. Top with **2 thick slices of bacon.** Bake in a moderate, 350° F. oven 30 to 40 minutes or until the bacon is crisp and brown and the beans are tender. Serves 4.

OPEN GATE FARM BEAN RABBIT

Melt **2 tablespoons fat** in the top of a double boiler. Dice **½ green pepper** and cook it in the fat for 5 minutes. Blend in **2 tablespoons flour.** Gradually add **1 cup hot milk,** stirring constantly until the boiling point is reached. Place over hot water and add **1 cup grated cheese.** Stir until the cheese is melted. Add **2 cups dried beans** which have been cooked until tender and pressed through a sieve. Mix and season to taste with about ½ **teaspoon salt** and ⅛ **teaspoon Cayenne pepper.** Serve on toast. Serves 4.

If the rabbit is too thick, thin it with additional milk.

SHOSHONE COUNTY SAUSAGE AND BEAN CASSEROLE

Cook **1 cup dried lima beans** until tender. Mix with **1 diced onion.** Place in a greased baking dish. Cover the top with **1 pound pork sausage** in patties or in links. Bake uncovered in a moderate, 350° F. oven until the sausage is thoroughly cooked and nicely browned, 40 to 60 minutes. Serves 4.

HARD-COOKED EGGS

Place **eggs** in a saucepan and add cold water to cover. Cover the pan with a lid and bring the water to a boil. When the boiling point is reached, reduce the heat and simmer 15 to 20 minutes. Plunge the eggs into cold water immediately and peel.

CREOLE EGGS

Dice and fry **2 strips bacon.** Remove bacon and add to the fat ¼ **diced onion** and ½ **small green pepper,** diced. Cook for 5 minutes. Add **1 cup tomatoes** and cook for 3 minutes. Beat **2 eggs** slightly. Beat in **2 tablespoons cream.** Add to the vegetable mixture. Return the bacon to the pan. Cook over a low fire, stirring constantly until the eggs are set. Season with about ½ **teaspoon salt** and ¼ **teaspoon pepper.** Serves 2 or 3.

OLD FARM PICKLED EGGS

Hard-cook **6 eggs.** Slice lengthwise. Bring to a boil **1 cup vinegar, 2 tablespoons butter, ½ teaspoon salt,** and **¼ teaspoon pepper.** Pour over the eggs. Serves 6.

LIGHT AND FLUFFY OMELET

Make **1 cup medium Cream Sauce.*** Separate **4 eggs.** Beat the whites of the eggs stiff but not dry with **¼ teaspoon salt.** Without washing the beater, beat the yolks with **⅛ teaspoon pepper.** Beat the cooked cream sauce into the yolks and gently fold in the egg whites. Grease a 10-inch frying pan. Pour the egg mixture in and cook over a low flame for about 5 minutes or until the bottom has had time to brown. Finish in a very moderate, 325° F. oven, baking until the top is nicely browned, 15 to 30 minutes. Sprinkle **1 tablespoon herbs or 4 tablespoons grated cheese** over the omelet. Serve portions from the pan or fold the omelet. Top each portion with a small pat of butter. Serves 4.

OMELET WITH VEGETABLES

Make **Light and Fluffy Omelet,** above, adding to the yolks **2 cups cooked peas, spinach, corn, or carrots.** Bake in a very moderate, 325° F. oven for about 30 minutes. Serves 4.

HUPPLE PUPPLE

Slice **4 medium potatoes** which have been cooked. Cook in **¼ cup fat** until nicely browned. Beat **6 eggs** slightly. Add to the potatoes and scramble over a low flame, stirring constantly until the eggs are firm. Season to taste with about **½ teaspoon salt** and **¼ teaspoon pepper.** Serves 4.

PINCH-PENNY CREAMED DISH

Make **Crooked Elm Farm Giblet Sauce.*** Hard-cook **2 eggs.** Mix and add to the sauce with **1 tablespoon chopped herbs,** parsley, chives, summer savory, etc. Serve on toast or rice.

CLEBURNE COUNTY BROWN PUFF CHEESE PUDDING

Cream **4 tablespoons butter.** Beat in **1 tablespoon parsley** or other herb which has been cut fine. Add **1 teaspoon onion juice.** Toast **six ½-inch-thick slices whole wheat bread** and spread with mixture. Cut each slice into four sticks. Grease a baking dish. Put some of the bread sticks on the bottom. Sprinkle with grated cheese. Alternate bread and cheese, ending with cheese. Use **2½ cups cheese** in all. Beat **3 eggs** slightly. Beat in **2½ cups milk.** Add **½ teaspoon salt.** Pour over the bread and cheese. Bake in a very moderate, 325° F. oven 40 to 60 minutes or until the custard is firm. Serves 6.

FRIED MUSH

Cooked, leftover cereals are good fried. If they are cooked especially for pan frying, the amount of water called for should be reduced by about ⅛. Turn the hot cooked cereal into long, narrow pans, jelly glasses, or baking powder tins which have been rinsed in cold water. Cover to prevent a crust from forming and let stand in a cold place until firm. Turn out and slice ¼ to ½ inch thick. Cereal may be dipped in corn meal, flour, or slightly beaten egg. Heat enough fat to cover the bottom of a spider and, when very hot, add the mush. Brown on one side, turn and brown on the other. It will take about 3 minutes for each side. The mush may be fried over a low flame for a greater length of time if it is liked crisp and dry. Serve with butter and syrup or with meat gravy, sorghum, or molasses.

Hominy grits, corn meal, rice, farina, etc., may be used.

Aunt Sleide says: "Uncle'd like winter better without the cold weather. And I'd like summer better without the hot weather."

HASTY PUDDING (CORN MEAL MUSH)

Place **6 cups water** in the top of a double boiler. Add **2 teaspoons salt.** Bring the water to a rapid, vigorous boil. Add **1 cup corn meal** slowly so the water does not stop boiling. Cook for 5 minutes. Place over hot water, cover, and cook 45 minutes to 1 hour. The corn meal may be cooked uncovered over direct heat for 30 minutes, but then it must be watched and stirred to prevent burning. Serve with hot or cold milk, butter, sugar, or syrup, or a combination of these. Serves 4 to 6.

Yellow or white, dry or moist corn meal may be used interchangeably in any recipe. Water-ground meal contains more fat and is more moist than meal which is milled by modern methods. Yellow corn meal is usually preferred above the Mason-Dixon line, white below it.

SCRAPPLE

Clean a **pig's head** (and feet, if desired) as for **Old Farm Headcheese*** and cover with cold water. Bring to a boil, then simmer until the flesh falls from the bones, 3 to 4 hours. Let cool in the water. Strip the meat from the bones, chop fine and weigh it. Remove fat from the water in which the head was cooked, strain the water and bring it to a boil. Sprinkle in **corn meal,** slowly, using 2 pounds meal to each 3 pounds meat. If the mush is too thick, thin with boiling water. Add meat and for each pound of meat add **2 teaspoons salt, 1/4 teaspoon pepper,** and **1 teaspoon onion juice.** Cook slowly for 20 minutes, stirring constantly. Cook over hot water 30 to 40 minutes longer.

Turn into a pan or mold. When cold, slice, coat as for **Bertha Lewis' Receipt for Breaded Veal Steaks and Potatoes*** and fry in **fat** until brown.

Other meat may be used.

SWIFT WATER FARM MOCK SCRAPPLE

Pour **1 cup corn meal** into **3 cups rapidly boiling water or stock** in which **½ teaspoon salt** has been dissolved. Pour the meal in slowly so that the liquid does not stop boiling. Cook over a low flame for 10 minutes. Add **2 cups cooked meat** which has been chopped, and cook 5 minutes longer. Turn into a greased loaf pan, 9 x 5 x 3 inches, and chill until firm. Slice 1½ inches thick and coat each slice as for **Bertha Lewis' Receipt for Breaded Veal Steaks and Potatoes.*** Fry in plenty of fat until brown. Serves 4 to 6.

HOMINY (HULLED CORN, SAMP, GRITS)

Hominy is a general name for ground corn which is made finer or coarser in different parts of the country. Whole kernel hominy is often called "samp," or "hulled corn." Hominy in smaller forms is called "grits."

To cook whole kernel hominy, soak overnight in cold water; drain, add fresh water, and proceed as for **Dried Vegetables.***

Place **4 cups water** in the top of a double boiler. Add **1 teaspoon salt.** Bring the water to a rapid vigorous boil. Add **1 cup hominy grits** so the water does not stop boiling. Cook over direct heat 5 minutes. Place over hot water, cover, and cook until tender, about 1 hour. Serve with melted butter or with meat gravy as a vegetable.

BULLOCH COUNTY BACON AND EGGS WITH HOMINY

Dice **4 slices bacon.** Fry until crisp. Remove the bacon and brown in the fat **2½ cups whole kernel hominy** cooked as above. (A Number 2 can of hominy, well drained, may be used.) When brown, add **¼ teaspoon pepper, ½ teaspoon salt,** and **4 eggs** which have been beaten slightly. Cook over a very low flame, stirring constantly until the eggs are cooked. Sprinkle bacon over each serving. Serves 4.

GOLDEN LEAF PLANTATION SAUSAGE AND HOMINY

Brown **½ pound pork sausage** in a skillet. Remove the sausage and brown **2 cups whole kernel hominy** cooked as for **Hominy*** in the fat. (A Number 1 tall can of hominy, well-drained, may be used.) Drain off the excess fat. Add **1 cup tomato juice.** Turn into a greased baking dish and mix with the sausage. Top with **½ cup bread crumbs** mixed with **3 tablespoons fat** from the sausage. Bake in a moderate, 350° F. oven 40 to 60 minutes or until the sausage is completely cooked and the top is nicely browned. Serves 4.

MACARONI, SPAGHETTI, NOODLES

Add **1 teaspoon salt** to **2 quarts water.** Bring the water to a rapid vigorous boil. Add **½ pound macaroni, spaghetti, or noodles** slowly and boil 20 to 30 minutes or until tender. Drain and pour **1 quart hot water** over them to rinse off the excess starch. One-half pound macaroni or spaghetti makes about 2 cups when cooked. One-half pound noodles makes about 7 cups when cooked. If noodles, macaroni or spaghetti are wanted whole rather than broken, hold the ends in the boiling water until they soften, then slide the entire piece into the water. Four ounces macaroni, spaghetti, or noodles will serve 2.

DINNER-IN-A-DISH

Cook **½ pound macaroni or noodles** as above. Mix with **2 cups chopped cooked ham** or other meat. Add **1 cup me-**

dium Cream Sauce.* Mix well and turn into a greased baking dish. Cover with ½ **cup grated cheese.** Bake in a very moderate, 325° F. oven until the cheese is melted and nicely browned, 15 to 30 minutes. Serves 4.

COCONINO COUNTY MACARONI LOAF

Break ½ **pound macaroni** in 1½- to 2-inch pieces and cook it. Add **2 teaspoons onion, 2 tablespoons pimiento,** and ½ **small green pepper** which have been diced fine. Scald **2 cups milk.** Add to **2 cups dry bread crumbs.** Add vegetables, macaroni, **4 beaten eggs,** ½ **teaspoon salt,** ⅛ **teaspoon pepper,** and **2 cups grated cheese.** Mix well. Turn into a greased loaf pan, 9 x 5 x 3 inches. Set in a pan of hot water. Bake in a very moderate, 325° F. oven 60 to 75 minutes. Serve with **Mushroom Sauce*** or **Osceola Farm Tomato Sauce.*** Serves 6.

BIG BAY FARM BAKED PORK AND NOODLES

Cook 1½ **pounds noodles.** Dice **1 small green pepper** and slice **1 medium onion.** Cook in **2 tablespoons fat** for 5 minutes. Add and brown **1 pound ground lean pork shoulder.** Add 1½ **cups tomatoes** and the noodles. Season to taste with about ½ **teaspoon salt** and ¼ **teaspoon pepper.** Mix and turn into a greased baking dish. Bake in a moderate, 350° F. oven 60 to 75 minutes or until the meat is completely cooked. Cover the top with ¼ **pound grated cheese.** Return to the oven and bake until the cheese is melted. Serves 4.

RICE

Place ½ **cup rice** in a sieve and wash it by allowing cold water to run over it. Add ½ **tablespoon salt** to **4 cups water.** Bring the water to a rapid, vigorous boil. Add the drained rice slowly so the water does not stop boiling. Boil for about 20 minutes or until tender. A small lump of butter placed in the water will keep it from boiling over.

The rice is tender if no hard spot can be felt when a kernel is crushed between the fingers. Drain the rice in a sieve (any water remaining may be used in soups), and pour **4 cups hot water** over it to remove excess starch. Return to the vessel in which it was cooked and set in a warm place to dry. One-half cup uncooked rice makes 1½ cups or more cooked rice.

WILD RICE

Prepare as above, allowing a longer time for cooking.

OSCEOLA FARM CHICKEN BAKED WITH RICE

Bring **4 cups strained stock,** made by cooking chicken as for **Huntington County Creamed Chicken Casserole,*** to a boil in a large pot. Add slowly **1 cup rice** which has been washed and picked over. Add the **hearts, necks, wings, giblets and feet,** cooked as for **Crooked Elm Farm Giblet Sauce,*** of any number of chickens available and **½ cup chicken fat** or other fat. Bake uncovered in a moderate, 350° F. oven 45 to 60 minutes or until the rice is tender. Serves 6.

6

BREAD

STRAIGHT YEAST DOUGH METHOD

Scald the liquid and set aside ¼ cup of it for softening the yeast. One cake of yeast weighs ½ ounce. Compressed yeast is generally used in this method. Cool the ¼ cup of liquid rapidly to lukewarm. It is lukewarm when a drop of the liquid tested on the inside of the wrist will feel neither hot nor cold. Add the yeast. Pour the remainder of the hot liquid over the sugar, fat, and salt. When this mixture cools to lukewarm, add the softened yeast. Add only half the total amount of flour to the dough, so that it may be beaten thoroughly. Then add the remainder of the flour or enough to make a stiff dough. All flours, except whole wheat, should be sifted before measuring. Then dip them lightly into the measure and level. Whole wheat flour and meals are stirred before measuring, then measured as other flours.

Now knead the dough. It may be kneaded in the mixing bowl. Use a large wooden spoon, push it under the dough, raise it and push it under the dough again, making a circle. Continue until the kneading is completed. The dough which clings to the sides of the bowl should be scraped down into the mass from time to time.

To knead by hand, turn the dough out on a clean floured surface. Use only a thin film of flour on the board, as the stickiness will disappear with kneading. Use the palm of the hand to press the dough, raise part of it with the fingers and fold it down, using a circular motion. Do not press heavily on the dough. Continue until the kneading is completed.

Knead rhythmically and at an even speed, whether kneading in the bowl or by hand. The dough has been kneaded sufficiently when it has a satin-smooth surface and when a floured knife will cut through it clean. Be careful not to overknead the dough. When the kneading process has been completed, shape the dough into a ball and place it in a bowl large enough to allow it to rise. To keep the surface of the dough from drying out, grease the bowl very sparingly with fat and turn the ball of dough over once or twice in the bowl. Cover the bowl with a clean cloth. Put in a warm place, 80° to 85° F., and let rise until about double in bulk. As the dough approaches this stage, test often, as the grain and lightness of the bread depend upon the degree to which it has risen. If the dough has risen sufficiently, a dent will remain when the surface is touched lightly with a finger. This test is used every time the dough is allowed to rise. If very strong flour is used, this stage will not be obtained until the dough has risen to about 2½ times its original bulk.

When the dough has risen sufficiently, it may be punched down and allowed to rise a second time. This will help to insure a fine texture. Punch in the center of the risen dough, pull the sides over, press them into the center, and turn the ball of dough over with the smooth side up. Cover the bowl and let rise to the same volume as before. The second rising will not take as long as the first.

After rising, the dough is ready to be placed in the pans. Divide the dough so that each piece will fill a baking pan about half full. For bread, a shallow pan is preferable to a deep pan, the best size for a 1- or 1½-pound loaf, for instance, being 8½ x 4 x 3 inches. The loaf bakes more quickly, is crusty all over, and makes a better-looking slice if baked in a pan of this size. Only the bottom of the pan needs greasing. After dividing the dough, round it into balls, sealing the cut surfaces, and allow it to stand for a few minutes.

To shape the balls into loaves, flatten each ball into an oblong on a board, and fold and seal the edges together with the palms of the hands. Repeat several times, folding a different way each time. Bring the sides together in the center the last time, and place the sealed edges of the loaf down in the greased pan. The top of the loaf is greased to prevent drying, or it may be brushed with lightly beaten egg, and sprinkled with seeds: poppy, caraway, sesame, etc.

Set the filled bread pans in a warm place, cover with a cloth, and allow the dough to rise about double in bulk again. Test by pressing lightly with the finger, as above.

Bake a pound loaf in an oven which has been preheated to moderately hot, 385° F. Bake larger loaves at a lower temperature, about 350° F. After 15 minutes, turn the pans around so the loaves will brown evenly, and reduce the temperature to moderate, 350° F. Continue baking for 30 to 45 minutes. The bread has finished baking when the loaves shrink from the sides of the pan, and when the bread gives out a hollow sound when tapped. For a tender, glossy crust, brush the loaves with milk or butter upon removing them from the oven. If crispness is desired, do not brush the crust.

If using glass or enamel pans, bake the bread at a lower temperature. (The exact temperature will vary, depending upon the lightness or heaviness of the container used. A little experimenting will determine the correct degree.)

Romove the bread from the pans immediately and place on a rack to cool. Do not cover the loaves until they are cold.

SPONGE METHOD

When dough is made with dried yeast, which takes longer to become active than compressed yeast, the sponge method is generally used. Except for the following exceptions, the dough is prepared and handled the same as in the straight-dough method. Make the sponge for the bread early in the morning or the night before it is to be baked. Break up the yeast cake and soak it in ¼ cup lukewarm water for about a half-hour, or until soft. If the sponge is to stand overnight, use only about half the quantity of yeast called for.

Mix the liquid, the yeast, and half the flour and let stand until a light, frothy sponge is formed. If time is short, the sponge may be made more rapidly by adding also the sugar called for in the recipe. If the sponge is to rise overnight, it may be kept at a temperature of 65° to 75° F. If made in the morning, keep the sponge at 80° to 85° F., as for the straight-dough method. When the sponge is light, stir it well and add the salt, melted shortening, sugar (if it was not added before), and the remainder of the flour, or enough to make a stiff dough. Mix the dough and proceed as for the straight-dough method.

Yeast dough made by either method may be stored in the ice box or other cold place and used as needed. Punch down after the first rising, brush the top with softened butter, cover tightly, and store until needed. Be sure that the bowl is large enough to hold the dough, as it will continue to rise in the ice box. Remove the dough when needed, discarding any crust which may have formed, shape it, let it rise until it is about double, and bake.

ROLLS

The same general methods as above are used for yeast rolls, the straight-dough method being the most convenient when rolls alone are made. The dough may or may not be allowed to rise twice. Roll it out thin, and either cut the rolls with a biscuit cutter or pinch off small pieces of the dough and shape them with the palms of the hands. Rolls which are placed close together in a tin will rise high but have very little crust. Place the dough 1½ to 2 inches apart for crusty rolls. If a soft crust is desired, brush the tops of the rolls with butter. Grease the pans on the bottom before putting in the rolls. Bake in a hot, 425° F. oven 10 to 30 minutes, depending upon the size of the rolls.

Rolls may be shaped in a variety of ways. For horn rolls, cut triangles rather than rounds, brush with softened butter and roll up, starting at the long side. For clover leaf rolls, shape three balls with the hands, place together in greased muffin tins, and brush between the balls with melted butter. For Parker House rolls, brush rounds of dough lightly with butter, crease deeply across the center of each with the handle of a table knife, fold over and press down the top. For plain rolls, pinch off pieces of dough, round into balls, and fill greased muffin tins two-thirds full.

Rolls may be shaped, placed in pans, and put in the ice box or other cold place until wanted. If the temperature has been low enough to check the rising very greatly, they should be kept in a warm place until almost doubled in bulk before being baked.

To freshen rolls or bread, place in a moderate, 350° F. oven for a few minutes. If very stale, slap a little water on the bottom before placing in the oven.

The hardest part of making bread and coffee cake is waiting for them to finish baking before digging in!

HARFORD COUNTY ANADAMA BREAD

Slowly sprinkle **½ cup yellow corn meal** into **2 cups rapidly boiling water.** Cook 5 minutes over a medium flame. Add **1 teaspoon salt, 3 tablespoons lard,** and **½ cup molasses.** Let cool to lukewarm. Dissolve **1 cake compressed yeast** in **½ cup lukewarm water.** Add to the lukewarm corn meal mixture. Add **2 cups sifted flour** and beat well. Add **3 cups sifted flour,** in addition, or enough to make a stiff dough. Knead, let rise, shape, let rise again, and bake. Makes two 1-pound loaves.

OATMEAL BREAD

Add **2 cups boiling water** to **1 cup oatmeal** and let stand for 1 hour. Add **½ cup molasses, 2 teaspoons salt, 2 tablespoons shortening,** and **1 cake compressed yeast** which has been dissolved in **½ cup lukewarm water.** Mix well and add **2½ cups sifted flour.** Beat thoroughly. Add **2½ cups sifted flour,** in addition, and knead. Let rise, shape, let rise again, and bake. Makes two 1-pound loaves.

OLD FARM MILK BREAD

Scald **2 cups milk.** Rapidly cool ¼ cup of it to lukewarm, then dissolve **1 cake yeast** in it. Add to the remainder of the milk **2 teaspoons salt, 3 tablespoons sugar,** and **3 tablespoons melted shortening.** When lukewarm, add the dissolved yeast and **3 cups sifted flour.** Beat well. Add **3 cups sifted flour,** in addition, to make a stiff dough. Knead, let rise, shape, let rise again, and bake. Makes two 1-pound loaves.

WHOLE WHEAT BREAD

Scald **2 cups milk.** Rapidly cool ¼ cup of it to lukewarm, then dissolve **1 cake compressed yeast** in it. Add to the remainder of the milk **2 teaspoons salt, ¼ cup molasses** (or ¼ cup sugar), and **1½ tablespoons melted fat.** When lukewarm, add the dissolved yeast, **1 cup sifted white flour,** and **2 cups whole wheat flour** which has been stirred before measuring. Beat well. Add, in addition, **3 cups whole wheat flour** (stir before measuring), to make a stiff dough. Knead, let rise, shape, let rise again, and bake. Rolls or bread are equally good made from this dough. Makes two 1-pound loaves.

RAISIN BREAD

With the last addition of flour used in the dough for **Old Farm Milk Bread*** or **Whole Wheat Bread,** above, mix **1 cup seedless raisins.**

EMANUEL COUNTY SALT-RISING BREAD

Scald **1 cup milk.** Stir in **1 tablespoon sugar, 7 tablespoons corn meal** (white is best), and **1 teaspoon salt.** Place in a large clean jar, cover and place in water as hot as the hand can stand. Keep in a warm place (115° F.) 6 to 7 hours, or until gas may be heard escaping. Add **2 cups flour, 2 cups lukewarm water, 2 tablespoons sugar,** and **3 tablespoons melted shortening.** Beat thoroughly, put the jar back in warm water (115° F.), and let rise until light and full of bubbles. Add **8½ cups sifted flour,** or enough to make a stiff dough. Knead 10 to 15 minutes. Divide into loaves, mold, place in greased pans and allow to rise 2½ times in bulk. Bake in a moderately hot, 385° F. oven for 10 minutes. Reduce heat to moderate, 350° F., and continue baking until done. Makes three 1-pound loaves.

BUTTERMILK ROLLS

Scald **2 cups buttermilk.** Rapidly cool ¼ cup of it to lukewarm, then dissolve **1 cake yeast** in it. Add to the remainder of the butter milk **1½ teaspoons salt, 6 tablespoons sugar,** and **4 tablespoons melted shortening.** When lukewarm, add the dissolved yeast and **3 cups flour** which has been sifted, then measured and resifted with **½ teaspoon soda** and **1 teaspoon baking powder.** Beat well. Add **3 to 4 cups sifted flour,** in addition, to make a stiff dough. Knead, shape, let rise again, and bake in a hot, 425° F. oven 10 to 25 minutes. Makes about 3½ dozen rolls.

SILVER FORK ROLLS

Scald **1 cup milk.** Rapidly cool ¼ cup of it to lukewarm, then dissolve **1 cake yeast** in it. Add to the remainder of the milk **1 teaspoon salt, ½ cup sugar,** and **½ cup melted shortening.** When lukewarm, add the dissolved yeast and **2 cups sifted flour.** Beat well. Add, in addition, **2 cups sifted flour** to make a stiff dough. Knead, let rise, shape, let rise again, and bake in a hot, 425° F. oven 10 to 25 minutes. Makes about 2 dozen rolls.

POTATO ROLLS

Peel, quarter and cook about 3 medium potatoes. Mash or rice them. To **1 cup mashed potato,** add **½ cup sugar, 1 cup milk** which has been scalded and cooled to lukewarm, **1 cup sifted flour,** and **1 cake yeast** which has been dissolved in **¼ cup lukewarm water.** Add **2 eggs** which have been beaten well. Mix, cover, and let rise until light and full of gas bubbles. Add **¾ cup shortening** which has been melted and cooled, **1½ teaspoons salt,** and **4½ cups sifted flour.** Mix well. Knead, let rise, roll ¼ inch thick, and cut with a biscuit cutter. Spread half the rolls with melted butter. Place the other half on top, sandwich fashion. Place on a greased baking sheet and let rise until about double. Bake in a hot, 425° F. oven 10 to 25 minutes. Makes 3 dozen rolls.

HAVEN FARM SQUASH ROLLS

To **½ cup scalded milk,** add **½ cup strained squash, ¼ cup sugar, ½ teaspoon salt,** and **¼ cup melted shortening.** Cool to lukewarm and add **¼ cake yeast** which has been dissolved in **¼ cup lukewarm water.** Then add **2½ cups sifted flour.** Cover and let rise overnight. Punch down, pinch off small pieces of dough and round each piece into a smooth ball. Place on a greased baking sheet and let rise until double. Bake in a hot, 425° F. oven 10 to 25 minutes.

GRAM'S COFFEE CAKE DOUGH

Scald **2 cups milk.** Rapidly cool ¼ cup of the scalded milk to lukewarm. Soften **1 cake yeast,** in it. Add to the remainder of the liquid **½ pound melted shortening, 1 teaspoon salt,** and **¾ cup sugar.** Add the softened yeast when the fat-sugar mixture has cooled to lukewarm. Add **2 well-beaten eggs** and **4 cups sifted flour,** and beat well. Add **3 to 4 cups flour,** in addition, or enough to make a stiff dough, and knead. Let rise, then use in any of the following recipes.

LARGE FILLED COFFEE CAKE

Brush a Turk's Head pan (tube pan with fluted bottom) all over with melted butter. Use enough dough, above, to fill the pan half full. Roll into an oblong 1 inch thick. Brush with melted **butter** and sprinkle with **sugar** and **cinnamon,** using 1 part cinnamon, or less, to 3 parts sugar. Broken nuts or seeded raisins may be added. Roll the dough up, and place the roll in the pan, encircling the tube. The ends may overlap slightly. Pinch the edges of the top end together and place it under the bottom end. Pinch the edges of that end together. Let rise, then bake in a moderately hot, 385° F. oven for 15 minutes. Reduce the heat to moderate, 350° F. and bake 30 to 45 minutes more. When the cake has finished baking, remove it from the pan, turn it right side up and slip it over the tube to cool.

CINNAMON BUNS

Grease the bottom of a pan. An 8-x-8-inch layer-cake tin is a good size to use. Roll the dough for **Gram's Coffee Cake** (two receipts above) into a rectangle. Brush with melted **butter** and sprinkle with **sugar** and **cinnamon** as above. Roll the dough and slice it down, making rolls 1½ inches thick. Place in the pan next to one another, with the filling vertical to the pan. Brush melted butter between the rolls. Let rise, then bake in a hot, 400° F. oven 15 to 20 minutes. As soon as they have finished baking, brush with **Plain Jane Icing*** made with either milk or water.

CRUMB COFFEE CAKE

Spread **Gram's Coffee Cake** dough* ¾ inch thick in 2 round 8-inch cake tins which have been greased on the bottom. Sprinkle with **4 tablespoons sugar, 1 teaspoon cinnamon, ¾ cup dry breadcrumbs,** and **5 tablespoons melted butter,** all of which have been mixed together. Let rise and bake in a moderately hot, 385° F. oven for 15 minutes. Reduce the heat to moderate, 350° F., and bake 30 to 45 minutes more.

CINNAMON COFFEE CAKE

Spread **Gram's Coffee Cake** dough* in pans as above. Let rise. Brush the top with melted **butter** and sprinkle heavily with **sugar** and **cinnamon,** using 3 parts sugar to 1 part cinnamon. Let rise, then bake in a moderately hot, 385° F. oven for 15 minutes. Reduce the heat to moderate, 350° F., and bake 30 to 45 minutes longer.

STREW COFFEE CAKE

Pat **Gram's Coffee Cake** dough* ¾ inch thick into a greased 8-x-8-inch pan. Sift, then measure **⅓ cup flour.** Mix with **⅓ cup sugar.** Cut in **3 tablespoons shortening.** Strew the mixture over the dough and top with **½ cup broken nuts.** Let rise and bake as above.

FRUIT ROUNDS

Roll **Gram's Coffee Cake** dough* 1 inch thick. Cut rounds with a biscuit cutter. Place them 1 to 1½ inches apart in greased pans and let rise. Make a deep depression in the center of each round. Fill with **cooked Dried Fruit*** which has been pressed through a strainer and sweetened to taste. Sprinkle with finely chopped **nuts.** Bake in a hot, 400° F. oven 15 to 20 minutes.

APPLE COFFEE CAKE

Spread **Gram's Coffee Cake** dough* ¾ inch thick in a greased pan, 9 x 13 x 2 inches. Peel and cut **6 sour apples** into eighths. Press the sharp edges of the apples into the dough in parallel rows lengthwise of the pan, placing them close together. Sprinkle the apples with a mixture of **½ cup sugar** and **1 teaspoon cinnamon.** Top with **3 tablespoons raisins.** Let rise and bake 40 to 60 minutes in a moderate, 350° F. oven. Cut in squares to serve. Top with whipped cream, if desired.

STICKIES

Grease muffin or pie tins with melted **butter.** Pat sifted **brown sugar** over the bottom and sprinkle with additional melted butter. Roll **Gram's Coffee Cake** dough* into an oblong ½ inch thick. Brush with melted butter and sprinkle with brown sugar. Drizzle additional butter over the sugar. Roll up and slice rolls that measure half the height of the sides of the pans. Place in the pans, cut side down. If using pie tins, brush between rolls with melted butter. Let rise and bake in a hot, 400° F. oven 15 to 20 minutes or more, depending upon the size of the muffin tins. If baking stickies in pie tins, bake in a moderately hot, 385° F. oven for 15 minutes. Reduce the heat to moderate, 350° F. and bake 30 to 45 minutes more. Remove from the pans as soon as they have finished baking and turn sticky side up. Rapidly spoon over them any syrup left in the pan.

Whole nuts may be placed on the sugar in the pans, rounded side down, and broken nuts may be sprinkled over the dough before it is rolled.

CHRISTMAS BREAD

After the dough for **Gram's Coffee Cake*** has risen, beat into it **½ pound citron,** sliced, **½ pound seeded raisins, ½ pound candied cherries, ½ teaspoon ground cardamom,** and **½ pound broken nuts.** Divide the dough into 6 equal parts. Roll each piece into a rope 10 to 12 inches long with the palms of the hands. Make 2 braids. Place in a greased pan one on top of the other. Brush the entire top of the loaf with melted **butter** and sprinkle with finely cut cherries and citron. Let rise and bake in a moderately hot, 385° F. oven for 15 minutes. Reduce the heat to moderate, 350° F. and bake 30 to 45 minutes more.

HOT CROSS BUNS WITH CURRANTS

Make half the dough for **Gram's Coffee Cake,*** sifting with part of the flour **½ teaspoon nutmeg, ½ teaspoon allspice,** and **1 teaspoon cinnamon.** Knead and let rise. Beat into the dough **½ cup currants** and **1 teaspoon grated lemon rind.** Roll 1 inch thick. Cut into rounds with a biscuit cutter. Place 1 to 1½ inches apart on a greased tin and bake in a hot, 400° F. oven 15 to 20 minutes. Make **Plain Jane Icing*** with milk or water. Using the icing, brush a cross on each roll after removing it from the oven.

Aunt Sleide says: "Gram and Gramp Stone came to America from Bohemia in 1887. They came because Gramp wanted to bring his young uns up in a free country. The Stones bought the old Wigger place near us. It was so run down that no one else would've taken it for a gift.

"The folks around here weren't very kind to the Stones at first. They said the Wigger place would probably look worse than ever, now that those 'furriners' had it. They laughed at the clothes the Stones wore and they giggled at the way they spoke English. It *was* kind of funny, I guess, because they'd learned most of it from an old mail-order catalogue they'd gotten hold of.

"But if the Stones minded the jeers and the snubs, they never said anything. Because even if their neighbors didn't welcome them, the Statute of Liberty had.

"Little by little, the old Wigger place began to look better. And in less than a year Gramp's acres were green and shining and Gram's farmhouse was clean and bright. Whenever there was sickness at a neighbor's farm, somehow Gram heard, and her steaming soup and her good coffee cake would be almost the first offerings to arrive. Then gradually, the Stones were accepted as our equals. Though privately I've always wondered if p'raps they weren't our betters.

"Gramp has passed on now and Gram is over eighty. But anyone looking for comfort or cheer knows he'll get it from Gram Stone. And, during homecoming week, the old Wigger place is always the first stop for the folks who've come back home for a visit."

MUFFINS

Prepare muffin tins before making the muffin batter. It is necessary to grease only the bottoms of the tins. Muffins are mixed just long enough to blend the liquid and the dry ingredients. Dry flour lumps must be dampened, but the batter, when mixed to the right stage, will appear lumpy and drop sharply from the spoon. Fill muffin tins ⅔ full of batter and bake 20 to 25 minutes in a hot, 400° to 425° F. oven.

What's good for biscuits is also good for muffins—take two and butter 'em while they're hot!

SWIFT WATER FARM MUFFINS

Sift, then measure **2 cups flour.** Resift with **2 tablespoons sugar, ½ teaspoon salt,** and **3 teaspoons baking powder.** Beat **1 egg.** Combine with **1 cup milk** and **¼ cup melted shortening.** Add to the dry ingredients all at once, and mix rapidly. Fill greased muffin tins ⅔ full and bake in a hot, 400° F. oven 20 to 25 minutes. Makes 12 muffins.

Squash Muffins. Add to the liquid ingredients ½ **cup squash** which has been cooked and pressed through a strainer. Sift ¼ **teaspoon allspice** with the dry ingredients. Add more flour if the squash is very moist.

Nut Muffins. Add ½ **cup broken nuts** to the dry ingredients.

Bacon Muffins. Dice bacon. Fry crisp and drain. Add ⅓ **cup bacon** to the batter.

Dried Fruit Muffins. Cut dried fruit— apricots, prunes, dates, etc.—with a knife or a scissors so the pieces will not stick together. Add ½ **cup dried fruit** to the dry ingredients.

Blueberry Muffins. Wash and dry **1 cup blueberries.** Add to the dry ingredients. Reduce the milk to ¾ cup and increase the sugar to ¼ cup.

Cranberry Muffins. Follow the recipe for **Blueberry Muffins,** above, substituting chopped cranberries.

Jelly Muffins. Fill muffin tins ¼ full of batter. Cover the batter with **1 teaspoon jam.** Fill the tins ⅔ full with batter. Or drop ½ **teaspoon jelly** into the center of each unbaked muffin.

OSCEOLA FARM APPLE SAUCE MUFFINS

Sift, then measure **2 cups flour.** Resift with **4 teaspoons baking powder,** ½ **teaspoon salt, 3 tablespoons sugar,** and ½ **teaspoon allspice.** Beat **2 eggs** well. Beat in **1 cup milk, 3 tablespoons melted butter,** and ½ **cup thick apple sauce.** Add to the dry ingredients. Stir rapidly just enough to mix well. Fill muffin tins ⅔ full and bake in a hot, 400° F. oven 20 to 25 minutes. Makes 12 muffins.

COOKED OATMEAL MUFFINS

Pour **1½ cups scalded milk** on **1 cup cooked oatmeal,** mixing it in. Add **2 eggs,** beaten well, and **2 tablespoons melted shortening.** Sift, then measure **1⅔ cups flour.** Resift with ½ **teaspoon salt, 3 teaspoons baking powder,** and **1 tablespoon sugar.** Add the liquid ingredients and stir rapidly just enough to mix well. Fill greased muffin tins ⅔ full. Bake in a hot, 400° F. oven 20 to 25 minutes. Makes about 12 muffins.

SEARSY COUNTY OATMEAL MUFFINS

Soak **1 cup oatmeal** in **1 cup sour milk** for 1 hour. Add **1 egg** and beat well. Mix in ½ **cup brown sugar** which has been packed firmly in the cup. Add ½ **cup melted shortening.** Sift, then measure **1 cup flour.** Resift with ½ **teaspoon salt, 1 teaspoon baking powder,** and ½ **teaspoon soda.** Add the liquid ingredients all at once. Stir rapidly just enough to mix well. Pour into greased muffin tins and bake in a hot, 400° F. oven 20 to 25 minutes. Makes 12 muffins.

OPEN GATE FARM SWEET POTATO MUFFINS

Cook **sweet potatoes,** mash and use 1 cup. Add **1½ cups milk, 2 eggs** beaten well, **2 tablespoons melted shortening,** and **2 tablespoons honey.** Sift, then measure **1 cup flour.** Resift with ¾ **teaspoon salt,** ¼ **teaspoon allspice,** and **4 teaspoons baking powder.** Add to the potato mixture and mix just enough to combine well. Fill greased muffin tins ⅔ full and bake in a hot, 400° F. oven 20 to 25 minutes. Makes about 12 muffins.

DOUGHNUTS

If doughnut, cruller, or fried cookie dough is chilled, it will be easier to roll. Use as little flour as possible for rolling. The dough should be rolled ⅓ inch thick. Cut with a floured cutter. Use hydrogenated vegetable fat or oil for deep-fat frying. Place the fat in a wide container with high sides and heat it to 360° to 370° F. A deep-fat thermometer or day-old bread cut in cubes 1 inch square may be used to test the temperature. The bread should brown in 60 seconds. If the fat is too hot, the doughnuts will burn before they are cooked through. If the fat is not hot enough, the doughnuts will absorb too much grease.

Drop the doughnuts into the fat, being careful not to splash it. Cook until they are brown on one side, then turn to brown the other side. This process will take about 3 minutes altogether.

Doughnuts should be turned only once. Do not prick them when turning, as the punctures will absorb fat. Remove the doughnuts when they have finished cooking, and drain on unglazed paper. Just before serving and when cool, shake in a sack with confectioner's sugar, granulated sugar, or sugar which has been mixed with cinnamon (1 part cinnamon to 3 parts sugar). The doughnuts may be iced rather than sugared. Store in a tin box to keep.

Some like them hot, some like them cold,
Some like them in coffee, no matter how old!

ANTELOPE COUNTY CRULLERS

Sift, then measure **3½ cups flour.** Resift with **½ teaspoon salt, ½ teaspoon soda, ½ teaspoon cream of tartar,** and **¼ teaspoon nutmeg.** Beat **4 eggs** well. Beat in gradually **⅔ cup sugar.** Combine **⅓ cup milk, ⅓ cup melted shortening,** and **¾ teaspoon grated orange rind.** Add to the egg mixture. Stir in the dry ingredients gradually and mix well. Knead lightly and roll the dough ¼ inch thick. Cut into strips 3 x 1 inches. Fry. Makes about 4 dozen.

SETTING HEN FARM FRIED CAKES

Sift, then measure **5 cups flour.** Resift with **4 teaspoons baking powder, 1 teaspoon salt, 1 teaspoon soda, ½ teaspoon cinnamon,** and **½ teaspoon nutmeg.** Cream **¼ cup shortening.** Add **1 cup sugar** gradually, and beat till light. Add **3 eggs,** one at a time, and beat well after each addition. Beat in **1½ teaspoons vanilla** and **¾ cup mashed**

banana (about 2 bananas). Add ½ **cup sour milk.** Add the sifted dry ingredients gradually and mix well. Knead lightly, roll, cut and fry.

OLD FARM POTATO DOUGHNUTS

Beat **2 eggs** well. Beat in **1 cup sugar.** Add **1 medium potato,** cooked and mashed. Stir in **¼ cup milk** and **1 tablespoon melted shortening.** Sift, then measure **2½ cups flour.** Resift with **2½ teaspoons baking powder, ¼ teaspoon salt,** and **½ teaspoon cinnamon.** Stir into the batter and blend well. Knead lightly, roll, cut, and fry. Makes about 4 dozen.

FRIED COOKIES

Beat **4 egg yolks** well. Two eggs may be used in place of the 4 egg yolks, but the latter makes more tender doughnuts. Beat in **1 cup sugar** gradually. Stir in **1 cup milk** and **2 tablespoons melted shortening.** Sift, then measure 3½ **cups flour.** Resift with **3 teaspoons baking powder, ½ teaspoon salt,** and **½ teaspoon cinnamon.** Add the dry ingredients to the batter gradually and beat until they are blended. Knead lightly, roll, cut, and fry. Makes about 4 dozen.

HILL 'N' DALE FARM RAISED DOUGHNUTS

Scald **1 cup milk.** Add **3 tablespoons fat.** When lukewarm, add **1 cake yeast** and **¾ cup sugar.** Stir in **1½ cups sifted flour.** Cover and let stand in a warm place until light and frothy. Add **1 egg** which has been beaten. Add **2 to 2½ cups sifted flour,** in addition, or enough to make a soft dough. The dough should not be as stiff as bread dough. Cover, set in a warm place and let rise until light. Roll ½ to ¾ inch thick on a lightly floured board. Cut rounds with a lightly floured biscuit cutter. Cover and set in a warm place until almost double. Fry the doughnuts in deep fat with the raised side down first, as in this way they will absorb less fat. When brown, drain and continue as for other doughnuts.

These doughnuts do not require kneading.

HILL 'N' DALE FARM JELLY DOUGHNUTS

Prepare the dough above and roll into a rectangle ¼ to ½ inch thick. Dot one half with teaspoonfuls of jelly—making 2 rows of 3 each, about 1½ inches apart. (Preserves or small pitted drained cooked prunes may be used instead of jelly or jam.) Fold the other half over the first half and cut rounds with a lightly floured biscuit cutter, making sure that the jelly is in the center of each doughnut. Cutting seals the doughnuts. Let rise and fry as above.

MARION COUNTY GINGERBREAD

Sift, then measure **2½ cups flour.** Resift with **1½ teaspoons soda, ½ teaspoon salt, 1 teaspoon cinnamon, 1 teaspoon ginger,** and **½ teaspoon cloves.** Cream **½ cup shortening.** Add **½ cup sugar** gradually, and beat until light and fluffy. Add **1 egg** and beat well. Beat in **1 cup molasses.** Add the dry ingredients to the batter alternately with **1 cup hot water,** beating well after each addition. Pour into a greased pan 9 x 13 x 2 inches. Bake in a moderate, 350° F. oven 30 to 40 minutes or until a tester thrust in the center comes out clean. Cut in squares and serve hot with butter, or cold with fruit.

SOUR MILK GINGERBREAD

Sift, then measure **3 cups flour.** Resift with **½ teaspoon salt, 1½ teaspoons soda, 1½ teaspoons ginger,** and **1 teaspoon allspice.** Cream **½ cup shortening.** Add **½ cup sugar** gradually, beating until the mixture is light and fluffy. Add **2 eggs,** one at a time, and beat well after each addition. Beat in **1 cup molasses.** Add the sifted dry ingredients to the batter alternately with **1 cup sour milk** and beat well after each addition. Grease a pan 9 x 13 x 2 inches, pour the batter in, and bake in a moderate, 350° F. oven 30 to 40 minutes. Top each serving with whipped cream and pass hot maple syrup.

SORGHUM GINGERBREAD

Substitute **sorghum** for molasses in **Sour Milk Gingerbread,** above, or **Marion County Gingerbread,** two receipts above.

AROOSTOOK COUNTY WHOLE WHEAT SCONES

Sift, then measure **½ cup white flour.** Resift with **2½ teaspoons baking powder, ½ teaspoon salt** and **1 tablespoon sugar.** Mix with **1½ cups whole wheat flour** which has been stirred before measuring. Cut in **¼ cup shortening.** Add **¾ cup milk** gradually, stirring it in to form a soft dough. Roll ½ inch thick. Cut in strips 3 inches wide. Make triangles out of the strips by making horizontal, then diagonal cuts. Brush the top of each scone with **cream.** Sprinkle with a little sugar, if desired. Place on a greased baking sheet and bake in a hot, 425° F. oven 15 to 20 minutes.

QUICK LOAF BREADS

Quick loaf breads are similar to muffins. Only the bottoms of the pans are greased for baking them. A moderate, 350° F. oven is used except for large loaves, which require a lower temperature, 300° to 325° F.

The bread has finished baking when the loaf is nicely browned and shrinks from the sides of the pan and when a tester inserted in the center will come out clean.

The bread is removed from the pans after baking, and turned out on a cake rack to cool.

CHAFFEE COUNTY BANANA BREAD

Cream ½ cup **shortening.** Add **1 cup sugar** gradually and beat until the mixture is light and fluffy. Add **2 eggs,** one at a time, and beat well after each addition. Add **1 teaspoon vanilla** and **3 tablespoons sour milk.** Sift, then measure **2 cups flour.** Resift with **1 teaspoon soda** and **½ teaspoon salt.** Add **1 cup broken nuts** to the dry ingredients. Add the dry ingredients to the batter and just beat until smooth. Add **3 medium-sized bananas** which have been pressed through a strainer. Pour into a greased loaf pan, 9 x 5 x 3 inches, and bake in a moderate, 350° F. oven 40 to 60 minutes.

BRAN FIG BREAD

Cream **¼ cup shortening.** Beat in gradually **¼ cup brown sugar** which has been packed firmly in the cup. Add **1 egg,** and beat well. Add **½ cup honey** and **1½ cups milk.** Sift, then measure **3 cups flour.** Resift with **1 teaspoon salt, ¼ teaspoon soda,** and **3 teaspoons baking powder.** Mix the dry ingredients with **1 cup bran** and **1 cup figs** which have been cut with a knife or a scissors. Add to the batter, stirring only until all the dry ingredients are dampened. Bake in a greased loaf pan, 9 x 5 x 3 inches, 40 to 60 minutes in a moderate, 350° F. oven.

One-half cup chopped nuts may be substituted for ½ cup of the figs.

BRAN DATE BREAD

Substitute for the figs in the recipe above **1 cup dates** which have been cut with a knife or a scissors, or use ½ cup dates and ½ cup nuts.

BRAN PEACH BREAD

Wash **1 cup dried peaches.** Pour boiling water over them and soak 15 minutes. Drain and cut coarsely with a knife or scissors. Sift, then measure **2 cups flour.** Resift with **2 teaspoons baking powder, ½ teaspoon salt, ½ teaspoon soda, ⅓ cup sugar,** and **¼ teaspoon allspice.** Add to the dry ingredients **1 cup bran flakes** and **½ cup chopped nuts.** Beat **1 egg.** Beat in **1¼ cup buttermilk** and 3 **tablespoons melted shortening.** Add to the dry ingredients and beat just enough to mix well. Add the peaches. Bake in a greased 9 x 5 x 3 inch loaf pan in a moderate, 350° F. oven 50 to 60 minutes.

HOOD COUNTY SOYBEAN BREAD

Sift, then measure **1½ cups flour** and **1 cup soybean flour.** Resift with **½ teaspoon salt, 3 teaspoons baking powder, ½ teaspoon allspice,** and **3 tablespoons sugar.** Beat **2 eggs** well. Beat in **1 cup milk** and **¼ cup melted shortening.** Add the dry ingredients to the liquid, mixing well. Add **1 cup soy nuts** which have been toasted and salted. If soy nuts are not available, any unsalted broken nuts may be used. Increase the salt in the recipe to 1 teaspoon if using unsalted nuts. Fill a greased loaf pan, 9 x 5 x 3 inches. Let stand 20 minutes. Bake in a moderate, 350° F. oven 50 to 60 minutes.

SWIFT WATER FARM CINNAMON BREAD

Sift, then measure 3 **cups flour.** Resift with **1½ teaspoon soda, ½ teaspoon salt,** and 3 **teaspoons cinnamon.** Cream **½ cup shortening.** Add **½ cup sugar** gradually and beat until light and fluffy. Add **2 eggs,** one at a time, and beat well after each addition. Add **1 cup honey** and **1 cup buttermilk,** beating them in. Add the sifted dry ingredients gradually, and beat vigorously. Pour into a greased pan, 9 x 13 x 2 inches. Bake in a moderate, 350° F. oven 40 to 60 minutes.

GRAHAM PRUNE BREAD

Sift, then measure **1 cup white flour** and **2 cups graham flour.** Resift with **1 teaspoon baking powder, 1 teaspoon soda,** and **½ teaspoon salt.** Cream **3 tablespoons lard.** Beat in **½ cup sugar.** Add **1 egg** and beat well. Combine **1 cup prune juice** with **¼ cup milk.** Add to the batter alternately with the sifted dry ingredients. Mix in **1 cup prunes,** which have been cooked and pressed through a strainer. Turn into a greased loaf pan, 9 x 5 x 3 inches, and let stand 10 minutes. Bake in a moderate, 350° F. oven 50 to 60 minutes.

GRAHAM APRICOT BREAD

Follow the recipe above, substituting **apricot pulp** and **apricot juice** for prune pulp and prune juice.

BISCATAQUIS COUNTY JOHNNY BREAD

Sift, then measure **3 cups flour.** Cut in **½ cup lard.** Dissolve **½ teaspoon salt** in **6 tablespoons milk.** Add to the flour mixture with enough additional milk to make a dough stiff enough to roll. Spread on a pan 8 x 8 inches. Bake in a hot, 400° F. oven 15 to 20 minutes or until nicely browned. Break, rather than cut, and eat piping hot with plenty of butter.

OLD-FASHIONED OATMEAL BREAD

Sift, then measure **1¼ cups flour.** Resift with **¾ teaspoon salt, 2½ teaspoons baking powder, ¼ teaspoon soda,** and **⅓ cup sugar.** Add **1 cup seedless raisins** and **1¼ cups oatmeal** (stirred before measuring), and mix together. Beat **1 egg** slightly. Add **2 tablespoons melted shortening** and **1 cup sour milk.** Pour into the dry ingredients all at once, and mix rapidly, stirring just enough to dampen them. The mixture should have a rough appearance. Turn into a greased loaf pan, 9 x 5 x 3 inches, and bake in a moderate, 350° F. oven 40 to 60 minutes.

QUICK CORN BREADS

SHORT'NIN' BREAD

Render about ½ pound fat by cutting it in small pieces and cooking it over boiling water in a covered double boiler. Stir occasionally. When melted, strain through a cheesecloth. Drain the crisp brown meat tissue or cracklings on unglazed paper. Cool the fat and store in a refrigerator or other cold place for frying, etc. The cracklings may be made from fowl, beef, or pork fat, or may be purchased in some butcher shops. The skin from fowl cracklings is used, but is removed from meat cracklings. To make short'nin' bread, pour **2 cups buttermilk** over **3 cups corn meal,** stirred. Mix with **1 teaspoon salt** and **1 teaspoon soda.** Mix in **1 cup cracklings** which have been put through a meat grinder or mashed with a rolling pin if they are larger than the first joint of the little finger. Add enough **boiling water** (up to 1 cup) to moisten and shape. Make cakes 4 x 2 x 1 inches. Place on a greased baking sheet and bake in a hot, 400° F. oven 20 to 30 minutes.

"Mammy's little baby loves short'nin' bread."

WILLOW FARM BROWN BREAD

Sift, then measure **1 cup flour.** Resift with **1 teaspoon salt, 4½ teaspoons baking powder.** Stir, then measure **1 cup corn meal** and **1 cup whole wheat flour** and mix with the dry ingredients. Add **⅔ cup molasses** to **1½ cups milk.** Add to dry ingredients and mix until smooth. Fill a greased mold ⅔ full and steam 3½ hours. Or bake in a greased loaf pan, 9 x 5 x 3 inches, in a moderate, 350° F. oven 40 to 60 minutes.

CATTO COUNTY HOMINY BREAD

Cook whole kernel hominy, or, if preferred, use well-drained canned hominy. To **1 cup hot hominy,** add **2 tablespoons shortening, ½ teaspoon salt,** and **2 eggs** beaten well. Mix well and add **¼ cup corn meal.** Pour into a greased casserole and bake in a very moderate, 325° F. oven for 12 minutes. Increase the heat to moderately hot, 375° F. and bake 20 to 25 minutes more. Serve like spoon bread.

CORN MEAL MUFFINS

Sift, then measure **¾ cup flour.** Resift with **3 teaspoons baking powder, ¾ teaspoon salt,** and **¾ cup corn meal.** Beat **1 egg** well. Beat in **¾ cup milk, 2 tablespoons light corn syrup,** and **3 tablespoons melted shortening.** Add to the dry ingredients and stir rapidly just enough to mix well. Fill greased muffin tins ⅔ full. Bake in a hot, 425° F. oven 15 to 25 minutes. Makes 16 muffins.

CORN STICKS

Grease corn-stick pans. Pour in the above batter. Bake in a hot, 425° F. oven 20 to 30 minutes.

MAGNOLIA HOUSE JOHNNY CAKE

Combine **½ cup sweet milk** and **½ cup sour milk.** Add **¾ teaspoon salt, ½ teaspoon soda,** and **1 tablespoon melted shortening.** Add **corn meal** to make a batter stiff enough to roll, about 4 cups. Spread in a greased 8 x 8 inch pan. Smooth it by pressing down with another pan the same size. Bake in a hot, 400° F. oven. When it begins to brown, in about 20 minutes, baste with melted butter. Baste again in 10 minutes. Bake until the crust is crisp and brown. The Johnny Cake will take about 40 minutes in all to bake. Break rather than cut Johnny Cake for serving. Serve hot with butter and honey or jelly. Serves 4 to 6.

Johnny Cake may be reheated in the oven. It keeps very well, as is evidenced by its name, which was originally Journey Cake. It was made to take on long trips because of its good keeping qualities.

BIBB COUNTY BUTTERMILK SPOON BREAD

Bring to a boil **1 cup sweet milk.** Stir in **½ cup corn meal** and cook for 5 minutes, stirring constantly. Remove from the fire and add **1 teaspoon baking powder, ½ teaspoon soda, 1 teaspoon salt,** and **3 tablespoons shortening.** Beat **2 egg yolks** well. Beat **1 cup buttermilk** into the yolks. Beat into the main mixture. Fold in gently **2 egg whites** which have been beaten stiff but not dry. Bake in a greased casserole in a moderate, 350° F. oven 30 to 40 minutes. Serve from the casserole. Serves 4 to 6.

McMINN COUNTY GREEN CORN SPOON BREAD

Remove the kernels from **6 medium ears of green corn** as for **Sweet Corn.*** Bring **1 cup milk** to a boil. Add the corn and stir in **⅓ cup corn meal** and **½ teaspoon salt.** Cook for 5 minutes, stirring constantly. Remove from the heat and beat in **¼ cup shortening** and **1 tablespoon sugar.** Beat **2 egg yolks** well. Beat **1 cup milk** into the yolks. Beat into the main mixture. Fold in gently **2 egg whites** which have been beaten stiff but not dry. Turn into a greased casserole and bake in a very moderate, 325° F. oven 40 to 60 minutes. This is especially good with chicken or ham. Serves 6.

PETTIS COUNTY SPIDER CORN BREAD

Sift, then measure **1 cup flour.** Resift with **½ teaspoon salt, 1 tablespoon sugar, 1 teaspoon soda,** and **1 cup corn meal.** Beat **2 eggs** well. Beat in **1¼ cup sour milk** and **2 tablespoons melted shortening.** Add to the sifted dry ingredients and beat only long enough to blend well. Pour into a greased, preheated 9-inch skillet. Bake in a moderate, 350° F. oven 50 minutes. Serves 6.

SANDWICH FILLINGS

Day-old bread slices best for sandwiches. Creaming the butter makes spreading the sandwiches easier. Spread the butter and the filling to the very edge of the bread. If crusts are to be removed, cut them off after spreading the sandwich with filling.

CAMDEN COUNTY COTTAGE EGG FILLING

Mince **2 hard-cooked eggs.** Add **1 teaspoon prepared mustard, ¼ teaspoon salt, 2 tablespoons chives** or other herb, and **1 cup creamed cottage cheese.** Mix well.

LADY CALLER SANDWICH FILLING

Cream **6 tablespoons cream cheese.** Beat in **1 tablespoon cream.** Add **4 tablespoons marmalade,** and **½ cup chopped salted nuts** and mix well. Add more cream if necessary to make the filling thin enough to spread easily.

TUSCARAWAS COUNTY SANDWICH FILLING

Spread **1 slice whole wheat bread** with **butter.** Spread a second slice with **tomato ketchup.** Add **¼ teaspoon onion,** which has been diced very fine, to enough **cold baked beans** to spread the bread.

POINTE COUPEE COUNTY LIVER SPREAD

Cook **1 diced onion** in **2 tablespoons fat** for 5 minutes. Add **⅔ pound liver** and cook slowly for 5 to 10 minutes. Press the liver and onion through a strainer with **3 hard-cooked eggs.** Add **2 tablespoons melted fat,** in addition, about **¾ teaspoon salt,** and **¼ teaspoon pepper** to taste, and mix lightly to a paste.

Any liver may be used but chicken livers are especially

good. Leftover cooked liver may be used in place of raw liver. Then omit frying.

HAVEN FARM SAVORY SPREAD

Run through a food grinder **8 slices bacon, 1 medium onion,** and **½ pound cheese.** Add **1 teaspoon dry mustard.** Mix well, and moisten with **2 to 3 teaspoons mayonnaise.** Toast **bread** on one side. Spread the untoasted side with the filling and place under the broiler of a slow, 300° F. oven. Broil until the cheese melts and the bacon is crisp.

This mixture may be stored in the refrigerator to be used as needed.

7

HOTCAKES AND FRITTERS

GRIDDLECAKES, PANCAKES, AND WAFFLES

Griddlecakes, pancakes, and waffles are all made by the same method. The liquid ingredients are added to the dry ingredients and they are combined rapidly with as few strokes as possible. There should not be any dry flour lumps in the batter, but it will have a lumpy appearance. The batter should not be so thin that it overspreads when placed on the griddle, nor so heavy that it heaps up and is thick when it rises. Add more flour to a batter which is too thin and additional liquid to a batter which is too heavy. It is easier to pour the batter from a pitcher than to spoon it onto the griddle.

Either a frying pan or a griddle may be used for frying pancakes or griddlecakes. A griddle is more convenient to use. For perfect cakes, the temperature of the pan or the griddle must be just right. If the pan is too hot, the cakes will burn before they finish cooking in the center. If the pan is not hot enough, the cakes will cook so slowly that they will lose too much air and flatten out. To test the pan or griddle for correct temperature, sprinkle a few drops of cold water on it. If the water dances around and disappears almost immediately, the pan is ready for use. It is not necessary to grease the pan or griddle unless specified in the recipe. If the griddle is greased, it is hot enough to use when the fat smokes slightly. If the cakes stick, it is because the pan was not the correct temperature.

When the edges of the cakes appear slightly dry, they

are ready to be turned. The cakes should be turned only once. They have finished cooking when they have settled to a practically level surface and are nicely browned.

The manufacturers' directions for using waffle irons should be followed.

Not even a lazybones will stay in bed if he smells griddle-cakes cooking!

Waffles, griddlecakes, and pancakes may be served with:

Butter and Maple Syrup
Buttered Honey*
Confectioners Sugar
Sugar and Cinnamon
Molasses
Shaved Maple Sugar
Sweetened Crushed Fruits
Dessert Sauces
Brown Sugar Sauce*
Corn Syrup

Griddlecakes may be fried all at once, buttered, sprinkled with shaved maple sugar and stacked. They are cut like a pie and sluiced with maple syrup. The cook can sit down and enjoy them too if they are prepared this way.

BUTTERED HONEY

Cream ½ **cup butter.** Add ¼ **cup honey** gradually, beating it in until the mixture is light and fluffy. Serve on hot waffles or pancakes.

BANNOCK COUNTY MOCK MAPLE SYRUP

Bring **2 cups water** to a boil. Add **3½ cups brown sugar** which has been packed firmly in the cup. Remove from the fire and stir until smooth. Add **1 teaspoon maple flavoring.** Bottle and let stand 24 hours before using.

OLD FARM BATTY CAKES

Sift, then measure **2 cups flour.** Resift with **2 teaspoons baking powder, ¼ teaspoon salt,** and **2 tablespoons sugar.** Beat **2 eggs** well. Beat in **1½ cups milk.** Add **6 tablespoons melted shortening.** Add to the dry ingredients and mix rapidly. Fry on a hot griddle. Serves 4.

CHEESE PANCAKES

Sift, then measure **1 cup flour.** Resift with **½ teaspoon salt** and **1 tablespoon sugar.** Beat **4 eggs** well. Beat in **1 cup sour cream.** Mix in **1 cup cottage cheese.** Add to the sifted dry ingredients and mix rapidly. Fry on a hot griddle. Serves 4.

LEAKE COUNTY CORN LACE CAKES

Beat **2 eggs** well. Beat in **2 cups milk.** Add **1 cup corn meal, ½ teaspoon salt,** and **6 tablespoons melted shortening.** Mix well and fry on a hot griddle, stirring the batter each time before dipping it up. The batter is very thin, but the cakes can be turned without difficulty as soon as they have finished cooking on one side. They are wonderful with syrup and butter. Serves 4.

CORN GRIDDLECAKES

Pour **1 cup boiling water** over **1 cup corn meal.** Add **¼ cup shortening** and stir until the shortening melts. Let cool. Sift, then measure **1 cup flour.** Resift with **2 teaspoons baking powder, 1 teaspoon salt,** and **2 tablespoons sugar.** Beat **2 eggs** well. Beat in **1 cup milk.** Add to the corn meal. Add to the dry ingredients and mix rapidly. Fry on a hot griddle. Serves 4.

BLUEBERRY GRIDDLECAKES

Sift, then measure **2 cups flour.** Resift with **¼ cup sugar, ½ teaspoon salt,** and **3 teaspoons baking powder.** Beat **2 eggs** well. Beat in **1 cup milk.** Add **¼ cup melted shortening.** Add to the dry ingredients and mix rapidly. Fold in **1½ cups blueberries or huckleberries** which have been washed and dried. Fry on a hot griddle. Serves 4 to 6.

LAKE FARM 'LASSES GRIDDLECAKES

Sift, then measure **2 cups flour.** Resift with **2 tablespoons sugar, ½ teaspoon salt,** and **3 teaspoons baking powder.** Beat **2 eggs** well. Beat in **1 cup milk, ¼ cup melted shortening,** and **3 tablespoons molasses.** Add to the dry ingredients gradually, and mix rapidly. Fry on a hot griddle. Serves 4.

CORA GILBERT'S RECEIPT FOR SOUR MILK GRIDDLECAKES

Sift, then measure **2½ cups flour.** Resift with **½ teaspoon salt, 1¼ teaspoons soda,** and **1 teaspoon baking powder.** Beat **1 egg** well. Beat in **2 cups sour milk.** Add to the dry ingredients gradually and mix rapidly. Fry on a hot greased griddle. Serves 4 to 6.

Aunt Sleide says: "Cora Gilbert says these cakes are so light that she's always afraid they're going to float right off of her griddle!"

GEAUGA COUNTY BUCKWHEAT CAKES

Sift, then measure **2 cups buckwheat flour.** Resift with **1½ teaspoons sugar** and **½ teaspoon salt.** Beat **1 egg.** Beat in **1¾ cups milk** and **2½ tablespoons melted fat.** (If serving with pork sausages, 2½ tablespoons of the drained fat may be used as the shortening in the recipe.) Add to the dry ingredients and mix rapidly. Fry on a hot greased griddle. Serves 4.

Geauga County is noted for its maple syrup. These good buckwheat cakes are served at the annual maple festival there.

RISEN BUCKWHEAT CAKES

Scald **2 cups milk** and pour over **½ cup bread crumbs.** When lukewarm, add **½ teaspoon salt** and **½ yeast cake** which has been dissolved in **½ cup lukewarm water.** Stir in enough sifted **buckwheat flour** to make a batter that will pour easily, about 1¾ cups. Cover and let stand overnight. The next morning, add **1 tablespoon molasses** and **½ teaspoon soda** which has been dissolved in **¼ cup lukewarm water.** Mix and fry on a hot greased griddle. Serves 4 to 6.

CROOKED ELM FARM CORN FRITTERS

Beat **2 egg yolks** well. Beat in **2 cups cooked fresh corn kernels** or drained can corn. Sift, then measure **¼ cup flour.** Resift with **1 teaspoon baking powder, 2 teaspoons sugar,** and **½ teaspoon salt.** Mix the dry ingredients with the yolk mixture. Add **3 tablespoons milk.** Fold in gently **2 egg whites** which have been beaten stiff but not dry. Fry on a greased griddle or in deep fat as for **Doughnuts.*** Serves 4.

ALACHUA COUNTY ORANGE FRITTERS

Sift, then measure **1 cup flour.** Resift with **1 teaspoon sugar, 1 teaspoon baking powder,** and **⅛ teaspoon salt.** Beat **1 egg** well. Beat in **1 cup milk.** Add to the dry ingredients gradually, stirring until smooth. Peel, slice and seed at least 2 oranges, removing all white membrane carefully. Dip in the batter. Fry as for **Doughnuts.*** Serve sprinkled with sugar. Serves 4.

MAGNOLIA HOUSE RICE FRITTERS

Sift, then measure **2 cups flour.** Resift with **1½ teaspoons baking powder, ½ teaspoon salt,** and **1 teaspoon sugar.** Beat **2 eggs** well. Beat in **1 cup milk** and **½ cup cooked rice.** Add to the dry ingredients gradually, stirring until smooth. Fry in deep fat as for **Doughnuts.*** Drain and serve mashed sugared fruit over them. Serves 4 to 6.

BROWN SUGAR WAFFLES

Sift, then measure **2 cups flour.** Resift with **3 teaspoons baking powder, ½ teaspoon salt,** and **3 tablespoons brown sugar** which has been packed firmly. Mix with **¾ cup broken nuts.** Beat **3 egg yolks** well. Beat in **1½ cups milk** and **6 tablespoons melted shortening.** Add to the dry ingredients and mix rapidly. Fold in **3 egg whites** which have been beaten stiff but not dry. Bake on a hot iron. Serves 4 or 5.

BUTTERMILK WAFFLES

Sift, then measure **2 cups flour.** Resift with **2 teaspoons baking powder, 1 teaspoon soda,** and **¼ teaspoon salt.** Beat **2 whole eggs** well. Beat in **2 cups buttermilk** and **6 tablespoons melted shortening.** Add to the dry ingredients and mix rapidly. Bake on a hot iron. Serves 4 or 5.

GINGERBREAD WAFFLES

Sift, then measure **2 cups flour.** Resift with **1 teaspoon soda, ½ teaspoon salt, 1 teaspoon baking powder, 2 teaspoons ginger,** and **1 teaspoon cinnamon.** Beat **2 whole eggs** well. Beat in **½ cup sour milk, 1 cup molasses,** and **½ cup melted shortening.** Add to the dry ingredients and mix rapidly. Bake on a hot iron. Serve with hot maple syrup and whipped cream as a dessert or with honey and bacon for breakfast. Serves 4 or 5.

RICH CREAM WAFFLES

Sift, then measure, **1½ cups cake flour.** Resift with **2 teaspoons baking powder, ½ teaspoon salt,** and **2 tablespoons sugar.** Beat **3 egg yolks** well. Beat in **1 cup cream, 1 cup milk,** and **½ cup melted shortening.** Add to the dry ingredients and mix rapidly. Fold in gently **3 egg whites** beaten stiff but not dry. Bake on a hot iron. Serves 4.

CROOKED ELM FARM SOUR CREAM WAFFLES

Sift, then measure **1 cup plus 2 tablespoons flour.** Re-sift with **¼ teaspoon salt, 1 teaspoon soda, 1 tablespoon sugar,** and **2 teaspoons baking powder.** Beat **3 egg yolks** well. Beat in **2 cups thick sour cream.** Add to the dry ingredients and mix rapidly. Beat **3 egg whites** stiff, but not dry. Fold them into the batter gently. Bake on a hot iron. Serves 4.

BACON WAFFLES

Fry **bacon** until crisp and crumble it into any plain waffle batter. Or place a half strip of bacon on top of the waffle before closing the iron, and bake.

8

SALADS AND SALAD DRESSINGS

All salads are more attractive and palatable if the ingredients used are fresh and crisp. Discolored or wilted ingredients should be discarded. Vegetables and fruit for salad are best when they are sliced or cut coarsely. If chopped, they lose their identity and look messy. Herbs are good in salads. Do not use them lavishly as they are strong in flavor.

If the salad is to be garnished, use only edible garnishes such as olives, carrot strips, pearl onions, sprigs of mint, radishes, hard-cooked egg slices, pickles, etc.

A cold salad should be served very cold.

ASPARAGUS SALAD

Cover **1 pound cold cooked asparagus** with **Cooked Sour Cream Dressing.*** Serves 4.

WILLOW FARM PICKLED BEET SALAD

Prepare the sauce for **Pickled Beets on Greens,*** and chill it. Mix **1 pound cold cooked beets** with the sauce. The beets may be sliced, cubed, or left whole if they are very small. Serve very cold on uncooked young beet greens or other greens. Or serve the beets in a bowl as a relish. Serves 4 to 6.

LIMA AND HAM SALAD

Dice ½ cup **celery.** Chop ½ **cup cooked ham.** Hard-cook **2 eggs** and chop coarsely. Mix with **2 cups cooked lima beans.** Add **1 teaspoon onion juice** and moisten with **Cooked Salad Dressing.*** Serve very cold on greens. Serves 4.

LENAWEE COUNTY KIDNEY BEAN SALAD

Dice ¼ **small green pepper, 1 small bunch celery,** and ½ **small onion.** Add ½ **cup cabbage,** shredded, **1 hard-cooked egg,** sliced, and **2 cups kidney beans,** canned or cooked. Season to taste with about ½ **teaspoon salt** and ⅛ **teaspoon pepper.** Mix and add any dressing. Serves 4.

KING COUNTY BLACK-EYE PEAS AND TOMATO SALAD

Soak and cook **2 cups black-eye peas** as for **Dried Vegetables.*** Drain. When cold, combine with **1 cup celery,** diced, **2 tablespoons green pepper,** diced, **1 small onion,** sliced, and **4 tomatoes,** quartered. Mix and season to taste with about ½ **teaspoon salt** and ⅛ **teaspoon pepper.** Add ¼ **cup vinegar,** or more if needed, to moisten. Serves 6 to 8.

STARK COUNTY CABBAGE APPLE SALAD

Mix equal parts **shredded cabbage** and unpeeled, diced **apple.** Season to taste with **salt** and **pepper** and very little **sugar.** Mix with **Cooked Salad Dressing*** or with vinegar. Serve on greens.

COLE SLAW

Shred **1 small head of cabbage** fine. Season to taste with about ½ **teaspoon salt** and ⅛ **teaspoon pepper.** Moisten with **Cooked Salad Dressing,*** or with ½ **cup sour cream** which has been thinned with **1 tablespoon vinegar.** Serves 4 to 6.

MERRIMACK COUNTY HOT COLE SLAW

Shred **1 small head of cabbage** fine. Season to taste with about **½ teaspoon salt, ⅛ teaspoon pepper,** and **1 teaspoon sugar.** Heat **2½ tablespoons bacon fat.** Add cabbage and cook until tender, 20 to 30 minutes. Break **1 egg** in a measuring cup. Beat slightly. Beat in **¼ cup water** and enough **vinegar** to fill the cup to the ¾ mark. Add to the cabbage and cook until slightly thickened, stirring constantly. Serves 4 to 6.

This may be used as a vegetable.

HI-HILL FARM DANDELION SALAD

Use only the leaves of young dandelions. Remove the hard and discolored parts from the leaves and wash thoroughly to remove all dirt. Dry gently but thoroughly. Season **2 cups greens,** to taste, with about **½ teaspoon salt, ⅛ teaspoon pepper,** and **¼ teaspoon sugar.** Add **¼ cup vinegar** or more to moisten. Serves 4.

OSCEOLA FARM WILTED CUCUMBERS

Peel and slice **2 medium cucumbers** about ⅛ inch thick. Dissolve **1 tablespoon salt** in **1 cup cold water** and soak the cucumbers in it for 15 minutes. Rinse with cold water and squeeze in a clean cloth to remove moisture. Mix with **Sour Cream Dressing.*** Dill is good with cucumbers. Use **¼ teaspoon dill seeds** or **2 tablespoons chopped fresh dill.** Serve on greens. Serves 4 to 6.

WILTED LETTUCE

Dice **5 strips bacon** and fry until crisp. Add to the pan about **¼ cup vinegar, ½ teaspoon salt, ⅛ teaspoon pepper** and **1 tablespoon sugar** to taste. Pour the hot dressing over **1 medium head lettuce** which has been shredded and mix well. Serves 4 to 6.

MARION COUNTY POTATO SALAD

Cook **6 medium potatoes** in their jackets. Peel immediately. Pull into pieces with two forks and add all the **mayonnaise*** they will absorb. Chill. Add **1 cup celery,** diced, **1 unpeeled cucumber,** sliced, **2 hard-cooked eggs,** chopped coarsely, **4 tablespoons green pepper,** diced, **1 small onion,** diced, about **½ teaspoon salt** and **¼ teaspoon pepper,** to taste, and additional mayonnaise which has been thinned slightly with **lemon juice or vinegar.** Serve very cold and garnish with quartered **tomatoes.** Serves 4 to 6.

HOT POTATO SALAD

Dice **5 strips bacon** and fry until crisp. Add to the pan **½ cup vinegar, 1 teaspoon salt, ¼ teaspoon pepper,** and **½ teaspoon sugar.** Additional seasoning or vinegar may be added, to taste. Dice **10 medium potatoes** which have been cooked and peeled, and chop **1 large onion** fine. Add the bacon-vinegar mixture and mix well. Serve hot. Serves 6 to 8.

MARIETTA BOBBITT'S RECEIPT FOR CHICKEN SALAD

Cut cooked chicken into chunks. Combine **2 cups chicken** with **1 cup diced celery** and **1 cup broken pecans.** Season to taste with about **¾ teaspoon salt** and **⅛ teaspoon pepper.** Whip **1 cup cream** stiff and fold it into **Cooked Salad Dressing.*** Mix with the chicken and the nuts. Serve very cold on greens. Serves 4 to 6.

Aunt Sleide says: "Marietta Bobbitt was a good cook before she was knee-high to a cucumber patch, and her cooking improved steadily. She took so many prizes at the county fair that people'd find out what she was entering and then make something else so they'd have a chance to win. It got so her entry would be the only one of its kind. The judges finally decided it wasn't fair. The next year they asked Marietta not to tell what she was entering. So she didn't. Lizzie Freel was going to enter a pie but she decided not to because maybe Marietta was. Polly Lyons was going to enter cookies, but she decided not to because maybe Marietta was. Bertha Lewis was going to enter a cake but she decided not to because maybe Marietta was. Meantime, Marietta got to thinking about the way she was always winning and maybe she'd ought to give someone else a chance, so she decided not to enter anything. But she forgot to tell anyone. That was the year that no baked goods was entered at the fair!"

SWIFT WATER FARM PORK SALAD

Shred **1 small head cabbage.** Chop coarsely **2 hard-cooked eggs.** Dice **½ cup celery, 2 tablespoons onion, 1 small green pepper,** and **1 tablespoon parsley.** Add to the cabbage mixture with **3 cups cold cooked pork.** Season to taste with about **¾ teaspoon salt** and **⅛ teaspoon pepper** and add approximately **½ cup mayonnaise*** to moisten. Serve cold on greens. Serves 6.

SALMON SALAD

Turn into a bowl the contents of a **1-pound can salmon.** Thinly slice **2 medium onions.** Add to the salmon, and toss with two forks to separate the salmon and break the onions into rings. Add about **½ cup vinegar,** to taste, and season with approximately **½ teaspoon salt** and **⅛ teaspoon pepper.** Serves 4.

COTTAGE EGG SALAD

Fill **lettuce leaves** with **Camden County Cottage Egg Filling.*** Makes 2 salads.

HERB GARDEN CHEESE

Add to **cottage cheese** a combination, in any proportion, of fresh herbs which have been cut fine with a scissors. Parsley, chives, tarragon, sage, summer savory, basil, marjoram, dill, rosemary, or any others available may be used. Season with **salt** and **pepper** to taste. Thin with sour cream, if desired. Quarter a **tomato** for each salad, but do not cut all the way through it, and cover with about ¼ cup of the cheese mixture. Serve on greens.

FRUIT SALAD

Prepare fruits by peeling, hulling, or pitting when necessary. Slice bananas and oranges, dice or make balls of melon, etc. Serve very cold on greens. Use any fruit dressing.

ASPIC SALADS

To turn out an aspic salad, hold the mold or molds in hot water for a second, being careful not to let the water touch the salad itself. Place the greens which are to be served with an aspic salad around, rather than under the salad, to avoid breaking it. Or tuck them under the edges of the aspic after it has been turned out.

BOX ELDER COUNTY JELLIED BEETS AND HORSERADISH

Cook **8 small beets.** Drain, reserving **1 cup liquid,** and dice the beets. Add to the beets **¾ cup diced celery, ½ teaspoon salt, 3 tablespoons vinegar,** and **3 tablespoons prepared horseradish.** Dissolve **2 packages lemon gelatin** in **2 cups hot water.** Mix with the beet water and the vegetables. Turn into a mold which has been rinsed with cold water. Chill until firm. Unmold. Serves 6 to 8.

HURRY-UP TOMATO ASPIC

Soak **1 tablespoon unflavored gelatin** in **¼ cup cold tomato juice** for 5 minutes. Dissolve in **1¾ cups tomato juice** which has been brought to the boiling point. Season highly with about **¾ teaspoon salt** and **¼ teaspoon pepper.** Add **1 tablespoon onion juice,** if desired, and **1 cup diced celery** or other vegetable. Canned or fresh crabmeat is good in this aspic. Chill until firm in molds which have been rinsed in cold water. Unmold. Serves 4.

JELLIED VEGETABLE SALAD

Soak **1 tablespoon unflavored gelatin** in **½ cup cold water** for 5 minutes. Dissolve in **1 cup boiling water or stock.** Add **¼ cup lemon juice** and season well with about **¾ teaspoon salt** and **⅛ teaspoon pepper.** Add onion juice to taste, if liked. Chill the aspic until it is about set. Then add **1 to 2 cups raw or cooked vegetables.** Use celery, diced; cauliflower, separated into flowerets; cabbage, shredded; carrots, cut lengthwise; peppers, diced; radishes, sliced; etc. Turn into a mold which has been rinsed with cold water. Chill until firm. Turn out and serve with **greens.** Serves 4 to 6.

RINGGOLD COUNTY ORANGE AND CRANBERRY JELLY

Pick over **4 cups cranberries** (1 quart). Wash **2 small oranges.** Quarter and peel the oranges, and remove the seeds. Run through a food chopper with the cranberries, using a medium knife. Do not drain. Dissolve **1 cup sugar** in **¼ cup water,** stirring over low heat. When hot, dissolve **1 package orange gelatin** in it. Add to the fruit with **1 cup chopped nuts.** Turn into a wet shallow pan and chill until firm. Cut in squares and serve on slices of **orange** which have been placed on **greens.** Serves 10 to 12.

This is an ideal salad for Thanksgiving.

SNOW WHITE MOLD

Press **3 cups cottage cheese** through a strainer. Blend in **1 teaspoon salt** and **1⅓ cup cream.** Soak **2 tablespoons unflavored gelatin** in **¼ cup cold milk** for 5 minutes. Dissolve over hot water. Stir in a portion of the cheese mixture, a tablespoon at a time. Return to the main mixture. Turn into individual molds which have been rinsed with cold water. Place slices of fruit, fresh or canned, on **greens.** Pineapple, melon, peach, or orange may be used. Turn the molds out on the fruit. Serves 6 to 8.

TWO HILLS PLANTATION JELLIED CHICKEN SALAD

Soak **1 tablespoon unflavored gelatin** in **¼ cup cold chicken stock** for 5 minutes. Dissolve it in **¾ cup chicken stock** which has been heated to the boiling point. Season well with about **½ teaspoon salt** and **⅛ teaspoon pepper.** Cool. Fold in **1 cup cream** which has been whipped stiff, **2 cups cooked chicken** which has been diced, and **½ cup celery,** diced. Turn into molds which have been rinsed with cold water. Chill until firm and turn out. Serve with greens. Serves 4.

WHITE CLOUD RANCH HAM SLAW SALAD

Soak **1 tablespoon unflavored gelatin** in **¼ cup cold water** for 5 minutes. Dissolve it in **¼ cup boiling water.** Add to **¾ cup mayonnaise** with **½ teaspoon salt, 1 tablespoon vinegar, 1½ cups cooked ham,** chopped, **1½ cups cabbage,** shredded, **½ onion,** chopped fine, and **3 sweet pickles,** chopped. Turn into molds which have been rinsed with cold water. Chill until firm, and turn out. Serve with **greens.** Serves 4.

VEGETABLE DRESSINGS

MIZ DEAN EDMISTON'S RECEIPT FOR BACON DRESSING

Dice **3 strips bacon** and fry crisp. Remove bacon and all but **1 tablespoon bacon fat.** Add **2 tablespoons vinegar, 1/8 teaspoon dry mustard, 1/8 teaspoon pepper,** and **1/4 teaspoon sugar.** Mix with **1/2 cup cream.** Heat and pour over shredded **cabbage or lettuce,** adding the bacon.

Aunt Sleide says: "Miz Dean Edmiston asked my great-niece Fern Sleide what she wanted to be when she grew up, and Fern told her, 'A mama, if someone asks me.' "

COOKED SALAD DRESSING

Beat **3 eggs** slightly in the top of a double boiler. Add **1 cup rich milk** and **1/4 cup lemon juice** to **1/2 teaspoon dry mustard, 1 tablespoon sugar, 1/2 teaspoon salt, 1 1/2 teaspoons flour,** and **1/4 teaspoon paprika,** stirring to make a smooth paste. Beat into the egg, and cook over hot water, stirring constantly until the mixture coats the spoon well. Add **2 tablespoons butter.** Cool and serve very cold.

COOKED SOUR CREAM DRESSING

When **Cooked Salad Dressing,** above, has cooled, fold in **1 cup thick sour cream.**

SOUR CREAM DRESSING

Dissolve the following in **3 tablespoons lemon juice: 1 teaspoon dry mustard, 1/2 teaspoon paprika, 1 teaspoon salt, 1 teaspoon sugar,** and **1/2 teaspoon pepper.** Add to **1 cup sour cream. One to 2 tablespoons herbs,** cut fine, may be added. Serve very cold.

GOLDENROD SOUR CREAM DRESSING

Mash **2 hard-cooked egg yolks.** Proceed as for **Sour Cream Dressing,** above, adding the ingredients slowly tc the yolks, and beating well.

HILL 'N' DALE FARM HONEY TOMATO DRESSING

Mix together in a large bowl **1 teaspoon onion juice, ½ teaspoon salt,** and **¼ cup honey.** Stir in **⅓ cup tomato ketchup,** adding it a tablespoon at a time. Beat in **1 cup oil,** adding a tablespoon at a time. Beat in **¼ cup vinegar,** a tablespoon at a time. Add **1 tablespoon seeds:** celery, dill, poppy, or caraway. Store in a jar in the refrigerator or other cold place. Shake well before using.

MAYONNAISE

Beat **1 egg yolk** well. (Do not use strictly fresh eggs.) Dissolve **¼ teaspoon dry mustard, ½ teaspoon salt, ¼ teaspoon paprika,** and **½ teaspoon sugar** in **2 tablespoons vinegar.** Beat the mixture into the egg yolk. Beat in **½ to 1 cup oil** until of the desired consistency, adding it a tablespoon at a time, and beating constantly. The dressing should not be too thick as it will become thicker on standing. When about half the oil has been added, larger quantities of it may be beaten in. If the mayonnaise separates, beat an egg yolk well and add the separated mayonnaise to it a little at a time, beating constantly. Continue until of the desired consistency. The recipe may be doubled.

When serving mayonnaise, add chopped hard-cooked eggs, olives, pickles, etc., for variety.

FRUIT DRESSINGS

HONEY DRESSING

Add **1 tablespoon lemon juice** (lime juice may be substituted) and **⅛ teaspoon salt** to **3 tablespoons honey.** Whip **1 cup cream** stiff. Fold into the honey mixture.

WINSTON COUNTY BANANA DRESSING

Press **2 large ripe bananas** through a strainer. Beat in **2 tablespoons honey, 1 tablespoon lemon juice** (lime juice may be substituted), and 1/8 **teaspoon salt.** Beat 1/2 **cup cream** stiff and fold into the banana mixture.

OPEN GATE FARM CREAM FRUIT DRESSING

Beat **2 eggs** slightly in the top of a double boiler. Beat in **3 tablespoons confectioners sugar,** 1/8 **teaspoon salt,** and 1/2 **cup fruit juice.** Fresh juice or juice from canned fruits may be used. Cook over hot water, stirring constantly, until the mixture coats the spoon well. Cool. Just before serving, fold in **1 cup cream** which has been whipped stiff. Serve very cold.

9

FRUITS

All fruits should be washed thoroughly before they are used, even if they are to be peeled. To wash soft fruits such as berries, add them to a container filled with cold water, then gently lift the fruits from the water. Repeat until the water is clean. Then remove caps or stems.

Peel or pit juicy fruits over a bowl to catch the juice. Use the juice with the fruit or, if the fruit is to be drained, the juice may be used as the base of a beverage.

DRIED FRUITS

Wash dried fruits, prunes, apricots, etc. Place in a saucepan and cover with hot water. Place over a very low flame. The water should remain hot, but should not boil. If using a thermometer, 176° F. is the correct temperature at which the fruit should cook. The fruit will be tender in about 2 hours. Add sugar to taste at the end of the cooking period. The amount of sugar needed will depend upon the tartness of the fruit. It is not necessary to presoak dried fruit when it is cooked by this method.

To purée the fruit, press it through a strainer.

GREENUP COUNTY APPLE RINGS

Peel and core **6 tart firm apples.** Cut into rings. Make a medium thick syrup by boiling together **3 tablespoons butter,** the juice of **1 orange, 1 cup brown sugar** which has been packed firmly in the cup, and **⅛ teaspoon salt.** Stir until the sugar is dissolved. Drop the apple rings into the syrup and simmer until they are tender. Test for tenderness with a clean broom straw or other tester. When the rings have finished cooking, arrange them neatly on a serving dish. If there is any syrup remaining in the pan, continue cooking it until it is quite thick but will still pour. Pour over the apples and chill. Serve with **1 cup cream** whipped, or pass cream with them. Serves 4.

HONEY APPLE RINGS

Peel, core and cut **6 apples** into rings. Place in a pan with **3 tablespoons butter** and **1 cup honey** which has been mixed with **2 teaspoons lemon juice.** Cook slowly, turning the rings until they are glazed. These may be served hot with meat. Serves 4 to 6.

APPLES IN GRAPE JUICE

Peel and core **4 medium-sized apples.** Slice into rings 1 inch thick. Cook gently in **1 cup grape juice** until tender. Serve with meat. Serves 4 to 6.

APPLE SAUCE

Wash and quarter **2½ pounds apples.** Add enough water, about 1 cup, to almost cover the apples. Cover the pan, and cook over a medium flame until tender. A few whole cloves or a half-stick cinnamon may be added to the apples while they are cooking. Press through a strainer. Return the apples to the pan. Add **sugar** to taste, about ½ cup, and cook, stirring, on a slow fire until the sugar melts. Sprinkle the apple sauce with **cinnamon** before serving. Makes about 1 quart of sauce.

BAKED APPLES

Wash **apples** and peel the upper fourth of each. Core, being careful not to cut all the way through. Fill the cavities, and bake in a moderate, 350° F. oven until the apples are tender enough to be pierced with a tester. Unless otherwise specified, place in the baking pan **1 tablespoon water** for each apple. Serve with whipped or plain cream if desired. Allow 1 apple for each person. Below are listed some of the many ways of preparing baked apples:

Fill the cavities with any **cranberry sauce** and put in the baking pan 1 tablespoon sauce for each apple. Serve with poultry or meat. Do not add water.

Fill with **honey,** dot with **butter.**

Fill with **maple syrup,** dot with **butter.**

Fill with **Waukesha County Mince Meat.***

Mix granulated **sugar** with **cinnamon, nuts,** and **raisins** and fill.

Pack the cavities hard with shaved **maple sugar** or **brown sugar.**

SUGAR ORCHARD FARM FRIED APPLES

Pare and core **8 tart apples.** Slice into eighths. Melt **3 tablespoons bacon drippings** or other fat in a heavy spider. Add the apples. Cover and cook very slowly, 10 to 15 minutes. If the apples are dry, add a little hot water. Sprinkle with **⅓ cup brown sugar** which has been packed firmly in the cup, and **⅛ teaspoon salt.** Cook uncovered until tender, 20 to 25 minutes. The apples are good with any pork dish such as bacon, pork chops, etc. Serves 6 to 8.

FRIED BANANAS

Peel and quarter **bananas.** Dredge them with **flour.** Heat **bacon drippings** or other fat in a heavy skillet. Fry the bananas in the fat until brown. Serve hot with meat. One large banana will serve 2.

FAIRFIELD COUNTY JELLIED WHOLE CRANBERRIES

Make a syrup by placing in a saucepan **2 cups water and 2 cups sugar.** Boil, stirring until the sugar is dissolved.

Add to the syrup **1 quart cranberries** which have been washed and picked over, and cook until clear. Add **1 tablespoon grated orange rind,** if desired. Turn into molds which have been rinsed in cold water. Put in the refrigerator or other cold place until firm. Unmold and serve. Serves 6 to 8.

THANKSGIVING CRANBERRIES

Tie in a cheesecloth **12 whole cloves** and a **3-inch stick of cinnamon.** Place in a saucepan **1 cup water, ½ cup vinegar,** and **2 cups sugar.** Add the spices. Bring to a boil, stirring until the sugar is dissolved, and add **1 pound cranberries** which have been picked over and washed. Cook until the cranberries stop popping, 2 to 5 minutes. Remove from the fire and add the juice and grated rind of **1 orange.** Makes 1 quart sauce. It will keep indefinitely if stored in the refrigerator or other cold place.

GLAZED PEACHES

Melt over a low flame in a heavy skillet **1 cup brown sugar** which has been packed firmly in the cup, and **3 tablespoons butter.** Add **8 large, fresh peaches** which have been peeled and sprinkled lightly with **lemon juice,** or use well-drained canned peaches. Keep turning until the peaches are glazed. Use a low flame. Serve hot with meat. Serves 6.

RED CHIMNEY FARM DESSERT PEACHES

Place **½ cup water** in a large saucepan. Add **½ cup sugar, ½ cup honey,** and **⅛ teaspoon salt.** Boil for 5 minutes, stirring until the sugar is dissolved. Peel and add **6 to 8 peaches,** depending upon their size, and cook until they are tender but not soft. Serve plain, or with puddings or ice creams.

SUGAR 'N' SPICE PEACHES

Peel **6 ripe peaches.** Stick each one with 2 cloves. Place in a baking dish. Add **½ to 1 cup sugar,** depending upon the tartness of the peaches. Dot with **2 tablespoons butter.** Add **1 teaspoon lemon juice** and **2 tablespoons water.** Sprinkle with **1 tablespoon cinnamon or nutmeg.** Cover and bake in a moderate, 350° F. oven 15 minutes. Uncover and bake until tender, about 10 minutes more. Serve hot with meat. Serves 4 to 6.

PLUMP RAISINS

Cover **large seeded raisins** with **grape juice** and place over a very low flame 10 to 15 minutes or until the raisins are plump. Serve hot with meat.

SPICY PRUNES

Cover **½ pound unpitted prunes** with **1½ cups hot water** and keep the water hot until the prunes are tender, about 2 hours. Add **2 tablespoons vinegar, 1 teaspoon cinnamon, 3 whole cloves,** and **2 tablespoons brown sugar.** Cook very slowly for 10 minutes more. Serve with meat. Serves 6.

CUYAHOGA COUNTY PIEPLANT AND STRAWBERRIES

Wash **1 pound pieplant** and cut in 1-inch dices. Peel if it is old. Place in an enamel saucepan. Sprinkle with **½ pound sugar.** Cook over low heat until the sugar is dissolved. Then cook over medium heat until the pieplant is tender. When the pieplant is almost tender, add **1 pint strawberries** and finish cooking. Serves 4 to 6.

BANANA CREAM

Mash the pulp of **6 bananas.** Gradually beat in **2 cups orange juice.** When the mixture is smooth, add **¼ cup**

cream and **⅛ teaspoon salt.** Mix well and chill. Serves 4 to 6.

CLOTTED CREAM

It is impossible to make clotted cream with pasteurized milk, so certified milk must be used. (It is dangerous to health to use fresh milk.) Place any amount of **certified milk** in a wide, shallow container and put over a very low flame for 2 hours. The milk must never reach the scalding point. Set in a cold place for 24 hours. Skim off the thick cream which has formed on top. Place it in a bowl, and beat it gently until it has a nice consistency for serving. It should be very thick and clotted. Serve cold on fresh fruit or with fruit pies or puddings.

10

CAKES

Standard measuring cups and spoons should be used when baking cakes. All ingredients are measured level. Brown sugar and maple sugar should be packed firmly enough in the cup to hold the shape of the cup when they are turned out.

Sift flour just before using it. Then measure it, spooning it gently into the measuring cup. Using a spatula or knife, cut the excess flour off the top of the cup sharply. Then sift it with the other dry ingredients: baking powder, spices, etc. If substituting cake flour for all-purpose flour, add 2 tablespoons more per cup. If substituting all-purpose flour for cake flour, remove 2 tablespoons per cup after sifting and measuring it.

All ingredients should be at room temperature unless otherwise stated in the recipe. Separate eggs when cold, but beat them at room temperature.

Solid shortening is preferable to liquid shortening for making butter cakes. Butter, margarine, vegetable shortening, lard, or a combination of these may be used.

To substitute butter or margarine for lard in a recipe, use 2 extra tablespoons of butter for each cup of lard. To substitute hydrogenated fat for lard, use 1½ extra tablespoons of hydrogenated fat for each cup of lard. If substituting lard for these fats, subtract, instead of adding, fat. Hydrogenated fat, margarine, or butter may be used measure for measure.

If eggs or egg yolks are beaten before they are added

to a batter, beat them very well, then add them gradually. Egg whites should be beaten until they are stiff, but not dry. This stage has been reached as soon as the egg whites will stand in firm peaks when the beater is withdrawn.

Sifted dry ingredients are added to a batter alternately with the liquid ingredients. Begin and end with the dry ingredients. The dry ingredients are usually added in 4 parts, the liquid in 3 parts. Beat the dry ingredients in. Stir the liquid ingredients in. Be careful not to overbeat, as the cake may fall. Work rapidly after the first addition of dry ingredients.

Cake tins should be prepared before the cake mixing is begun. The flavor of the cake will be better if butter is used for greasing the tins. Grease the bottom of the tins only. If the tins are old and it has proved difficult to remove cakes from them, grease the bottom of the tins, then sift a small quantity of flour over them. Shake out the excess flour. Another trick to insure easy removal of the cake is to grease the bottom of the tin, cut a piece of waxed paper to fit the bottom, put it in place and grease the paper lightly. The paper is peeled from the cake as soon as it is turned out of the tin.

Sizes of tins are given in each recipe. However, any tin which approximates the given size may be used. Fill cake tins ⅔ full of batter.

Turn the batter into the prepared tins and gently push it up into the corners of the tin so that it is slightly hollow in the center. This helps to insure a level cake. Put the cake in an oven which has been pre-heated to the temperature called for in the recipe. Cake tins should be placed in the center of the oven. If more than 1 tin is used, it should not touch other tins or touch the sides of the oven. It is unwise to bake other foods such as potatoes, meat, etc., at the same time a cake is being baked. Care must be taken not to disturb the cake during the first quarter of the baking period. Slamming or banging in the kitchen at this time may cause the cake to fall.

The cake should be tested for "doneness" 5 minutes before the time called for in the recipe. To test the cake, pierce it in the center with a clean broom straw, a toothpick, or a cake tester. If these come out clean with no particles of cake adhering to them, the cake has finished baking. Other indications of "doneness" are: The cake pulls away from the sides of the pan; the cake when pressed lightly with a fingertip springs back into place immediately.

When a butter cake has finished baking, remove it from the oven and allow it to remain in the tin for 5 minutes. Then turn it out on a cake rack or a cake cooler to cool.

When chocolate is used, melt it over boiling water, as it may burn if melted over direct heat. One ounce bitter chocolate equals 1 square. Nuts, raisins, other dried fruits, etc., should be perfectly clean before they are added to cake or any other batter. To be sure that they are, pour boiling water over them and let them dry completely before incorporating them in a cake. When they are dry, they may be broken, cut, etc., as desired. Nuts and raisins are added to the dry ingredients so they will not fall to the bottom of the pan.

Cakes which contain no shortening are called sponge-type cakes. Eggs are separated for use in these cakes. Whole eggs or egg yolks are beaten until they are thick and lemon colored. Egg whites are beaten stiff, but the peaks which form may bend slightly when the beater is withdrawn.

A gentle folding motion is used to incorporate sugar, flour and egg whites in a sponge-type cake. Ingredients to be added are sprinkled over the surface. Only 2 tablespoons of sugar should be added to the batter at a time. Flour should also be added very gradually.

It is preferable to bake sponge-type cakes in ungreased

tube pans. When the cake has finished baking, it is removed from the oven and turned upside down to hang until it is perfectly cold. It should not be subject to drafts or sudden changes in temperature while it is cooling. If the cake has not fallen out of the pan when it is cold, loosen around the sides and the tube carefully with a spatula. It may have to be prized out gently. The cake will come out more easily if a piece of waxed paper cut to fit the bottom is placed in the tin. Do not grease the tin or the paper.

Good luck!

SPONGE CAKES

OPEN GATE FARM MARBLE ANGEL CAKE

Sift, then measure ½ **cup cake flour.** Resift 3 times with ⅛ **teaspoon salt.** Sift, then measure ½ **cup cake flour.** Resift 3 times with **3 tablespoons cocoa** and ⅛ **teaspoon salt.** Keep these separate. Beat **1¼ cups egg whites** (10 to 12 eggs) to a froth. Sprinkle **1 teaspoon cream of tartar** over the surface and beat until the mass will form soft peaks which curl slightly when the beater is withdrawn. Fold in ½ **teaspoon almond extract** and ½ **teaspoon vanilla.** Fold in gently **1¼ cups sugar,** adding no more than 2 tablespoons at a time. Divide the mixture in half. Add the plain flour to half the mixture and the flour mixed with cocoa to the other half of the mixture. Fold the flour in gently and add it gradually. Fill an ungreased 9-inch tube pan with alternate spoonfuls of the batter, being careful not to stir them together. Bake in a slow, 325° F. oven 40 to 60 minutes. Let hang until cold.

CHOCOLATE ANGEL FOOD CAKE

Sift, then measure ¾ **cup cake flour.** Resift 6 times with ¼ **cup cocoa** and ⅛ **teaspoon salt.** Beat **1¼ cups egg whites** (10 to 12 eggs) to a froth. Add **1 teaspoon cream of tartar** and beat until the whites will form soft peaks which curl slightly when the beater is withdrawn. Fold in **1½**

cups sugar gently, adding only 2 tablespoons at a time. Fold in the sifted dry ingredients gradually. Bake in an ungreased 9-inch tube pan in a slow, 325° F. oven 45 to 60 minutes. Let hang until cold.

DAFFODIL CAKE

Beat **6 egg whites** with **½ teaspoon salt** until they froth. Add **½ teaspoon cream of tartar** and beat until the egg whites will form soft peaks which curl slightly when the beater is withdrawn. Add **½ teaspoon almond extract.** Sift, then measure **½ cup cake flour.** Resift several times. Sift **¾ cup sugar** and fold it into the egg whites, adding no more than 2 tablespoons at a time. Add the flour gradually. Make the second part of the mixture as follows: Beat the yolks of **6 eggs** with **¼ cup hot water** until thick and lemon colored. Add **¾ cup sifted sugar** gradually, beating it in well. Add **½ teaspoon vanilla.** Sift, then measure **¾ cup cake flour.** Resift it several times with **⅛ teaspoon salt.** Add this to the yolk mixture gradually, beating it in well. Place alternate spoonfuls of the batter in a 9-inch ungreased tube pan, being careful not to stir them together. Bake the cake in a slow, 325° F. oven 45 to 60 minutes. Let hang until cold.

WARREN COUNTY CHOCOLATE SPONGE CAKE

Beat the yolks of **6 eggs** with **⅓ cup cold water** until thick and lemon colored. Add **1¾ cups sugar** gradually and beat well. Sift, then measure **1 cup cake flour.** Resift several times with **2 tablespoons cocoa, ½ teaspoon allspice, 1 teaspoon cinnamon,** and **¼ teaspoon salt.** Add to the egg mixture gradually and mix well. Fold in **6 egg whites** beaten stiff but not dry and **½ cup broken nuts** which have been dredged with a little of the flour from the recipe. Bake in a slow, 325° F. oven in an ungreased 9-inch tube pan 45 to 60 minutes. Let hang until cold.

MAPLE SYRUP SPONGE CAKE

Sift, then measure **1 cup cake flour.** Resift 3 times with **½ teaspoon salt** and **1 teaspoon baking powder.** Boil **1½ cups maple syrup** to 238° F. or until it will form a long thread when dropped from the tines of a fork. Beat **6 egg whites** stiff but not dry, and gradually add the cooked syrup to the whites, beating it in as it is added. Beat the mixture until it is cool. Beat **6 egg yolks** until they are thick and lemon colored. Fold the sifted dry ingredients into the yolks gradually. Fold gently into the egg white-syrup mixture. Bake in a 9-inch ungreased tube pan in a slow, 325° F. oven 45 to 60 minutes. Let hang until cold.

LIZZIE FREEL'S RECEIPT FOR ORANGE SPONGE CAKE

Beat **6 egg yolks** until they are thick and lemon colored. Sift **1 cup sugar** and add it gradually to the yolks, beating constantly. Beat in the juice of **½ lemon** and the juice of **½ orange** plus **2 tablespoons grated orange rind.** Sift, then measure **1 cup cake flour.** Resift several times with **1 teaspoon baking powder** and **¼ teaspoon salt.** Add to the yolks gradually. Beat **6 egg whites** stiff but not dry. Fold them into the batter gently. Bake the cake in an ungreased 9-inch tube pan in a slow, 325° F. oven 40 to 60 minutes. Let hang until cold.

Aunt Sleide says: "Lizzie Freel stopped keeping company with her beau from the city. She baked him a cake that was higher than a silo and he said he hoped she wasn't always that extravagant with eggs."

SKILLET CAKES, COFFEE CAKES, AND FRUIT CAKES

SUMMER FRUIT CAKE

Place in a bowl **⅔ cup lard, 1 cup sugar, 3 teaspoons cinnamon, 1 teaspoon ground cloves, 1 whole nutmeg,** grated (or 1½ teaspoons ground nutmeg), and **1 egg.** Sift, then measure **3 cups flour.** Resift with **1 teaspoon soda,** and **½ teaspoon salt.** Add to the bowl. Add **1 cup seeded raisins** and **1 cup warm water.** Beat thoroughly and turn into a large loaf pan, 10 x 6 x 3 inches, which has been greased all over. Bake in a slow, 300° F. oven 1 hour or more.

Aunt Sleide says: "This was my grandmother's receipt. She wrote it in her Receipt Book and dated it 1880. When I was a little girl, my job was to grate the nutmeg for the cake."

HI-HILL FARM WHITE FRUIT CAKE

Cream **½ cup shortening.** Add **1 cup sugar** gradually and beat until the mixture is light and fluffy. Sift, then measure **1½ cups cake flour.** Resift several times with **1 teaspoon baking powder** and **½ teaspoon salt.** Add to the first mixture gradually, beating well after each addition. Add **½ cup chopped almonds, ¾ cup grated coconut, ½ cup citron,** cut fine, and **½ cup seeded raisins,** all of which have been dredged with **¼ cup sifted cake flour.** Add **½ teaspoon vanilla** and **½ teaspoon almond extract.** Gently fold in **5 egg whites** which have been beaten stiff but not dry. Bake in a greased 9-inch tube pan 1 to 2 hours in a slow, 300° F. oven. Ice, and decorate with holly sprigs.

TUTTI FRUTTI CAKE

Cream **1½ cups shortening.** Add gradually **2 cups sugar** and beat until the mixture is light and fluffy. Gradually stir in **6 tablespoons strained honey** and **6 well-beaten eggs.** Add **½ cup strong black coffee** and **¼ cup grape juice.** Sift, then measure **3½ cups flour.** Resift with **1 teaspoon soda, 3 teaspoons baking powder, ½ teaspoon salt, 2 teaspoons cinnamon, 1 teaspoon cloves,** and **½ teaspoon nutmeg.** Add the dry ingredients to the batter. Dredge the following with **½ cup sifted flour,** and add: **1 cup blanched**

almonds, chopped, **1 cup hickory nuts, ¼ pound candied orange peel,** cut fine, **1 pound currants, 1 pound raisins, ¼ pound candied cherries, ½ pound citron,** and **¼ pound candied lemon peel,** cut fine. Mix all the ingredients well and turn into a very large loaf pan (or several small pans) which has been greased and lined with heavy waxed paper. Place in a pan filled with 1 inch of hot water and bake in a slow, 300° F. oven for 1 hour. Remove the pan of water and continue baking the cake for 2 more hours.

Bake the cake at least a month before using it. To be sure that it will remain moist, and to make it extra good, dampen a cloth with whiskey and wrap the fruit cake in it. Store in a tin box. Examine every week or so to be sure that the cloth is moist. Dampen it again if it dries out. Keep the cloth around the cake until the last delectable morsel is gone.

WHITE CLOUD RANCH COFFEE CAKE

Sift, then measure **2½ cups flour.** Resift with **¼ teaspoon salt.** Measure **2 cups brown sugar** by packing it firmly into the cup. Mix with the flour. Cut in **⅔ cup shortening.** Reserve ½ cup of the mixture to use as a topping. Add to the remainder, **2 teaspoons baking powder, ½ teaspoon soda, ½ teaspoon allspice,** and **½ teaspoon cinnamon.** Add **2 eggs** and **1 cup sour milk** and beat vigorously until the batter is well mixed. Turn into 2 greased 8-x-8-inch tins. Sprinkle with the topping. Bake in a moderately hot, 375° F. oven 25 to 30 minutes.

PERFECTION COFFEE CAKE

Sift, then measure **2 cups flour.** Resift with **3 teaspoons baking powder, ¼ teaspoon salt,** and **1 cup sugar.** Break **2 eggs** in a measuring cup. Fill with **milk** to the 1-cup mark. Add **½ teaspoon vanilla.** Cut **4 tablespoons shortening** into the dry ingredients. Remove 3 tablespoons of it for a topping, and mix it with **¼ teaspoon cinnamon.** Add

A find: Hidden apricot cake

THE FOLLOWING CAKE was developed in The Tribune test kitchen by Beverly Dillon to use up a surplus of fresh apricots. It was devoured by the tasters. Serve the cake warm for rave reviews.

Hidden apricot cake

Six servings
Preparation time: 15 minutes
Baking time: 40 minutes

- 1½ **pounds fresh apricots, about 8 large**
- 2 **tablespoons butter**
- 1 **cup flour**
- 2 **teaspoons baking powder**
- ¾ **cup granulated sugar**
- 2 **eggs**
- ¾ **cup half-and-half**
- 2 **tablespoons apricot brandy**
- ½ **cup coarsely ground almonds**
- ¼ **cup packed brown sugar**
- **Whipped cream**

1. Heat oven to 350 degrees. Cut apricots in half; remove and discard pits. Butter an 11 by 7-inch baking pan with 2 tablespoons butter. Arrange apricots, cut side down, in pan.
2. Sift together flour, baking powder and granulated sugar in large bowl. Stir in eggs, half-and-half and brandy until dry ingredients are moistened. Pour mixture evenly over apricots in pan.
3. Sprinkle top with almonds and brown sugar. Bake until puffed and golden, about 40 minutes. Cool on wire rack until warm. Serve with whipped cream, if you wish.

AKE A WISH COME TRUE"
TAKES ENTRY FORM

ZIP:

IN BY 4 P.M. WEDNESDAY SEPTEMBER 5,
se. You must be 18 or over to win. Enter as
se no entries other than official entry blanks.
ill not be eligible.
TIFIED BY PHONE

milk, eggs and vanilla to the remainder, and beat well. Turn into 2 greased 8-x-8-inch cake tins. Sprinkle the topping over the coffee cake. Strew with **½ cup broken nuts** and bake in a moderately hot, 375° F. oven 20 to 25 minutes. The receipt may be halved.

Aunt Sleide says: "The first cake I ever baked was so durned awful that my father sneaked it out before anyone could see it. That night a freight train jumped the track near our farm. My father said it was right where he had put my cake."

CHERRY SKILLET CAKE

Melt **⅓ cup butter** in a heavy 10-inch skillet. Sprinkle over it **½ cup sugar, 1 cup broken nuts,** and **2 cups sour pitted cherries.** Put it aside while mixing the cake. To make the batter, cream **⅔ cup shortening.** Add **1½ cups sugar** gradually and beat until the mixture is light and fluffy. Add **2 eggs,** one at a time, and beat well after each addition. Sift, then measure **2½ cups cake flour.** Resift with **3 teaspoons baking powder** and **¼ teaspoon salt.** Add **1 teaspoon vanilla.** Add the dry ingredients to the batter alternately with **⅔ cup milk.** Beat well after each addition of dry ingredients and stir in the milk. Pour the batter over the cherry mixture in the skillet and bake in a moderate, 350° F. oven 50 to 60 minutes. As soon as it has finished baking, turn out on a large serving plate. If using canned cherries, make **Cherry Sauce*** with the liquid in the can.

CAMBRIA COUNTY APPLE CAKE

Cream **3 tablespoons shortening.** Add **½ cup sugar** gradually, and beat the mixture until it is light and fluffy. Add **2 eggs,** one at a time, and beat well after each addition. Add **¼ teaspoon vanilla.** Sift, then measure, **1 cup flour.** Resift with **¼ teaspoon salt** and **½ teaspoon baking powder.** Add to the batter gradually, beating it in well.

Spread the batter into a greased 8-x-8-inch tin. Peel, core and slice about **3 medium apples.** Stick the slices into the batter close together, with the core end down. Dot with **1 tablespoon butter.** Sprinkle with **2 tablespoons sugar** and shake about **1 teaspoon cinnamon** over the top. Bake in a moderate, 350° F. oven 40 to 60 minutes.

CUP CAKES OR CUP COOKIES

The same general directions given for cakes are to be followed for cup cakes. In fact, any cake batter may be used to make cup cakes. Cup cakes may be baked in muffin tins or in special paper cups which may be purchased. Fill any container used ¾ full of batter. The bottoms of muffin tins require greasing. Paper cups are not greased. The filled paper cups may be placed on baking sheets.

OLD FARM MINCEMEAT CUP CAKES

Cream **⅓ cup shortening.** Add **⅓ cup sugar** gradually, and beat the mixture until fluffy. Add **2 eggs,** one at a time, and beat well after each addition. Beat in **1 cup mincemeat** and **½ teaspoon vanilla.** Sift, then measure **2 cups flour.** Resift with **1 teaspoon baking powder, ½ teaspoon soda,** and **¼ teaspoon salt.** Add the dry ingredients to the batter alternately with **⅓ cup sour milk.** Beat well after each addition of dry ingredients and stir in the liquid. Bake in a moderately hot, 375° F. oven 20 to 30 minutes. Makes 24 cakes if paper cups are used, 12 cakes if muffin tins are used.

ANGEL CUP COOKIES

Melt **2 tablespoons shortening.** Add **½ cup milk,** scalded, and **1 cup sugar.** Sift, then measure **1 cup cake flour.** Resift twice with **1 teaspoon baking powder** and **½ teaspoon salt.** Add the dry ingredients to the milk mixture slowly to avoid lumps, beating them in. Add **½ teaspoon almond extract.** Beat **4 egg whites** until foamy. Add **¼ teaspoon**

cream of tartar. Continue beating the egg whites until stiff but not dry. Fold them gently into the batter. Bake in a moderately hot, 375° F. oven 15 to 20 minutes. Yield: 12 feather light cup cakes in paper cups, 6 in muffin tins.

BROWN SUGAR CUP CAKES

Beat **2 eggs** until they are thick and lemon colored. Gradually add **1 cup brown sugar** which has been packed firmly in the cup, beating it in. Add **½ teaspoon vanilla.** Sift, then measure **½ cup cake flour.** Resift with **¼ teaspoon baking powder** and **½ teaspoon salt.** Add **1 cup broken nuts** to the dry ingredients. Add to the egg mixture gradually and beat well. Bake in a moderately hot, 375° F. oven 15 to 20 minutes. Yield: 12 cup cakes in paper cups, 6 in muffin tins.

BUTTERCUP COOKIES

Cream **½ cup butter** or other shortening. Add **1⅔ cups sugar** gradually, beating until the mixture is light and fluffy. Add **2 eggs,** one at a time, and beat well after each addition. Sift, then measure **3 cups cake flour.** Resift with **¼ teaspoon salt** and **3 teaspoons baking powder.** Add the dry ingredients to the batter alternately with **1 cup milk** and beat well after each addition of dry ingredients and stir in the milk. Bake in a moderately hot, 375° F. oven 20 to 30 minutes. Yield: 1½ dozen cakes in muffin tins, 3 dozen cakes in paper cups.

FILLED CUP COOKIES

Prepare the above recipe. When the cup cookies are cool, cut off the tops and with a spoon, make a cavity in each. Fill the cavities with **lemon butter** as in **Lottie Herbel's Receipt for All-Purpose Lemon Butter,*** or **Orange Filling.*** Replace the tops and ice with **Snow White Icing.***

MARSHMALLOW TOPPING FOR CUP CAKES OR CUP COOKIES

Remove cup cakes from the oven after baking and turn out the fire. Place a very fresh marshmallow on each cup cake and put back in the oven. Remove when the marshmallows have partially melted and are light brown.

BUTTER CAKES

BANANA CAKE

Cream ¼ **cup shortening.** Add 1½ **cups sugar** gradually and beat until the mixture is light and fluffy. Add **2 egg yolks,** one at a time, and beat until the batter is light and fluffy. Add **2 large, ripe bananas** which have been pressed through a strainer. Add ½ **teaspoon vanilla.** Sift, then measure **2 cups cake flour.** Resift with **1 teaspoon baking powder, 1 teaspoon soda,** and ½ **teaspoon salt.** Add the dry ingredients to the batter alternately with **1 cup sour cream,** beating well after each addition of dry ingredients and stirring in the liquid. Fold in **2 egg whites** which have been beaten stiff but not dry. Bake in 2 greased 8-x-8-inch layer cake tins in a moderate, 365° F. oven 25 to 35 minutes. Ice with **Banana Icing*** if desired.

CHOCOLATE HONEY CAKE

Melt **3 ounces bitter chocolate.** Add ⅔ **cup honey.** Cool to lukewarm. Cream ½ **cup shortening.** Add ½ **cup sugar** gradually, and beat the mixture until it is light and fluffy. Add the chocolate-honey mixture and **1 teaspoon vanilla** and blend. Add **2 eggs,** one at a time, and beat well after each addition. Sift, then measure 1¾ **cups cake flour.** Resift with **1 teaspoon soda** and ½ **teaspoon salt.** Add the sifted dry ingredients to the batter alternately with ⅔ **cup milk.** Beat well after each addition of dry ingredients and stir in the milk. Bake in 2 greased 8-x-8-inch layer cake tins in a moderate, 365° F. oven 25 to 35 minutes.

CHOCOLATE WONDER CAKE

Cream ½ cup **shortening.** Add 1½ **cups sugar** gradually and beat until the mixture is light and fluffy. Add **2 eggs,** one at a time, and beat well after each addition. Add **1 teaspoon vanilla** and **2 ounces bitter chocolate,** melted, and beat the batter until it is fluffy. Sift, then measure **2¼ cups cake flour.** Resift 3 times with **1 teaspoon soda** and **½ teaspoon salt.** Add to the batter alternately with **½ cup buttermilk,** beating well after each addition of dry ingredients and stirring in the milk. Add **½ cup boiling water** all at once and stir the batter until it is smooth. Bake in 2 greased, 8-x-8-inch pans in a moderate, 365° F. oven 25 to 35 minutes.

This is a rich, moist cake.

SOUR MILK CHOCOLATE CAKE

Cream **½ cup shortening.** Add **1⅓ cups sugar** gradually, and beat the mixture until it is light and fluffy. Add **3 eggs,** one at a time, and beat well after each addition. Add **½ teaspoon vanilla** and **3 ounces bitter chocolate,** melted. Sift, then measure **2 cups cake flour.** Resift 3 times with **¾ teaspoon soda** and **½ teaspoon salt.** Add the sifted dry ingredients to the batter alternately with **¾ cup sour milk.** Beat well after each addition of dry ingredients and stir in the milk. Bake in 2 greased, 8-x-8-inch tins in a moderate, 365° F. oven 25 to 35 minutes.

Aunt Sleide says: "Whenever I ask Uncle what he wants me to bake for him, he says chocolate cake with chocolate icing with chocolate nuts."

WILLOW FARM DEVIL'S FOOD CAKE

Place **3 ounces bitter chocolate, ¼ cup sugar, ⅔ cup water,** and **⅛ teaspoon salt** in a saucepan. Cook until the mixture is thick and smooth, stirring occasionally. Let stand until cold, stirring occasionally. Add **1 teaspoon**

vanilla. Sift, then measure **2 cups cake flour.** Resift with **¼ teaspoon salt** and **½ teaspoon soda.** Cream **⅔ cup shortening.** Add **1 cup sugar** gradually and beat until the mixture is light and fluffy. Add **3 eggs,** one at a time, and beat well after each addition. Blend in the cold chocolate mixture. Add the sifted dry ingredients to the batter alternately with **⅓ cup sour milk.** Beat well after each addition of dry ingredients and stir in the milk. Pour the batter into 2 greased, 9-x-9-inch layer cake tins. Bake in a moderate, 365° F. oven 25 to 35 minutes.

MOWRER COUNTY CHOCOLATE CAKE

Melt **¼ ounce bitter chocolate** over hot water with **1 tablespoon shortening.** Add **1 cup sugar** and **1 teaspoon vanilla** and beat for 5 minutes. Sift, then measure **1 cup flour.** Resift with **1 teaspoon baking powder** and **¼ teaspoon salt.** Break **1 egg** into a measuring cup. Fill with **milk** to the 1-cup mark. Beat the egg and milk into the chocolate mixture. Add the dry ingredients gradually and mix well. Bake in a greased, 8-x-8-inch tin in a moderate, 365° F. oven 20 to 35 minutes.

BLUE RIBBON POTATO CAKE

Cream **1 cup shortening.** Add **2 cups sugar** gradually and beat until the mixture is light and fluffy. Add **4 egg yolks,** one at a time, and beat well after each addition. Add **4 ounces bitter chocolate,** melted. Beat in **1 cup mashed potatoes** and **2 teaspoons vanilla.** Sift, then measure **1¾ cups cake flour.** Resift with **½ teaspoon salt** and **2 teaspoons baking powder.** Add **1 cup broken nuts** to the dry ingredients. Add to the batter alternately with **½ cup milk.** Beat after each addition of dry ingredients and stir in the milk. Fold in **4 egg whites** which have been beaten stiff but not dry. Bake in a greased, 9-inch tube pan in a moderate, 325° F. oven 40 to 45 minutes.

POSEY COUNTY GINGER CAKE

Cream ½ cup **shortening.** Add ½ cup **sugar** gradually, and beat until the mixture is light and fluffy. Beat in ½ cup **molasses.** Sift, then measure 1¾ cups **cake flour.** Resift with ½ teaspoon **soda,** ¼ teaspoon **salt,** 1 teaspoon **cream of tartar,** and 1 teaspoon **ginger.** Add to the batter alternately with ½ cup **sour milk,** beating well after each addition of dry ingredients and stirring in the milk. Fold in gently the whites of 2 **eggs** which have been beaten so that they form soft curled peaks when the batter is withdrawn. Bake in a greased pan, 9 x 13 x 2 inches, in a moderate, 365° F. oven 25 to 35 minutes.

This is similar to gingerbread, but finer. The receipt is almost one hundred years old.

OPEN GATE FARM GOLD CAKE

Cream ⅔ cup **shortening.** Add 2 cups **sugar** gradually, and beat the mixture until it is light and fluffy. Add 2 **egg yolks,** one at a time, and beat well after each addition. Add 1 teaspoon **vanilla.** Sift, then measure 3 cups **cake flour.** Resift with 3 teaspoons **baking powder** and ½ teaspoon **salt.** Add to the shortening-sugar mixture alternately with 1 cup **milk.** Beat well after each addition of the dry ingredients, and stir in the milk. Fold in gently 2 **egg whites** which have been beaten stiff but not dry. Bake in 2 greased, 9-x-9-inch layer cake tins in a moderate, 365° F. oven 25 to 35 minutes.

CREAM CAKE

Fill **Gold Cake,** above, with **Sour Cream Filling.*** Frost with **Snow White Icing.***

GRANT COUNTY DELICATE CAKE

Cream ½ cup **shortening.** Add 1 cup **sugar** gradually and beat the mixture until it is light and fluffy. Add

½ teaspoon almond extract. Sift, then measure **2 cups cake flour.** Resift with **1 teaspoon baking powder** and **¼ teaspoon salt.** Add the dry ingredients to the batter alternately with **½ cup milk,** beating well after each addition of dry ingredients and stirring in the milk. Fold in gently **4 egg whites** which have been beaten stiff but not dry. Bake in a moderate, 365° F. oven in 2 greased 8-x-8-inch layer cake tins 25 to 35 minutes.

CREAM CAKE WITH FRUIT

Bake **Delicate Cake,** above, in 3 layers. Cut **¾ cup figs** and **¾ cup seeded raisins** with a knife or a scissors. Double the recipe for **Snow White Icing.*** Add the figs and raisins to two-thirds of the icing. Spread between the layers of the cake. Cover the top and sides with the remaining third of the icing, peaking it on top.

HICKORY NUT CAKE

Cream **½ cup shortening.** Add **1 cup sugar** gradually, and beat the mixture until it is light and fluffy. Add **1 teaspoon vanilla.** Sift, then measure **2 cups cake flour.** Resift with **2 teaspoons baking powder** and **¼ teaspoon salt.** Add **½ cup broken hickory nuts** to the dry ingredients. Add the dry ingredients to the shortening-sugar mixture alternately with **¾ cup milk,** beating well after each addition of dry ingredients; stirring in the milk. Fold in gently **3 egg whites** which have been beaten until they are stiff but not dry. Pour the batter into 2 greased, 8-x-8-inch tins and bake in a moderate, 365° F. oven 25 to 35 minutes. Fill with jelly and ice with **Plain Jane Icing*** for a real treat!

FIG MARBLE CAKE

Cream **¾ cup shortening.** Add **1½ cups sugar** gradually, and beat until the mixture is light and fluffy. Add **1 teaspoon vanilla.** Sift, then measure **3 cups flour.** Resift with **½ teaspoon salt** and **4 teaspoons baking powder.** Add to the batter alternately with **1 cup milk.** Beat well after each addition of dry ingredients and stir in the milk. Fold in gently **4 egg whites** which have been beaten stiff but not dry. Cut **1 cup figs** with a knife or a scissors. Add **1 teaspoon cloves** and **1 tablespoon molasses.** Add this mixture to ⅔ of the batter. Grease a 9-inch tube pan and add the plain mixture and the fig mixture to the pan alternately, being careful not to stir them together. Bake in a very moderate, 325° F. oven 40 to 45 minutes.

Mmmm!

POUND CAKE

Cream **1 pound butter.** Add **1 pound sugar** gradually, and beat until the mixture is light and fluffy. Gradually add **10 egg yolks** beaten until thick and lemon colored, **1 pound flour, ½ teaspoon salt,** and **2 tablespoons orange juice.** Beat vigorously for 5 minutes. Fold in gently **10 egg whites** beaten stiff but not dry. Line a tube pan completely with waxed paper, turn the batter in and bake in a slow, 300° F. oven 1 to 1¼ hours.

Aunt Sleide says: "My great-niece, Fern Sleide, raced over the other day to tell me that their dog Toby had just had ten puplets!"

SEED CAKE

Soak **½ cup poppyseed** in **1 cup milk** overnight. Sift, then measure **2 cups cake flour.** Resift with **2 teaspoons baking powder** and **¼ teaspoon salt.** Cream **¾ cup shortening.** Add **1½ cups sugar** gradually, beating until the mixture is light and fluffy. Add the dry ingredients to the fat-sugar mixture alternately with the milk and poppyseed, beating in the former, stirring in the latter. Fold in gently **3 egg whites** which have been beaten stiff but not dry. Bake in 2 greased tins, 8 x 8 inches, in a moderate, 365° F. oven 25 to 35 minutes. Fill with **Orange**

Filling* or **Custard Filling.*** Shake confectioners sugar over the top of the cake, or ice it.

JAM CAKE

Cream **½ cup shortening.** Add **¾ cup sugar** gradually and beat until the mixture is light and fluffy. Add **3 egg yolks** and **1 egg white** and beat well. Sift, then measure **1¾ cups cake flour.** Resift with **½ teaspoon salt, 1 teaspoon soda, 1 teaspoon cinnamon, 1 teaspoon cloves,** and **1 teaspoon allspice.** Add the dry ingredients to the first mixture alternately with **3 tablespoons sour cream** and **¾ cup blackberry jam,** beating in the former, stirring in the latter. Any jam may be used, but black raspberry is extra good. Bake in 2 greased, 8-x-8-inch tins in a moderate, 365° F. oven 25 to 35 minutes. Spread more of the jam between the layers or use **Open Gate Farm Jam Filling*** and ice with **Snow White Icing,*** if desired.

This is a moist, dark cake.

BROWN NUT CAKE

Cream **⅓ cup shortening.** Add **1 cup sugar** gradually, and beat until the mixture is light and fluffy. Add **1 egg** and beat thoroughly. Add **1 teaspoon vanilla.** Sift, then measure **2 cups cake flour.** Resift twice with **1 teaspoon baking soda, 2 tablespoons cocoa, ¼ teaspoon salt, 1 teaspoon cinnamon,** and **½ teaspoon allspice.** Add **½ cup seeded raisins** and **½ cup broken nuts** to the dry ingredients. Add the dry ingredients to the batter alternately with **1 cup sour milk,** beating well after each addition of dry ingredients and stirring in the liquid. Bake in a greased loaf pan, 9 x 5 x 3 inches, in a very moderate, 325° F. oven 40 to 45 minutes. This cake does not require an icing.

BENNINGTON COUNTY MAPLE NUT CAKE

Cream **½ cup shortening.** Add gradually **1 cup maple sugar** which has been packed firmly in the cup, and beat the mixture until it is light and fluffy. Add **2 eggs,** one at a time, and beat well after each addition. Sift, then measure **2 cups cake flour.** Resift with **3 teaspoons baking powder** and **½ teaspoon salt.** Add **1 cup seeded raisins** and **1 cup broken nuts** to the dry ingredients. Add them to the batter alternately with **½ cup milk.** Beat well after each addition of dry ingredients and stir in the liquid. Bake in a greased pan, 9 x 13 x 2 inches, in a moderate, 365° F. oven 25 to 35 minutes. The cake may be left in the pan. It may be iced or it may be served with a topping of whipped cream. If using whipped cream, pass hot maple syrup.

APPLE SAUCE CAKE

Cream **½ cup lard.** Add gradually **1 cup brown sugar** which has been packed firmly in the cup, and beat well. Add **1 egg** and beat thoroughly. Sift, then measure **2½ cups cake flour.** Resift with **2 teaspoons soda, ¼ teaspoon salt,** and **1 teaspoon cinnamon.** Add **½ cup seeded raisins** to the dry ingredients. Mix **¼ cup hot water** with **1½ cups thick sweetened apple sauce.** Add to the batter alternately with the dry ingredients, beating well after each addition of the dry ingredients and stirring in the apple sauce. Turn into a greased loaf pan, 9 x 5 x 3 inches, and bake in a very moderate, 325° F. oven 40 to 45 minutes.

This is a rich, moist cake.

BAKED-ON-ICING SPICE CAKE

Cream **½ cup shortening.** Add gradually **1 cup brown sugar** which has been packed firmly in the cup. Beat the mixture until it is light and fluffy. Add **1 egg** and **1 egg yolk** and beat thoroughly. Add **½ teaspoon vanilla.** Sift, then measure **1⅓ cups cake flour.** Resift with **½ teaspoon each of baking powder, soda, salt, cinnamon, and cloves.** Add the sifted dry ingredients to the batter alternately with **½ cup sour milk,** beating in the former, stirring in the latter. Turn into a greased, 9-x-9-inch pan. Make the following icing rapidly: Beat **1 egg white** until it is frothy. Beat in **⅛ teaspoon salt.** Add **½ cup brown sugar** which has been packed firmly in the cup, beating in not more than 2 tablespoons at a time. Beat until stiff, and fold in **½ cup broken nuts.** Spread the icing over the batter and bake in moderate, 350° F. oven 25 to 35 minutes.

HOT JUMBLE CAKE

Sift, then measure **2 cups cake flour.** Resift with **1 teaspoon baking powder, ½ teaspoon soda, ½ teaspoon salt, 1 teaspoon cloves, 1 teaspoon cinnamon, 1 teaspoon ginger,** and **½ teaspoon allspice.** Add **1 cup seeded raisins** and **1 cup broken nuts** to the dry ingredients. Beat **3 eggs** until they are thick and lemon colored. Add **1 cup sugar** gradually and beat well. Add **1¾ cups thick sour cream** and mix well. Add the sifted dry ingredients gradually, beating well. Bake in a greased pan, 9 x 13 x 2 inches, in a moderate, 365° F. oven 25 to 35 minutes. The cake may be served hot, without icing.

PRUNE SPICE CAKE

Cream **½ cup shortening.** Add **1½ cups sugar** gradually and beat the mixture until it is light and fluffy. Add **2 eggs,** one at a time, and beat well after each addition. Sift, then measure **2½ cups cake flour.** Resift with **1 teaspoon soda, ½ teaspoon salt, 1 teaspoon baking powder, 1 teaspoon cinnamon, 1 teaspoon cloves,** and **1 teaspoon allspice.** Add to the batter alternately with **1 cup sour milk,** beating well after each addition of the dry ingredients and stirring in the liquid. Add **1 cup prune pulp,** cooked as for **Dried Fruits,*** and mix well. Turn into 2 greased, 9-x-9-inch tins and bake in a moderate, 365° F. oven 25 to 35 minutes.

11

ICINGS AND FILLINGS

Icings made by cooking sugar and water to a syrup (boiled icings) sometimes prove tricky. If the icing will not harden, place it over hot water and beat it until it reaches the correct spreading consistency. Be careful not to let the hot water touch the bowl which contains the icing.

If the icing hardens too rapidly, beat in a teaspoonful of boiling water at a time to soften it to the correct spreading consistency.

The cooked syrup should not be poured onto the egg whites while it is still boiling hot. Wait until the syrup stops bubbling before adding it.

All extra ingredients—raisins, nuts, etc.—should be added to the icing at the last possible minute.

When icing a cake, it is best to use the bottom of the cake for the top, as it has a smoother surface. To be sure that the surface is perfectly smooth, lightly brush off any loose crumbs with a soft pastry brush. Heap the icing on the cake with a spoon, then smooth it with a spatula. It is best to ice the sides of the cake first and the top last. A soft icing looks more attractive if it is peaked on top with a spatula or knife.

Wait until the cake is cold if icing it with cooked icing.

If using an uncooked icing, it may be put on while the cake is still warm. If uncooked icing has hardened too rapidly and the top surface is rough, it may be smoothed with a spatula which has been dipped in hot water.

Confectioners sugar must always be sifted before it is added to icings.

Icings may be used as fillings.

COOKED ICINGS

SNOW WHITE ICING (Boiled Icing)

Place in a saucepan **½ cup water, 1/16 teaspoon cream of tartar,** and **1 cup sugar.** Cook over moderate heat, stirring until the sugar is dissolved, about 5 minutes. Cover the pan and boil for 4 minutes. Remove the cover. Use a wet pastry brush or a fork with a cloth wrapped around the tines to remove any sugar crystals which may have formed on the sides of the pan. Keep removing them as they form and cook the syrup to 240° F. or until it will form a long, wavy thread when dropped from the tines of a fork, 7 to 10 minutes. The syrup should be removed from the fire for each test, as it may overcook while it is being tested. Test frequently.

When the syrup has cooked to the correct stage, wait until it stops bubbling, then pour it on **2 egg whites** which have been beaten with **⅛ teaspoon salt** until they are stiff but not dry. Pour the syrup on the whites in a fine stream and beat constantly with a rotary beater. Continue beating until the icing is cold and thick, about 5 minutes. Overbeating at this stage is not harmful to the icing. To test the icing, lift a spoonful and drop it back into the bowl. If it holds its shape, it is ready to be spread. Beat in **1 teaspoon flavoring** and use.

CREOLE ICING

Follow the above recipe, but substitute for the granulated sugar **brown sugar** which has been packed firmly in the cup. The syrup will have to be cooked slightly longer to reach the long-thread stage. Omit the flavoring.

HONEY SATIN ICING

Place **1½ cups honey** in a large pan. Cook to about 240° F. or until it will spin a long, wavy thread when dropped from the tines of a fork. When the honey has stopped bubbling, pour it on **1 egg white** which has been beaten with **⅛ teaspoon salt** until stiff but not dry. Pour the honey on the egg white in a fine stream and beat constantly with a rotary beater. Beat until of the correct spreading consistency. Beat in **½ teaspoon vanilla.**

MAPLE ICING

Substitute **1 cup maple syrup** for the honey in the recipe above. Omit the flavoring.

CHOCOLATE POUR ICING

Melt **2 ounces bitter chocolate** over hot water. Stir in **3 tablespoons boiling water.** Add **6 tablespoons confectioners sugar,** sifted, and **⅛ teaspoon salt,** and stir until smooth and glossy. Add more confectioners sugar, to taste, if the icing seems too bitter. Pour the icing over cake prepared as in **Abbie Reit's Receipt for Reese Roll,*** or **Cream Puffs*** which have been placed on a cake rack. Scrape up the icing which runs off, reheat it and use it again.

RIVER VIEW FARM CHOCOLATE ICING

Melt **3 ounces bitter chocolate** over hot water. Add **3 tablespoons boiling water, ¼ cup butter, ¼ teaspoon salt,** and **1½ cups confectioners sugar,** sifted. Stir until the icing is smooth and well blended. If the butter tends to separate out, add more sifted confectioners sugar. Remove from the fire, cool the icing, and beat in **1 teaspoon vanilla.**

NEWCASTLE COUNTY FUDGE ICING

Boil ¼ cup water. Add **1 ounce bitter chocolate** and **2 tablespoons sugar.** Stir over low heat until the mixture boils. Remove from the fire and add **1 tablespoon butter.** Beat in **1½ cups confectioners sugar,** sifted, **⅛ teaspoon salt,** and **½ teaspoon vanilla.** Double the receipt for an 8-x-8-inch layer cake. This is an excellent icing for a 9-x-13-x-2-inch sheet cake. Broken nuts may be scattered over it and pressed down gently before the icing hardens.

UNCOOKED ICINGS

COFFEE ICING

Add **3 tablespoons strong hot coffee** to **3 tablespoons dry cocoa.** Stir until smooth. Add **1 cup confectioners sugar,** sifted, **¼ teaspoon salt,** and **½ teaspoon vanilla** and beat until of the correct spreading consistency. Add more confectioners sugar if necessary.

BANANA ICING

Press ripe bananas through a strainer. To **½ cup banana pulp** add **⅛ teaspoon salt, 1 teaspoon lemon juice,** and **⅛ teaspoon vanilla.** Beat in enough sifted **confectioners sugar** (about 1¾ cups) to give the icing the correct spreading consistency.

BERRY ICING

Crush **2 cups strawberries or raspberries.** Add confectioners sugar, to taste, and set aside until the sugar is dissolved. Drain the pulp and add it to the following mixture: Beat **4 egg whites** with **⅛ teaspoon salt** until they are stiff but not dry. Beat in **¼ cup confectioners sugar,** sifted. Add the fruit pulp and spread on angel food or sponge cake just before serving.

Use the drained juice as a base for a fruit drink.

LAKE FARM CREAM CHEESE ICING

Cream **6 ounces cream cheese** with **2 tablespoons cream.** Beat in **½ teaspoon vanilla.** Add **2 cups confectioners sugar,** sifted and beat. Add more confectioners sugar until the icing is of the correct spreading consistency.

CHOCOLATE WHIPPED CREAM ICING

Mix **1 cup cream, 1 cup confectioners sugar,** sifted, **6 tablespoons cocoa,** and **⅛ teaspoon salt,** and put in the refrigerator or other cold place for 1 hour. Remove and whip until the cream is thick. Add **¼ teaspoon vanilla.** Spread just before serving the cake.

This is delicious on sponge-type cakes, but must be used at once.

CHOCOLATE WONDER ICING

Melt **3 ounces bitter chocolate** with **2½ tablespoons water.** Add **1½ cup confectioners sugar** which has been sifted. Add 3 **egg yolks,** one at a time, and beat well after each addition. Add **¼ cup softened butter,** a tablespoon at a time, beating it in. Beat in **¼ teaspoon vanilla.** If necessary, add more confectioners sugar.

FRUIT ICINGS

Strawberry. Mix **2 cups confectioners sugar,** sifted, with **⅛ teaspoon salt,** and **¼ cup crushed strawberries.** Add a little **lemon juice** if the icing is too firm to spread.

Prune or Apricot. Mix **2 cups confectioners sugar,** sifted, with **¼ cup cooked dried fruit pulp,** cooked as for **Dried Fruits.*** Add a little **lemon juice** if the icing is too firm to spread.

Lemon or Orange. Mix **2 cups confectioners sugar,** sifted, with **3 tablespoons unstrained fruit juice** (lemon or orange), **⅛ teaspoon salt,** and **¾ teaspoon grated fruit rind.** Add more juice if the icing is too stiff.

Pineapple. Mix **2 cups confectioners sugar,** sifted, with **¼ cup crushed pineapple,** drained, and **⅛ teaspoon salt.** Add **lemon juice** to give the icing the correct spreading consistency.

LEMON BUTTER ICING

Cream **2 tablespoons butter.** Beat in **1 cup confectioners sugar,** sifted. Add **⅛ teaspoon salt, 1 teaspoon grated lemon rind, 1 tablespoon water** and enough **lemon juice** to give the icing the correct spreading consistency.

ORANGE BUTTER ICING

Cream **2 tablespoons butter.** Beat in **1 cup confectioners sugar,** sifted. Add **⅛ teaspoon salt, 1 teaspoon grated orange rind,** and enough **orange juice** to give the icing the correct spreading consistency.

PLAIN JANE ICING

Add **⅛ teaspoon salt** to **2 cups confectioners sugar,** sifted. Stir in **milk, water, or fruit juice,** a teaspoon at a time, until the icing is of the correct spreading consistency. Stir in **¼ teaspoon vanilla or almond extract.**

SPICE ICING

Follow the recipe for **Plain Jane Icing.*** Sift **½ teaspoon spice** with the sifted confectioners sugar. Cinnamon, cloves, nutmeg and ginger are all good. Omit the flavoring.

CROOKED ELM FARM SYRUP ICING

Place in a large bowl **1 cup light corn syrup, 1 egg white,** and **⅛ teaspoon salt.** Beat with a rotary beater until the icing is snowy white and of the correct spreading consistency. Beat in the preferred flavoring. Use this icing very soon as it does not keep well.

Vanilla. Beat in 1 teaspoon vanilla.

Orange. Beat in 1 tablespoon orange juice and 1 teaspoon grated orange rind.

Lemon. Beat in 1½ teaspoons lemon juice and 1 teaspoon grated lemon rind.

CAKE FILLINGS

Any sweet spread such as jams, jellies, marmalades, or conserves may be used between the layers of cakes.

Do not fill cakes until both cakes and fillings are cold.

For additional information on custard fillings see **Desserts.***

CARAMEL FILLING

Melt **½ cup sugar** in a heavy frying pan. Use a low flame and stir constantly. Stir in gradually **1½ cups hot milk.** Mix **½ cup sugar** with **⅓ cup flour,** and **¼ teaspoon salt.** Stir the first mixture into this. Cook until it thickens, stirring constantly. Add a portion of the mixture to **1 egg yolk,** beaten slightly. Return to the main mixture and cook 1 to 2 minutes more, stirring constantly. Cool, and add **½ teaspoon vanilla.**

CUSTARD FILLING

Beat **4 egg yolks** slightly in the top of a double boiler. Add **½ cup sugar** and **⅛ teaspoon salt.** Stir in **1 cup milk.** Cook the mixture over hot water, stirring constantly until it coats the spoon well. Cool the custard and add **¼ teaspoon vanilla or almond extract.**

This filling may be used as a sauce.

CREAM COFFEE FILLING

Beat **3 egg yolks** slightly in the top of a double boiler. Stir in **2 tablespoons flour, ½ cup sugar,** and **⅛ teaspoon salt** which have been mixed together. Add **⅓ cup cream** and **½ cup strong black coffee.** Cook over hot water, stirring constantly until the mixture coats the spoon well.

Cool. Add ¼ **teaspoon vanilla** and fold in ½ **cup cream** which has been whipped stiff.

OPEN GATE FARM JAM FILLING

Whip ½ **cup cream** until it is stiff. Fold into it ½ **cup any jam.** Spread thickly between layers of cake just before serving it, and use immediately.

ORANGE FILLING

Beat **3 egg yolks** slightly in the top of a double boiler. Add slowly **2 tablespoons flour,** ½ **cup sugar,** and ¼ **teaspoon salt** which have been mixed together. Add ½ **cup orange juice,** 1½ **teaspoons lemon juice,** ⅓ **cup water,** and **1 teaspoon grated orange rind.** Cook over hot water, stirring constantly until the mixture coats the spoon well.

PEACH FILLING

Mix together **3 tablespoons cornstarch,** ½ **cup sugar,** and ¼ **teaspoon salt.** Add **1 cup chopped peach pulp,** using either fresh, canned, or dried peaches. Add ¼ **cup peach juice** and ¼ **teaspoon almond extract.** Stir until smooth. Cover, and cook for 10 to 20 minutes, or until there is no taste of raw starch, stirring frequently.

ANOKA COUNTY RAISIN FILLING

Cut **1 cup seedless raisins** with a knife or scissors. Add **1 cup water,** ⅔ **cup sugar,** ⅛ **teaspoon salt,** and **1 cup light corn syrup.** Cook in the top of a double boiler until the raisins are soft. Remove from the fire and add **1 egg,** beaten slightly. Place over hot water and cook until the mixture will coat a spoon well, stirring constantly. Cool and add ½ **teaspoon vanilla.**

SOUR CREAM FILLING

Place in the top of a double boiler **1 cup sour cream** and **1 cup sugar.** Cook over hot water for 5 minutes. Place

4 teaspoons cornstarch in a bowl with **1/8 teaspoon salt.** Add **2 tablespoons cold water,** or more, gradually, and mix to a smooth paste. Add to the cream-sugar mixture, stirring until smooth. Cook covered for 15 to 20 minutes or until there is no taste of raw starch. Cool slightly and add **1/2 teaspoon vanilla.** When cold, fold in **1/2 cup hickory nuts, walnuts, or butternuts** which have been chopped fine.

VANILLA CREAM FILLING

Combine **3/4 cup sugar, 1/3 cup flour,** and **1/8 teaspoon salt.** Stir in **2 cups cream.** Beat **4 egg yolks** slightly in the top of a double boiler. Pour the cream mixture over them and cook over hot water, stirring constantly, until the mixture coats the spoon well. Cool, and add **1/2 teaspoon vanilla.**

CHOCOLATE CUSTARD FILLING

Add **2 ounces melted chocolate** to **Vanilla Cream Filling,** above, adding it with the cream.

12

COOKIES

Cookies are made by the same general methods used for cakes. It is not necessary to use cake flour for cookies unless specified. There are many types of cookies. **Drop Cookies** are dropped from a teaspoon onto a greased baking sheet. Drop them about 2 inches apart on the pan to allow room for spreading. The pan should be greased lightly for baking the first pan of cookies. It will probably not be necessary to grease it for baking the rest of the cookies in the batch.

Rolled Cookies are rolled and cut into shapes with cutters. Test the dough to see if enough flour has been added by touching it lightly with floured fingers. If it does not feel sticky, it contains sufficient flour. If the dough is chilled thoroughly, the cookies will be easier to roll and handle. The dough may remain in the refrigerator or other cold place for several days without spoiling. Use as little flour as possible on the board and on the rolling pin when rolling the cookies. For further directions on rolling, see **Pastry.*** For a very crisp cooky, roll the dough thin. Otherwise roll it ¼ to ⅛ inch thick. Cut desired shapes with a cutter which has been dipped lightly in flour. It is not necessary to grease the cooky sheet for rolled cookies. Rolled cookies spread very little in baking, so they need only be placed about ½ inch apart.

Filled Cookies are rolled and cut as above.

Slice (Refrigerator) Cookies may be placed ¾ inch to

1 inch apart on a baking sheet. The sheet will not require greasing.

If a cooky sheet is not available, any pan turned upside down may be used for baking cookies. Large-sized pans are the best to use.

Cookies should be baked on the top rack of the oven for fast browning.

They have finished baking when they are nicely browned. Cookies which contain molasses burn easily, so watch them carefully.

Cookies should be removed from the pans as soon as they are baked. Use a spatula for removing them. If the cookies break or crumble when being removed, wait a minute or two until they harden before taking them off the pan. It is not wise to stack cookies until they cool, as they may stick together.

Cookies are always more interesting if they are decorated. Candied fruits cut in small pieces, perfect nut meats, a sprinkling of finely chopped nuts, raisins, caraway or poppy seed, cinnamon drops, or any suitable decoration may be used. To make chopped nuts, caraway seeds, or the like stick on, glaze each cooky with lightly beaten egg white or yolk before adding the decoration. The egg may be brushed on with a pastry brush. All decorations are put on before the cookies are baked.

Cookies may be iced rather than decorated. It is easiest to use an uncooked icing which is soft enough to brush on with a pastry brush before hardening.

Cooky recipes may be halved or doubled.

Cookies will keep well if stored in a tin box or a cooky jar. To store them in a tin box, make a waxed paper cut out for the bottom of the box and overlap the cookies in rings.

Trying to *save* cookies is another matter. The only suggestion for that is a double lock on the pantry door!

SHAPED COOKIES

FORK COOKIES

Cream **1 pound shortening.** Gradually add **1 cup sugar** and beat until the mixture is light. Add **1 teaspoon vanilla.** Sift, then measure **5 cups flour.** Resift with **1 teaspoon baking powder** and **½ teaspoon salt.** Add the dry ingredients to the batter gradually, beating them in. Shape with the hands into balls the size of a walnut and press down with a fork. Place 1½ to 2 inches apart on a greased baking sheet and bake in a moderately hot, 375° F. oven 15 to 18 minutes.

This recipe makes a large batch of very good, rich cookies.

OLD FARM GINGER CRINKLES

Cream **¾ cup shortening.** Gradually add **1 cup brown sugar** which has been packed firmly in the cup and beat well. Add **1 egg** and beat well. Beat in **¼ cup molasses.** Sift, then measure **2¼ cups flour.** Resift with **2 teaspoons soda, ¼ teaspoon salt,** and **1½ teaspoons ginger.** Beat the dry ingredients into the batter gradually. Chill the dough one hour or more. With the hands, shape the dough into small balls. Dip the top of each ball into granulated sugar. Then sprinkle each cooky with 2 or 3 drops of water. Place 2 inches apart on a greased baking sheet and bake in a moderately hot, 375° F. oven 10 to 12 minutes.

FUSS CAKES

Cream **½ cup shortening.** Beat in **2 tablespoons sugar.** Add **1 teaspoon vanilla.** Grind or chop fine **1 cup nuts.** Hickory nuts, black or English walnuts, pecans, or almonds may be used. Sift, then measure **1 cup cake flour.** Resift with **½ teaspoon salt** and add it to the nuts. Stir into the first mixture. Blend all the ingredients well. Shape the dough into small balls with the hands. Bake on a lightly greased baking sheet in a moderately slow, 325° oven until they are light brown, 20 to 30 minutes. While the balls are still warm, roll them in confectioners sugar. For variety, shape some of the dough into crescents.

LADIES' AID COOKIES

Cream ½ **cup shortening.** Gradually add ¾ **cup sugar** and beat until fluffy. Add **1 teaspoon vanilla.** Add 3 **egg yolks,** one at a time, and beat well after each addition. Sift **1 cup flour.** Resift with ½ **teaspoon salt.** Add it to the batter gradually, beating it in. Add up to 1 cup additional flour, enough to make a dough that can be shaped into small balls with the hands. Shape. Dip a clean thimble in flour and dent each cookie with it. Fill the dent with any thick jam or preserves. Place the cookies on a greased baking sheet and bake in a moderately hot, 375° F. oven 15 to 18 minutes.

FLORENCE RINK'S RECEIPT FOR PEANUT BUTTER COOKIES

Cream together ½ **cup shortening** and ½ **cup peanut butter.** Gradually add **1 cup brown sugar** which has been packed firmly in the cup and beat until the mixture is fluffy. Add **1 egg** and beat well. Sift, then measure **1¼ cups flour.** Resift with ½ **teaspoon salt,** ½ **teaspoon baking powder,** and ¾ **teaspoon soda.** Add the dry ingredients to the batter gradually, beating them in well. Chill the dough thoroughly, then shape into balls the size of a walnut. Place the balls on a greased baking sheet and flatten them with a fork lightly dipped in flour. Bake the cookies in a moderately hot, 375° F. oven 15 to 18 minutes.

Aunt Sleide says: "Florence Rink lets her children shape and flatten these cookies and she says she always comes out with heavily floured cookies and lightly floured children."

DROP COOKIES

RED CHIMNEY FARM APPLE SAUCE COOKIES

Cream ½ cup **shortening.** Gradually add **1 cup sugar** and beat until the mixture is light and fluffy. Add **1 egg** and beat well. Sift, then measure **1¾ cups flour.** Resift with **1 teaspoon soda, ¼ teaspoon salt, 1 teaspoon cinnamon, ½ teaspoon cloves** and **½ teaspoon nutmeg.** Add **1 cup bran** to the dry ingredients. Add them to the batter alternately with **1 cup sweetened apple sauce** which is fairly thick. Beat well after each addition. Add **½ cup broken nuts** and **½ cup seeded raisins,** stirring them in. Drop from a teaspoon onto a greased baking sheet and **bake in a** moderately hot, 375° F. oven 15 to 18 minutes.

BANANA OATMEAL COOKIES

Cream **¾ cup shortening.** Gradually add **1 cup sugar** and beat until the mixture is light and fluffy. Add **1 egg** and beat thoroughly. Stir in **1 cup banana pulp.** Two or 3 bananas forced through a strainer will make 1 cup of pulp. Sift, then measure **1½ cups flour.** Resift with **½ teaspoon soda, ½ teaspoon salt,** and **1 teaspoon cinnamon.** Mix **1¾ cups oatmeal** with the dry ingredients. Add to the batter gradually, beating them in well. Add **½ cup broken nuts.** Drop from a teaspoon onto a greased baking sheet. Sprinkle each cooky with a little oatmeal, if desired, and bake in a moderately hot, 375° F. oven 15 to 18 minutes.

LICKING COUNTY FUDGE COOKIES

Cream **1 cup shortening.** Gradually add **1 cup brown sugar** which has been packed firmly in the cup, and **1 cup granulated sugar** and beat until the mixture is fluffy. Add **2 eggs,** one at a time, and beat well. Stir in **4 ounces bitter chocolate,** which has been melted. Add **½ teaspoon vanilla** and **⅓ cup sour milk.** Sift, then measure **4¼ cups cake flour.** Resift with **½ teaspoon salt, 1 teaspoon baking**

powder, and **½ teaspoon soda.** Add the dry ingredients to the batter gradually, beating them in well. Mix in **2 cups broken nuts.** Drop from a teaspoon onto a greased baking sheet and bake in a moderately hot, 375° F. oven 15 to 18 minutes.

CHOCOLATE OATMEAL COOKIES

Cream **½ cup shortening.** Gradually add **1 cup sugar** and beat the mixture until it is light and fluffy. Add **1 egg** and beat until the batter is very light. Stir in **2 ounces bitter chocolate,** melted, **1 teaspoon vanilla,** and **¼ cup milk.** Sift, then measure **1 cup flour.** Resift with **1 teaspoon baking powder** and **½ teaspoon salt.** Add **1½ cups oatmeal.** Add the dry ingredients to the batter gradually, mixing them in well. Drop from a teaspoon onto a greased baking sheet and bake in a moderately hot, 375° F. oven 15 to 18 minutes.

CRYBABY COOKIES

Cream **2 tablespoons shortening.** Gradually add **1 cup sugar** and beat until the mixture is light and fluffy. Add **2 eggs,** one at a time and beat well after each addition. Beat in **1 cup molasses** and **1 cup sour milk.** Sift, then measure **4 cups flour.** Resift with **1 teaspoon salt, 1 teaspoon soda, ½ teaspoon cinnamon, ¼ teaspoon ginger, ½ teaspoon nutmeg** and **¼ teaspoon allspice.** Add **1 cup seeded raisins** to the dry ingredients. Add the dry ingredients to the batter, gradually, mixing them in well. Drop from a teaspoon onto a greased baking sheet. Flatten each cooky with a knife dipped in cold water. Bake in a moderately hot, 375° F. oven 10 to 12 minutes.

Aunt Sleide says: "Uncle always wants to know if these are called Crybaby Cookies because a baby'll stop crying if you give him one or start crying if you don't."

LEA COUNTY DATE DROPS

Pour 1/3 **cup boiling water** over **1 cup dates** which have been pitted and cut fine with a knife or scissors. Set aside to cool. Cream 1/3 **cup shortening.** Gradually add **1 cup brown sugar** which has been packed firmly in the cup and beat until the mixture is fluffy. Add the cooled date mixture. Add 1/2 **teaspoon vanilla.** Sift, then measure **1 3/4 cups flour.** Resift with **1 teaspoon soda,** 1/2 **teaspoon salt** and **2 teaspoons baking powder.** Add the dry ingredients to the batter gradually, beating them in well. Mix in 1/2 **cup broken nuts.** Drop from a teaspoon onto a greased baking sheet and bake in a moderately hot, 375° F. oven 15 to 18 minutes.

FRUIT CAKE COOKIES

Cream 1/4 **cup shortening.** Gradually add **1 1/2 cups brown sugar** which has been packed firmly in the cup and beat the mixture until it is fluffy. Add **3 eggs,** one at a time, and beat well after each addition. Add 1/2 **teaspoon vanilla.** Sift, then measure **2 1/2 cups flour.** Resift with **1 teaspoon soda,** 1/2 **teaspoon salt, 1 teaspoon cloves, 1 teaspoon cinnamon,** and 1/2 **teaspoon nutmeg.** Add the dry ingredients to the batter gradually, beating them in well. Mix in **1 1/2 cups seeded raisins** and 1/2 **cup broken nuts.** Drop from a teaspoon onto a greased baking sheet, and bake in a moderately hot, 375° F. oven 15 to 18 minutes.

BIG BAY FARM HERMITS

Cream 1/2 **cup shortening.** Gradually add **1 1/2 cups sugar** and beat the mixture until it is light and fluffy. Gradually add **2 eggs** which have been well beaten and mix thoroughly. Beat in 1/2 **cup sour milk.** Sift, then measure **3 cups flour.** Resift with **1 teaspoon soda,** 1/2 **teaspoon salt,** and 1/2 **teaspoon each of nutmeg, cloves, cinnamon, and allspice.** Add 1/2 **cup broken nuts** and 1/2 **cup seeded raisins** to the dry ingredients. Add the dry ingredients to the batter gradually, beating them in well. Drop from a teaspoon onto a greased baking sheet. Bake in a moderately hot, 375° F. oven 15 to 18 minutes.

MINCEMEAT JUMBLES

Cream 1/4 **cup shortening.** Add 1/2 **cup sugar** gradually and beat the mixture until it is light and fluffy. Add **1 egg** and beat well. Beat in **1 cup mincemeat.** Sift, then measure **1 1/4 cups flour.** Resift with **2 teaspoons baking powder, 1/4 teaspoon salt,** and **1/4 teaspoon nutmeg.** Add the dry ingredients to the batter gradually, mixing them in well. Drop from a teaspoon onto a greased baking sheet. Bake in a moderately hot, 375° F. oven 15 to 18 minutes. Each cooky may be decorated with a plump seeded raisin.

PEANUT COOKIES

Cream 1/2 **cup shortening.** Gradually beat in **1 cup molasses.** Gradually add **2 eggs** which have been beaten until they are thick and lemon colored. Sift, then measure **2 cups flour.** Resift with **1/4 teaspoon salt** and **3 teaspoons baking powder.** Add the dry ingredients to the batter gradually, beating them in well. Stir in **1 cup roasted unsalted peanuts.** Drop the batter from a teaspoon onto a greased baking sheet. Bake in a moderately hot, 375° F. oven 10 to 12 minutes or until brown.

ROCKS

Cream 1/2 **cup shortening.** Gradually add **1 1/2 cups brown sugar** which has been packed firmly in the cup and beat the mixture well. Add **3 well-beaten eggs** gradually. Add **1/4 cup milk.** Sift, then measure **3 1/4 cups flour.** Resift with **1/2 teaspoon salt, 1 teaspoon soda, 1/2 teaspoon allspice, 1/2 teaspoon cloves** and **1 teaspoon cinnamon.** Add to the dry ingredients **1/4 pound dates** which have been cut with a knife or a scissors and **1/2 cup broken nuts.** Add the dry ingredients to the batter gradually, and mix thoroughly. Drop from a teaspoon onto a greased baking sheet and bake in a moderately hot, 375° F. oven 15 to 18 minutes.

SWIFT WATER FARM SPICE COOKIES

Cream ½ cup **shortening.** Add ¾ cup **brown sugar** which has been packed firmly in the cup and beat well. Add **1 egg** and beat well. Sift, then measure **1½ cups flour.** Resift with **¼ teaspoon salt, 1 teaspoon baking powder, 1 teaspoon cinnamon, ¼ teaspoon nutmeg, ¼ teaspoon allspice,** and **¼ teaspoon cloves.** Add the dry ingredients to the batter alternately with **¼ cup milk,** beating well after each addition of dry ingredients and stirring in the liquid. Fold in **½ cup seeded raisins** and **½ cup nuts.** Drop from a teaspoon onto a greased baking sheet and bake in a moderately hot, 375° F. oven 15 to 18 minutes.

TEACHER'S PET COOKIES

Cream ⅓ cup **shortening.** Gradually add **1 cup brown sugar** which has been packed firmly in the cup and beat the mixture until it is light and fluffy. Add **2 eggs,** one at a time, and beat well after each addition. Add **½ teaspoon vanilla** and **2 ounces bitter chocolate,** melted. Sift, then measure **2¾ cups flour.** Resift with **½ teaspoon soda, ½ teaspoon salt,** and **½ teaspoon cinnamon.** Add the dry ingredients to the batter alternately with **¾ cup sour cream.** Mix in **1 cup broken nuts.** Drop from a teaspoon onto a greased baking sheet and bake in a moderately hot, 375° F. oven 15 to 18 minutes. If desired, brush **Plain Jane Icing*** made with milk and confectioners sugar over the top of each cooky while it is still warm.

Aunt Sleide says: "Lucky teacher!"

ROLLED COOKIES

REGIMENT COOKIES

Sift, then measure **8 cups flour.** Resift with **2 teaspoons baking powder** and **½ teaspoon salt.** Measure **3 cups sugar.**

Sift the flour with the sugar. Cut **1 pound butter** into the dry ingredients. Add **4 egg yolks** and **4 whole eggs,** one at a time and beat well after each addition. Beat in the **grated rind of 2 lemons and 1 orange** and the **juice of 1 orange and 1 lemon, ½ cup cream** and **1 teaspoon vanilla.** Roll the dough on a floured board and cut in shapes. Brush the top of each cooky with lightly-beaten egg white. Finely chopped nuts may be sprinkled on if desired. Bake on a baking sheet in a moderately hot, 375° F. oven 10 to 15 minutes.

This receipt makes at least 200 cookies that keep perfectly in tin boxes.

COUNTY FAIR BUTTER COOKIES

Cream **1 cup shortening.** Add **1 cup sugar** gradually and beat the mixture until it is light and fluffy. Add **3 eggs,** one at a time, and beat well after each addition. Add **1 teaspoon vanilla.** Sift, then measure **½ cup flour.** Resift with **2 teaspoons cream of tartar, 1 teaspoon soda,** and **¼ teaspoon salt.** Add to the batter with enough additional flour, about 3 cups, to make a dough stiff enough to roll. Roll the cookies on a floured board and cut in desired shapes. Bake on a baking sheet in a moderately hot, 375° F. oven 10 to 15 minutes.

WHOPPERS

Cream **1 cup shortening.** Add **2 cups sugar** gradually, and beat until the mixture is light and fluffy. Gradually add 3 eggs beaten until they are thick and lemon colored, and **½ teaspoon vanilla.** Beat them in. Add **2 tablespoons milk.** Sift, then measure **1 cup flour.** Resift with **1 teaspoon baking powder, ½ teaspoon salt, 1 teaspoon nutmeg, ½ teaspoon cloves,** and **½ teaspoon cinnamon.** Mix well. Add enough additional flour to make a stiff dough, about 3 cups. Roll the dough thin on a floured board. Cut out 4-inch cookies. Sprinkle the top of each cooky with sugar mixed with cinnamon (3 tablespoons sugar to 1 tablespoon cinnamon), if desired. Bake on a baking sheet in a moderately hot, 375° F. oven 10 to 15 minutes.

RIVER VIEW FARM SAND TARTS

Cream **¾ cup shortening.** Add **1 cup sugar** gradually, and beat until the mixture is light. Add **1 egg** and **1 egg yolk** and beat well. Add **½ teaspoon vanilla.** Sift, then measure **3 cups flour.** Resift with **⅛ teaspoon salt** and add it to the batter gradually, beating it in. Roll the dough thin on a floured board. Cut the cookies in desired shapes and place on cooky sheets. Brush the tops of each cooky with lightly beaten egg white. Sprinkle the cookies with sugar. Bake on a baking sheet in a moderately hot, 375° F. oven 10 to 15 minutes.

SUMOR COOKIES

Sift, then measure **1 cup flour.** Resift with **¼ teaspoon salt** and **½ teaspoon soda.** Cream **½ cup shortening.** Add **¾ cup sugar** gradually and beat until the mixture is light and fluffy. Add **2 egg yolks,** one at a time and beat well after each addition. Beat in **½ teaspoon vanilla** and **⅓ cup sour cream.** Beat in the sifted dry ingredients gradually. Add enough extra flour, about 1 cup, to make a dough stiff enough to roll. Roll thin on a floured board and cut into shapes. Brush with lightly beaten egg white, sprinkle with sugar or caraway seeds and place a raisin in the center of each cooky. Place on a baking sheet and bake in a moderately hot, 375° F. oven 10 to 15 minutes.

DAWSON COUNTY GINGER DELIGHTS

Cream **1 cup shortening.** Add **¾ cup sugar** gradually and beat the mixture until it is light. Add **1 egg yolk** and beat well. Beat in **1 cup molasses** and **½ cup sour milk** to which has been added **1 teaspoon vinegar.** Sift, then measure **1 cup flour.** Resift with **1 teaspoon soda, ½ teaspoon salt, 1 teaspoon cloves, ½ teaspoon allspice,** and **1**

teaspoon ginger. Add to the batter gradually and beat it in well. Add enough more flour to make a dough stiff enough to roll, about 3 cups. Roll on a floured board and cut in desired shapes. Place on a baking sheet and bake in a moderately hot, 375° F. oven 10 to 12 minutes.

Gingerbread men may be made from this recipe. Cut seeded raisins in half and make eyes, nose and mouth and give the gentlemen 3 waistcoat buttons.

LOUISE GRIEST'S RECEIPT FOR MOLASSES SNAPS

Melt **1 cup shortening.** Add **1 cup molasses** and mix together. Blend in gradually **1 egg** beaten until it is thick and lemon colored. Sift, then measure **4½ cups flour.** Resift with **1 teaspoon soda, ½ teaspoon salt, 2 teaspoons ginger,** and **1 teaspoon cloves.** Add the dry ingredients to the batter gradually and beat well. Roll the dough on a floured board. Cut in desired shapes and bake in a moderately hot, 375° F. oven 10 to 12 minutes.

Aunt Sleide says: "Louise Griest is neighbor to the Swezeys. Miz Swezey never buys anything she can borrow, and nothing is ever returned. Once when Miz Swezey came over for sugar to make cookies, Louise thought she'd fix her. She gave her this receipt for Molasses Snaps and said, why didn't she bake them, because they didn't take any sugar at all. Miz Swezey said, good, she would. Twenty minutes later she was back to borrow the molasses."

DESHA COUNTY SUGAR COOKIES

Cream **½ cup shortening.** Add **1 cup sugar** gradually and beat until light. Add **1 egg** and beat well. Beat in **¼ cup milk.** Sift, then measure **1¾ cups flour.** Resift with **3 teaspoons baking powder** and **½ teaspoon salt** and add to the batter gradually, mixing well. Beat in **1 teaspoon vanilla.** Add more flour, if necessary, to make a dough stiff enough to roll. Roll on a floured board and cut in desired shapes. Place on a cooky sheet. Sprinkle each cooky with sugar. Bake in a moderately hot, 375° F. oven 10 to 15 minutes.

FILLED AND SLICE (REFRIGERATOR) COOKIES

APPLE-FILLED COOKIES

Cream 1/3 **cup shortening.** Add **1 cup sugar** gradually, beating it in well. Add **1 teaspoon vanilla.** Beat in 1/2 **cup buttermilk.** Sift, then measure **3 cups flour.** Resift with **1 teaspoon soda** and 1/4 **teaspoon salt.** Add to the batter and beat well. Roll 1/8 inch thick on a floured board and cut with a round cooky cutter. Place 1 teaspoon filling on half the cookies, cover with the other half and press together with the tines of a lightly floured fork. Bake on a baking sheet in a moderately hot, 375° F. oven 10 to 15 minutes.

Filling. Cook for 3 minutes **1 cup unsweetened apple sauce, 2 tablespoons sugar, 1 tablespoon flour,** 1/4 **teaspoon nutmeg,** and 1/4 **teaspoon cinnamon.** Cool and use.

KANKAKEE COUNTY BUTTERSCOTCH SLICE COOKIES

Cream 1/2 **cup shortening.** Add gradually **1 cup brown sugar** which has been packed firmly in the cup, and beat until the mixture is light. Add **1 egg** and 1/2 **teaspoon vanilla** and beat well. Sift **1¾ cups flour.** Resift with **2 teaspoons baking powder** and 1/2 **teaspoon salt.** Add 1/2 **cup broken nuts** to the dry ingredients. Add the dry ingredients to the batter gradually and beat them in well. Shape the batter into a roll 1½ inches in diameter, wrap it in waxed paper, and chill it thoroughly. Slice thin cookies from the roll, and place them on a baking sheet. Bake the cookies in a moderately hot, 375° F. oven 15 to 18 minutes.

Spice Icing* is good on these cookies.

ORA ZORGER'S RECEIPT FOR DATE-FILLED OATMEAL COOKIES

Cream ½ **cup shortening.** Add **1 cup sugar** gradually and beat until light. Sift, then measure **2 cups flour.** Resift with **1 teaspoon soda** and ½ **teaspoon salt.** Add to the batter alternately with ½ **cup sour milk,** beating in the dry ingredients, stirring in the liquid. Beat in **2 cups oatmeal.** Roll the dough ⅛ inch thick on a floured board and cut with a round cutter. Place a teaspoon of the filling on half of the rounds. Cover with the remaining rounds and press together all around with the tines of a lightly floured fork. Bake on a baking sheet in a moderately hot, 375° F. oven 10 to 15 minutes.

Filling. Stone and cut ½ **pound dates** with a knife or scissors. Place **1 cup water** in a saucepan. Add ½ **cup brown sugar** and the dates. Cook until the mixture thickens, stirring until the sugar is dissolved, then occasionally, to prevent burning. Add **1 tablespoon lemon juice** and **1 teaspoon grated lemon rind.** Cool and use.

Aunt Sleide says: "Ora Zorger's littlest one had always heard about the lake but she'd never seen it. When she finally did, she reported to me, 'I saw the lake, Auntie, and it's *full* of water!' "

MAPLE SLICE COOKIES

Cream **1 cup shortening.** Add gradually **1 cup maple sugar** which has been packed firmly in the cup, and beat until the mixture is fluffy. Add **1 egg** and beat well. Add **1 teaspoon vanilla.** Sift, then measure **3 cups flour.** Resift with ½ **teaspoon soda** and ½ **teaspoon salt.** Add the dry ingredients to the batter gradually, and beat well. Shape the batter into a roll 1½ inches in diameter. Spread **1 cup broken nuts** on a flat surface and roll the batter over the nuts, pressing them in just enough to make them stick to the dough. Wrap in waxed paper. Chill the dough thoroughly. Slice thin and place the cookies on a baking sheet and bake in a moderately hot, 375° F. oven 10 to 15 minutes.

MOLASSES SLICE COOKIES

Cream ½ cup **shortening.** Add ½ **cup sugar** gradually and beat the mixture until it is light and fluffy. Add **1 egg** and beat well. Beat in ½ **cup molasses.** Sift, then measure **2⅔ cups flour.** Resift with ¼ **teaspoon salt** and ½ **teaspoon soda.** Add the dry ingredients to the batter gradually, mixing them in well. Shape the dough into a roll about 1½ inches in diameter. Wrap it in waxed paper and chill it thoroughly. Slice the dough when ready to bake and place the cookies on a baking sheet. Bake in a moderately hot, 375° F. oven 8 to 12 minutes.

RED CHIMNEY FARM RAISIN-FILLED COOKIES

Cream **1 cup shortening.** Add **2 cups sugar** gradually and beat until light. Beat in **2 eggs,** one at a time, and beat well after each addition. Add **1 cup milk,** beating it in. Sift, then measure **1 cup flour.** Resift with **1 teaspoon soda,** ½ **teaspoon salt** and **4 teaspoons baking powder.** Beat the dry ingredients in and add enough additional flour to make a dough that is stiff enough to roll, about 3 cups. Roll the dough on a floured board. Cut rounds. Put 1 teaspoon filling on half the rounds and cover with the other half, pressing them together with the tines of a lightly floured fork. Bake on a baking sheet in a moderately hot, 375° F. oven 10 to 15 minutes.

Filling. Place in a saucepan **1 cup water, 1 teaspoon vinegar** and ½ **cup sugar** which has been mixed with ¼ **cup flour** and ½ **pound seeded raisins.** Cook until the filling is thick, stirring until the sugar is dissolved, then occasionally, to prevent burning. Cool and use.

SQUARES AND BARS AND KISSES

MOLASSES NUT SQUARES

Cream **1/3 cup shortening.** Add **1/3 cup sifted confectioners sugar** gradually and beat until light. Beat in gradually **1 well-beaten egg.** Add **1/3 cup molasses.** Sift, then measure **1 cup cake flour.** Resift with **1/4 teaspoon salt, 1/8 teaspoon soda,** and **1/2 teaspoon allspice.** Add the dry ingredients to the batter gradually, beating them in. Turn the batter into a greased pan and arrange **1 cup nuts** in rows on top of it. Bake in a greased 8-x-8-inch tin in a moderate, 350° F. oven 20 to 35 minutes. Cut into squares while still warm.

BELL COUNTY PRESERVE BARS

Beat **4 egg yolks** until they are thick and lemon colored. Beat in **1 pound brown sugar.** Sift, then measure **2 cups flour.** Resift with **2 teaspoons baking powder** and **1/2 teaspoon salt.** Add to the egg-sugar mixture, beating it in. Fold in gently **4 egg whites** which have been beaten stiff but not dry, **1/2 cup broken nuts,** and **1/4 cup quick preserves.*** (Other preserves may be substituted.) Turn the batter into a sheet, 9 x 13 x 2 inches, and bake in a moderate, 350° F. oven for about 40 minutes. Sprinkle with confectioners sugar when finished baking and cut into bars.

CHOCOLATE PRUNE BARS

Wash **1 cup prunes** and soak in cold water for 1 hour. Stone and cut into small pieces with a knife or scissors. Melt **2 ounces bitter chocolate.** Sift, then measure **3/4 cup flour.** Resift with **1/4 teaspoon baking powder, 1/4 teaspoon soda,** and **1/4 teaspoon salt.** Cream **1/2 cup shortening.** Add gradually **1 cup sugar,** beating the mixture until it is light and fluffy. Add **2 eggs,** one at a time, and beat well after each addition. Add the melted chocolate. Beat in the sifted dry ingredients, adding them gradually. Mix in the chopped prunes. Turn into a greased 9-x-9-inch pan and bake in a moderate, 350° F. oven 30 to 40 minutes.

These keep well.

FRUITED HONEY SQUARES

Beat **3 eggs** until they are thick and lemon colored. Beat in gradually **1 cup honey.** Add **½ teaspoon vanilla.** Sift, then measure **1¼ cups flour.** Resift with **1 teaspoon baking powder** and **½ teaspoon salt.** Add **1 cup broken nuts, ½ cup candied citron,** and **½ cup seeded raisins** to the dry ingredients. Add the dry ingredients to the egg mixture gradually, beating them in well. Pour the batter into a greased tin, 9 x 9 inches, and bake in a moderate, 350° F. oven 15 to 20 minutes. Let the cakes stay in the pan for 5 minutes after removing them from the oven. Then turn out on a cake rack or cooler. When cold, sprinkle with confectioners sugar and cut in squares.

YUM YUMS

Cream **1 cup shortening.** Add **½ cup confectioners sugar** gradually and beat the mixture until it is light and fluffy. Add **1 egg yolk** and **½ teaspoon vanilla** and beat the batter light. Sift, then measure **2½ cups cake flour.** Resift with **½ teaspoon salt.** Add the dry ingredients to the batter gradually, and mix well. Turn into a greased 9-x-9-inch pan. Smooth the batter by pressing it down with another pan of the same size. Chill for at least 1 hour. Cover the batter thickly with any **jam or jelly.** Beat **1 egg white** until frothy. Sprinkle **a few grains of salt** over the surface and beat it in. Add **¼ cup sugar,** 2 tablespoons at a time, beating constantly. Add **1 teaspoon cinnamon** and beat the mixture until it is stiff. Spread the meringue over the jelly and sprinkle with **¼ cup chopped nuts.** Bake in a moderate, 350° F. oven 20 to 30 minutes. Allow the bars to cool in the pan.

Aunt Sleide says: "You'll add a few more 'yums' after you taste these!"

CARAMEL CHEWS

Beat **1 egg white** until it is stiff but not dry. Beat in **1 cup brown sugar,** which has been packed firmly in the cup, beating in 2 tablespoons at a time. Add ¼ **teaspoon salt,** ½ **teaspoon vanilla,** and **1 cup broken nuts** and mix the batter well. Drop from a teaspoon onto a heavily greased baking sheet. Bake in a slow, 300° F. oven 20 to 30 minutes.

OLD FARM CHOCOLATE KISSES

Beat 3 **egg whites** until they are foamy. Add ⅛ **teaspoon salt** and ⅛ **teaspoon cream of tartar** and continue beating until the whites are stiff but not dry. Add ½ **cup sugar,** 2 tablespoons at a time, and beat well after each addition. Fold in **2 ounces bitter chocolate,** grated. Drop from a teaspoon onto a baking sheet covered with heavy paper, or drop on floured tins. Bake in a slow, 300° F. oven 25 minutes or until done. Remove the kisses from the pan while they are still slightly warm.

13

PASTRY

All-purpose flour is superior to cake flour for making pastry. It produces a dough which is more flaky and easier to handle. The same kind of flour used in making the pastry should be used for rolling it.

Any solid shortening with good flavor may be used for pastry. If the fat is to be worked into the flour with the fingertips, it is better to use cold fat. The water used should be cold, but it need not be ice-cold. The salt may be added to the flour or it may be dissolved in the water. Some bakers think that the salt is distributed more evenly if it is dissolved in the water and that the crust will be more tender if the salt is added in this way.

Sift, then measure the flour. Mix with the salt or dissolve the salt in the water. Cut the fat into the flour with the fingertips. (Be careful not to let the mixture go above the fingertips. The hands are warm there, and will melt the fat.) A pastry blender, two knives, or two spatulas may be used instead of the fingertips. The fat is cut in enough when the particles are the size of peas. However, if a very flaky crust is desired, the cutting in may be continued until the particles resemble coarse corn meal.

Add as little water as possible by sprinkling some of it over the surface of the dough. Combine the dampened parts into a dough. Continue adding water gradually, until the mixture becomes a stiff dough which will hold together when pressed into a ball. Use a fork in tossing.

If there is time, wrap the dough in waxed paper and put it in the refrigerator or other cold place to ripen. Fifteen to 20 minutes is sufficient, but a well-chilled dough requires less flour for rolling and is easier to roll. The dough will keep for at least a week in the refrigerator, so large quantities may be made up and used as needed.

The dough may be rolled on a lightly floured marble slab, porcelain table top, board, or on a pastry cloth which has had flour worked into it. A floured rolling pin may be used, or one covered with a cotton stocking which has had flour worked into it.

Roll the dough from the center out, using light, even strokes. Raise the pin at the edges of the dough, to keep the crust of uniform thickness. If the dough sticks, lift it with a spatula and add more flour where it stuck. The dough should be rolled ⅛ to ¼ inch thick.

Double-Crust Pies. Roll the upper and the lower crust separately when making a double-crust pie. The bottom crust is larger than the top crust, so use a little more than half the dough for rolling it. To place the crust in the pan, fold it in half or roll it around the rolling pin. Fit the crust into the tin carefully, patting it in place to exclude air bubbles, but being careful not to stretch it. Put in a cold place while preparing the filling. Place the filling in the crust and moisten the rim of the dough. Roll the upper crust from the remainder of the dough, allowing an extra half-inch around the edge. Fold the dough in half and cut a few gashes through both thicknesses of the dough near the center to allow the steam to escape. Place on the pie, unfold and press lightly around the edge of the pan. If the filling is very juicy, allow enough dough to fold under the top crust, for a more perfect seal. Lift the pan to trim off the surplus dough, holding the knife underneath the pan and slanting it to cut off the excess. Flute the edge of the dough with the fingers or press it down with the tines of a fork to make a design. A key with a round ward pressed straight down is traditional for mince pie in many localities.

One tablespoon quick-cooking tapioca may be sprinkled on the bottom crust of a fruit pie to absorb some of the juice if the fruit is very juicy.

To prevent the bottom crust from becoming soggy, a coating of melted butter may be painted on it with a pastry brush before the filling is added. A perforated pie tin will ensure a well-baked under-crust. Several small holes may be drilled in the bottom of an ordinary tin, or a perforated tin may be purchased.

The pie may be glazed. Paint the top of the pie with melted butter and allow the butter to harden before baking the pie.

Double-crust fruit pies are baked in a hot, 425° F. oven for 35 minutes or until the fruit is tender and the crust is nicely browned.

Single-Crust Pies. Pat the rolled-out dough into the pie tin and trim off the excess dough as above, cut the edge away, but leave enough dough to turn under. Turn it under, flute the edge as above, and add the filling. To make a lattice top for a fruit pie, roll out the surplus pastry into an oblong and cut half-inch strips. Moisten the rim and place the strips across the filling one-half inch apart. Weave additional strips through these. Trim the ends even with the edge of the tin, fasten the strips by pressing them down securely and flute the edge of the crust. Bake at the same temperature as for double-crust fruit pies.

Custard-Type Pies are baked without a top crust of any kind. Pour the raw custard into the unbaked crust and bake in a hot, 450° F. oven for 15 minutes. Reduce the heat to moderately slow, 325° F., and continue baking for 40 to 50 minutes, or until the tip of a paring knife inserted in the center will come out clean and the custard does not feel excessively sticky. Care must be taken not to overbake custard-type fillings as they will separate and become watery. Custards which are to be cooked, then placed in the pastry, are cooked over hot rather than boiling water to avoid overcooking. For further information on custards, see **Desserts.***

To bake a **Pastry Shell**, place it in the pan as above and prick the dough every 2 or 3 inches over the bottom and the sides. Bake in a hot, 425° F. oven 10 to 15 minutes or until delicately browned.

Unbaked Custard-Type Fillings may be baked in a prebaked crust. Bake in a moderate, 350° F. oven for 25 minutes or until the tip of a paring knife inserted in the center will come out clean.

Fruit Fillings may be baked in a prebaked crust. Use a moderately hot, 375° to 400° F. oven and bake 25 to 30 minutes, or until the fruit is tender.

If too much filling has been made for custard-type pies, the excess may be baked in custard cups. Set the cups in a pan of water and bake in a moderate, 350° F. oven until the tip of a paring knife inserted in the center will come out clean.

Meringues make decorative toppings for single-crust pies. If a meringue is not used, the pie may be topped with whipped cream. Whip about 1 cup cream for a 9-inch pie.

A 9-inch double-crust pie will serve 4 to 6.

Pies are a blessing for farm women because a quantity of dough may be made up and stored to be turned into pies in a jiffy. And who is there to say that a good pie is not a blessing to the eaters thereof.

MERINGUE, CRUSTS, BISCUITS, AND SHORTCAKES

MERINGUE TOPPING

Beat **1 egg white** until it is frothy. Sprinkle a **few grains of salt** over the surface. Beat it in. Add **2 tablespoons sugar** and beat until the mixture is stiff, beating in 1/8 tea-

spoon flavoring, if desired. For a sweeter meringue, beat in **1 tablespoon additional sugar.** Never beat in more than 2 tablespoons of sugar at a time. Always add it by sprinkling it over the surface. If using more than 1 egg white, increase the other ingredients proportionately. Pile the meringue gently on the pie, covering the filling completely. A rough meringue is more attractive than a smooth one, so peak the meringue with a spatula or knife. Bake in a moderate, 350° F. oven 12 to 18 minutes, depending upon the depth of the meringue. The meringue has finished baking when it is delicately browned.

PASTRY FOR A 9-INCH DOUBLE-CRUST PIE

2½ cups flour
¾ cup shortening
1 teaspoon salt
5 to 6 tablespoons water

Combine the ingredients as described in the general directions for **Pastry.***

PASTRY FOR AN 8-INCH DOUBLE-CRUST PIE

2 cups flour
⅔ cup shortening
¾ teaspoon salt
4 to 5 tablespoons water

Combine the ingredients as described in the general directions for **Pastry.***

AMADOR COUNTY HOT WATER PIE CRUST

Dissolve **¼ teaspoon salt** in **¼ cup boiling water.** Pour the water over **½ cup shortening.** Stir until creamy. Cool slightly and add **1½ cups flour** which has been sifted, then measured. Mix lightly with a fork. Wrap in waxed paper, place in the refrigerator or other cold place for at least 15 minutes and roll. Makes one 9-inch pastry shell. This pie crust receipt never fails to produce good results.

SUGAR ORCHARD FARM COOKY CRUST

Sift, then measure **1 cup flour.** Resift with **⅛ teaspoon salt, ½ teaspoon baking powder,** and **¼ cup sugar.** Cut in **1 tablespoon butter.** Add **1 beaten egg** and enough **milk** to make a stiff dough, 1 to 2 tablespoons. Chill and roll ¼ inch thick. This is excellent with all fruits. Makes one two-crust or two single-crust 7-inch pies.

COTTAGE CHEESE CRUST

Sift, then measure **1 cup flour.** Mix with **½ teaspoon salt.** Cut in **¼ cup shortening.** Stir in **½ cup cottage cheese.** Press against the sides of the bowl so all ingredients will cling together. Chill before rolling. Makes a single crust for a 9-inch pie.

CRUMB CRUST

Crush fine **7 ounces zwieback, graham crackers, or vanilla, lemon, chocolate, or ginger cookies.** (Seven ounces makes 2 cups.) Mix the crumbs with **1 teaspoon cinnamon, ½ cup sugar,** and **¼ teaspoon salt.** Add **½ cup melted butter** and stir until all the crumbs are well coated. Pat into a 9-inch pie tin or a 10-inch spring form which has been greased. The shell may be used immediately or held in the refrigerator or other cold place overnight. Usually part of the crumb mixture is reserved for sprinkling over the top of the filling.

MARICOPA COUNTY CORN MEAL CRUST

Sift, then measure **1½ cups flour.** Resift with **¼ cup corn meal.** Cut in **½ cup shortening.** Dissolve **½ teaspoon salt** in **5 tablespoons water.** Add water to make a dough. Roll and bake. Makes two 9-inch shells. If individual shells are desired, fit the dough in, or over, muffin tins. Makes 8 individual shells. Serve as a base for creamed foods such as **Pinch Penny Creamed Dish,*** etc.

RIZ BISCUITS (BAKING POWDER BISCUITS)

Sift, then measure **2 cups flour.** Resift with **3 teaspoons baking powder** and **1 teaspoon salt.** Cut in **4 tablespoons fat.** Make a hollow and pour in enough **milk** to make a fairly moist dough, about ⅔ cup. Stir gently to dampen the flour. Then stir vigorously until a soft dough is formed. Knead lightly. Pat or roll ¾ inch thick. Cut biscuits with a floured biscuit cutter or use a small floured drinking glass. Place biscuits 1½ inches apart if a crisp crust is liked. If soft biscuits are desired, place the biscuits closer together. Dot each biscuit with butter if desired, or, for a varnished crust, paint each with slightly beaten egg yolk. Bake in a hot, 450° F. oven 12 to 15 minutes. Makes approximately 20 biscuits 2 inches in diameter.

DROP BISCUITS

Follow receipt for **Riz** or other biscuits, adding enough additional liquid to be able to drop the biscuits from a spoon. Drop onto a greased baking sheet, allowing room for spreading, and bake as above. Before baking, if desired, sprinkle each biscuit with sugar, and top with a plump seeded raisin.

OLD FARM SALERATUS BISCUITS (BUTTERMILK BISCUITS)

Sift, then measure **2 cups flour.** Resift with **1 teaspoon baking powder, ½ teaspoon salt,** and **½ teaspoon soda.** Cut in **4 tablespoons shortening.** Add **¾ to 1 cup buttermilk** to make a fairly moist dough. Knead, roll or pat, and bake as for **Riz Biscuits,*** or add more buttermilk and drop them. Makes about 20 biscuits 2 inches in diameter.

CREAM BISCUITS

Sift, then measure **2 cups flour.** Resift with **2 teaspoons baking powder, 1 tablespoon sugar,** and **½ teaspoon salt.**

Make a hole in the dry ingredients and pour in **⅞ cup cream** (1 cup minus 2 tablespoons) all at once. Stir gently to dampen the flour. Then stir vigorously. Drop from a teaspoon onto a greased baking sheet, allowing room for spreading. Bake in a hot, 450° F. oven 12 to 15 minutes. Makes 20 biscuits 2 inches in diameter.

CINNAMON ROLLS

Make the dough for **Riz Biscuits,*** adding **1 tablespoon butter** in addition to the shortening called for. Roll the dough into a sheet ¼ to ⅓ inch thick. Cream **3 tablespoons butter** and spread over the dough. Mix **½ teaspoon cinnamon** with **⅓ cup brown sugar** which has been packed firmly in the cup. Sprinkle over the dough. Roll up. Cut into slices 1 inch thick and place on a greased pan, cut side down. Bake in a hot, 425° F. oven 20 minutes. Serve hot or cold. Makes about 2 dozen rolls.

OATMEAL BISCUITS

Sift, then measure **1½ cups flour.** Resift with **3 teaspoons baking powder, ¼ teaspoon salt,** and **¼ cup sugar.** Cut in **⅓ cup shortening.** Add **1 cup oatmeal** and about **1 cup milk** to make a fairly moist dough. Roll and bake as for **Riz Biscuits.***

WHOLE WHEAT BISCUITS

Stir, then measure **2 cups whole wheat flour.** Sift **1 teaspoon soda, 2 teaspoons baking powder,** and **½ teaspoon salt.** Stir into the whole wheat flour. Cut in **4 tablespoons shortening.** Add just enough **buttermilk** to make a soft dough (about ⅔ cup). Continue as for **Riz Biscuits.***

PIKE COUNTY BISCUIT SHORTCAKE

Sift, then measure **2 cups flour.** Resift with **4 teaspoons baking powder, 1 teaspoon salt,** and **1 tablespoon sugar.** Cut in **5 tablespoons shortening.** Add up to **¾ cup top**

milk to make a fairly moist dough. Shape and bake as for **Rich Shortcake**, below.

OLD FARM RICH SHORTCAKE

Substitute **sour cream** for buttermilk in **Old Farm Saleratus Biscuits.*** Make individual biscuits or pat one-half the dough into a pie tin, brush it with softened **butter** and top with the other half of the dough. Pat the top half into shape. Bake in a hot, 450° F. oven 12 to 15 minutes. Split. It will come apart easily where it was buttered. Spread the bottom with additional butter, cover with crushed sweetened **fruit** (strawberries, blueberries, raspberries, bananas, peaches, etc.) and put the top in place. Pass rich cream, or top the shortcake with whipped cream. Have the fruit in readiness when the shortcake is removed from the oven, as the dessert should be served warm. Serves 4 to 6.

OSCEOLA FARM SHORT CAKE

Cream ⅓ **cup shortening.** Add ⅓ **cup sugar** and beat the mixture until it is light. Add **1 egg** and beat well. Sift, then measure **1 cup flour.** Resift with **2 teaspoons baking powder** and ⅛ **teaspoon salt.** Add the sifted dry ingredients to the batter alternately with ⅓ **cup milk,** beating in the former, stirring in the latter. Grease a round 8½-inch cake tin, turn the batter in and bake in a moderate, 350° F. oven 10 to 20 minutes or until a tester inserted in the center will come out clean. Cut in half and put crushed sweetened **fruit** (strawberries, blueberries, raspberries, bananas, peaches, etc.) between the layers. Top with **whipped cream** and decorate with whole perfect strawberries, blueberries, etc. This is not quite a cake and not quite a biscuit. But it *is* quite delicious. Serves 4.

FRUIT PASTRIES

APPLE PAN DOWDY

Make 1½ times the receipt for **Pastry for a 9-Inch Double-Crust Pie.*** Roll it out. Line a baking dish with it. Peel, core and slice **8 cooking apples** and put them in the dish. Mix together **½ cup sugar, ½ teaspoon cinnamon, ½ teaspoon cloves,** and **⅛ teaspoon salt.** Cover the apples with the mixture. Dot with **¼ cup butter.** Pour over **½ cup molasses** which has been mixed with **¼ cup water.** Cover with a top crust, gash it, crimp the edges of the two crusts together and press to the sides of the baking dish. Bake in a hot, 450° F. oven 15 minutes. Reduce the heat to moderate, 350° F., and bake until lightly browned. Remove from the oven and chop together the filling and the crust. Add more water and molasses if dry, return to a moderately slow, 325° F. oven and bake 1½ hours. Serve hot and pass a pitcher of **Old Farm Heavy Cream.*** Pan Dowdy improves with reheating. Serves 6.

APPLE SLUMP

Place in a greased casserole the apple mixture used for **Apple Pan Dowdy,** above. Cover with a crust made as for **Pike County Biscuit Shortcake.*** Gash the crust and bake in a hot, 425° F. oven 35 minutes, or until the apples are tender and the crust is browned. Invert on a heated serving dish and pass a pitcher of rich **cream.** Serves 4 to 6.

BLUEBERRY SLUMP

Pick over and wash **1 quart fresh blueberries.** Place in a saucepan with **1 cup water, ¼ teaspoon salt,** and **1½ cups sugar** and cook until the blueberries are slightly soft, just a few minutes. Place the mixture in a greased casserole, cover with a crust, bake, and serve as for **Apple Slump,** above. Serves 4 to 6.

BANBURY TARTS

Mix **1 cup seedless raisins, 1 cup sugar, 1 egg** beaten slightly, **2 tablespoons cracker crumbs, 2 tablespoons lemon juice, 1 tablespoon grated lemon rind,** and **1/8 teaspoon salt.** Make one-half the receipt for **Pastry for a 9-Inch Double-Crust Pie,*** roll into an oblong and cut into 5-inch squares. Put 2 teaspoons filling on each square. Fold into triangles and moisten the lower edge lightly with water. Press the edges together with the tines of a fork. Prick the tarts several times, place on a baking sheet and bake in a hot, 450° F. oven 15 to 20 minutes. Serves 4 to 6.

APPLE DUMPLINGS

Peel, core and chop **6 cooking apples.** Add **1 cup sugar, 1 teaspoon cinnamon, 1/8 teaspoon salt,** and **2 tablespoons melted butter.** Mix well. Place 2 teaspoons of the mixture on 5-inch circles of pastry as for **Open Gate Farm Pieplant Dumplings.*** Prick several times with a fork. Bake on a baking sheet in a hot, 425° F. oven 35 minutes. Serve with **Custard Sauce.*** Serves 6.

CHELAN COUNTY PEAR DUMPLINGS

Cut pastry into 5-inch squares, or larger if necessary as for **Banbury Tarts.*** Use **5 canned pears** and place 1/2 pear on each square of pastry. Fill the hollow in each pear with **1 teaspoon brown sugar** and **1 teaspoon butter.** Fold the pastry over after moistening the edges, press the edges together with the tines of a fork, prick several times, and bake in a hot, 425° F. oven 35 minutes. Serves 4 or 5.

OPEN GATE FARM PIEPLANT DUMPLINGS

Sift, then measure **3 cups flour.** Resift with **3 teaspoons baking powder** and **1/2 teaspoon salt.** Cut in **1/2 cup shortening.** Add **3/4 cup milk** gradually and mix to form a fairly moist dough. Stir, then knead lightly. Divide the dough into 6 pieces. Roll each piece ¼ inch thick. Cut **3 cups pieplant** into 1-inch pieces. Peel the pieplant if it is old. Put ½ cup pieplant in the center of each piece of dough. Wrap the dough around it, pinching the ends together tightly. Place the balls in a large baking dish. Pour over **3 cups boiling water** in which has been dissolved **½ cup butter** and **3 cups sugar.** Bake in a moderately hot, 375° F. oven 35 to 40 minutes. Serve hot with the sauce in the dish. Serves 6.

ALL-FRUITS COBBLER

Prepare **2 cups fresh fruit** by hulling strawberries, peeling apples, etc. Combine **½ cup sugar** (depending upon the sweetness of the fruit) with **1 tablespoon cornstarch** and **⅛ teaspoon salt.** Add to **1 cup water.** Add the fruit. Cook the mixture until it comes to a boil, stirring until the sugar is dissolved. Continue cooking 5 to 10 minutes or until there is no taste of raw starch. Stir occasionally. Pour into a greased baking dish. Cover the fruit with a crust, using one-half the receipt for **Riz Biscuits.*** Gash the crust. Bake in a hot, 450° F. oven 12 to 15 minutes, or until crust is nicely browned. Serves 4.

FRIED APPLE PIES

Make one-half the receipt for **Pastry for a 9-Inch Double-Crust Pie.*** Cut into 5-inch squares. Fill each with 1 teaspoon of the filling made for **Apple Dumplings.*** Moisten the edges and press together with the tines of a fork. Fry in deep fat, hot enough to brown an inch cube of bread in 60 seconds, 360° to 370° F., until nicely browned. Drain on unglazed paper. Shake gently in a sack in which there is **½ cup confectioners sugar** mixed with **2 teaspoons cinnamon.** Makes 8 individual pies.

APPLE ROLY POLY

Roll **Pike County Biscuit Shortcake*** ½ inch thick. Spread it with **5 apples** which have been peeled, cored, and chopped, and mixed with **1 cup seedless raisins, ½ cup sugar, ¼ teaspoon cinnamon,** and **¼ teaspoon nutmeg.** Roll up, pinch the edges together, place in a small baking pan, spread with **¼ cup melted butter,** and bake in a hot, 425° F. oven 35 minutes. Baste with the sauce in the pan and serve hot with cream or **Custard Sauce.*** Serves 4 to 6.

Jam, marmalade, or any fruits may be substituted for apples. Omit the raisins, add sugar to taste and any desired combinations of spices. Dredge very juicy fruits lightly with flour after draining off the juice. Use the juice for basting.

Roly Poly Puddings may be steamed as for **Bag Puddings.*** Steam them for 1 hour.

HONEY APPLE PIE

Line a 9-inch pie tin with pastry. Peel **6 medium apples.** Core and cut them into thin slices. Place on the pastry. Place over the apples **1 quince** which has been peeled and sliced thin. Sprinkle with **½ teaspoon cinnamon** and **½ teaspoon cloves.** Dot with **2 tablespoons butter.** Cut a hole ½ inch in diameter in the center of the top crust but do not gash it. Cover the apples with the crust and glaze it. Bake in a hot, 450° F. oven 15 minutes. Reduce the heat to moderate, 350° F., and continue baking 25 to 40 minutes. Remove from the oven. Use a funnel and carefully pour into the hole in the top crust **1 cup honey** which has been mixed with **2 tablespoons lemon juice.** Serve the pie cold, when the fruit will have had time to absorb the liquid.

HOOSIER APPLE PIE

Line a 9-inch pie tin with any pastry. Add **6 apples** which have been peeled, cored, sliced thin, and mixed with **½ cup sugar, ⅛ teaspoon salt, ½ teaspoon cinnamon,** and **¼ cup flour.** Pour over **1 cup cream.** Cover with a top crust, glaze it if desired, and bake in a hot, 425° F. oven 25 to 35 minutes.

CHERRY GLAZE PIE

Sprinkle **1¼ to 2 cups sugar,** to taste, over **4 cups pitted sour red cherries.** Let stand in a cold place for 2 hours. Drain the cherries and boil the juice until thick, 5 to 10 minutes. Mix the cherries with **⅛ teaspoon salt** and **½ teaspoon almond extract.** Place in a 9-inch pie tin which has been lined with any pastry and pour the cooked juice over them. Bake in a hot, 425° F. oven 30 minutes.

SUGAR ORCHARD FARM OCTOBER PIE

Peel, core, and slice thin **5 cups apples.** Pick over and cut in half **2 cups cranberries.** Sift, then measure **7 tablespoons flour.** Resift with **¼ teaspoon salt, 2 cups sugar, 1 teaspoon cinnamon,** and **2 teaspoons grated orange rind.** Add to the fruit and mix well. Line a 10-inch pie tin with any pastry and add the filling. Make lattice strips for the top. Bake in a hot, 425° F. oven 35 minutes.

GOOSEBERRY PIE

Pick over and hull **2 cups gooseberries.** Add **1 cup seeded raisins.** Place in a 9-inch pie tin which has been lined with any pastry. Mix **1¼ cups sugar** with **1 tablespoon cornstarch, ⅛ teaspoon salt, ½ teaspoon cinnamon,** and **½ teaspoon cloves** and sprinkle over the fruit. Dot with **2 tablespoons butter.** Cover with a top crust or make lattice top. Bake in a hot oven, 425° F. oven 35 minutes.

RILEY COUNTY GREEN TOMATO PIE

Core **6 large green tomatoes.** Slice very thin. Sprinkle with **½ teaspoon salt.** Let stand for 30 minutes. Line a 9-inch pie tin with any pastry. Sprinkle the crust with **1 tablespoon quick-cooking tapioca.** Put in **½ cup sugar.** Arrange the tomatoes in the pie. Pour over the tomatoes **2 tablespoons vinegar.** Add **½ cup sugar** and **1 teaspoon cinnamon** and dot with **2 tablespoons butter.** Cover with a top crust, glaze it and bake in a hot, 425° F. oven 35 minutes.

WAUKESHA COUNTY MINCEMEAT

Cook the following ingredients slowly for 2 hours, stirring frequently: **1 peck apples,** peeled, sliced and cored, **5 pounds lean beef,** chopped, **2½ pounds suet,** chopped, **2 pounds seeded raisins, 2 pounds currants, 1½ pounds citron,** the **juice and rind of 1 orange, 1 tablespoon cloves, 1 tablespoon cinnamon, 1 tablespoon allspice, 2 grated nutmegs or 1 tablespoon ground nutmeg, 2½ pounds sugar, 1 cup molasses,** and **3 quarts cider.** When cooked, add **1½ gallons whiskey** and completely fill sterile jars immediately. Seal and store. This will keep indefinitely. It should not be used until a week after it is cooked. Makes about 10 quarts. The receipt may be halved.

MINCE PIE

Line a pie tin with any pastry. Fill the pastry with **Mincemeat,** above. Cover with an upper crust, glaze it if desired, and bake in a hot, 425° F. oven 35 minutes. Serve hot.

CREAM PIES

APPLE CREAM PIE

Place over hot water **1½ cups hot unsweetened apple sauce, ½ cup scalded milk, 1 tablespoon butter, 3 egg yolks,** beaten slightly, and **1 cup sugar** which has been mixed with **1 tablespoon flour, 1/8 teaspoon salt, 1/2 teaspoon cinnamon,** and **1/2 teaspoon nutmeg.** Cook until the mixture coats the spoon well, stirring constantly. Remove from the heat and cool rapidly. When cold, turn into a baked, cooled **9-inch Pastry Shell.*** Make a **Meringue Topping*** with **3 egg whites.**

OTTER DALE COUNTY BUTTERSCOTCH PIE

Mix to a smooth paste **1 tablespoon cornstarch** and **1/4 cup cold milk.** Scald **3/4 cup milk** with **2 tablespoons butter** in the top of a double boiler. Add **1 cup brown sugar** which has been packed firmly in the cup and **1/8 teaspoon salt** and stir until the sugar is dissolved. Add the milk-cornstarch mixture slowly and cook over hot water, stirring constantly until thick and smooth. Cover and cook 15 to 20 minutes longer, or until no taste of raw starch remains, stirring occasionally. Beat **2 egg yolks** slightly. Beat in a portion of the hot liquid. Return to the main mixture and cook 1 to 2 minutes, stirring constantly. Cool rapidly and add **1/2 teaspoon vanilla.** When cold, turn into a baked, cooled **7-inch Pastry Shell.*** Cover with a **Meringue Topping*** made with **2 egg whites.**

DEER LODGE COUNTY CARROT PIE

Cook **carrots** until tender. Press through a strainer and measure 1 cup. Add **1/2 cup sugar, 1/2 teaspoon salt, 1/2 teaspoon cinnamon, 1/4 teaspoon allspice, 1/2 teaspoon ginger, 1/4 teaspoon cloves,** and **1 tablespoon cornstarch.** Beat **2 eggs** slightly. Beat in **1 1/2 cups top milk.** Add to the carrot mixture, and beat as it is poured into an unbaked **9-inch Pastry Shell.*** Bake in a hot, 450° F. oven 15 minutes. Reduce the heat to moderately slow, 325° F., and continue baking 30 to 40 minutes or until the tip of a paring knife inserted in the center will come out clean.

CROOKED ELM FARM CHERRY JERRY PIE

Pit **1 quart sour red cherries.** Sprinkle with **½ to 2 cups sugar,** to taste. Let stand until the sugar has dissolved. Beat **2 eggs** slightly. Add **½ cup milk, ½ cup juice drained from the cherries** (save the rest of the cherry juice to be used as the base for a beverage), **⅛ teaspoon salt, 2 tablespoons rum,** and **2 tablespoons brandy.** Pour over the drained cherries which have been placed in an unbaked **9-inch Pastry Shell.*** Sprinkle the top with **1 teaspoon nutmeg.** Bake in a hot, 450° F. oven 15 minutes. Reduce the heat to moderately slow, 325° F., and continue baking 30 to 45 minutes or until the tip of a paring knife inserted in the center will come out clean.

MIZ HEAVY TROOK'S RECEIPT FOR CHESS PIE

Cream **½ cup butter.** Gradually beat in **1 cup sugar.** Beat in **2 eggs.** If a meringue is desired, use only the egg yolks in the pie and make a **Meringue Topping*** with the whites. Add **1 teaspoon vanilla, ¼ cup cream, 1 cup seeded raisins,** and **¼ teaspoon salt.** Turn into an unbaked **9-inch Pastry Shell*** and bake in a hot, 450° F. oven 15 minutes. Reduce the heat to moderately slow, 325° F., and continue baking 20 to 45 minutes or until the tip of a paring knife inserted in the center will come out clean.

Aunt Sleide says: "They say that Heavy Trook got that way from eating Chess Pie. One night his wife—a wonderful cook—served it to him and he said it was too bad she couldn't make a chess pie like his mother's. So for two weeks she gave him chess pie at every meal. When he asked her why, she said, 'Eat it! I'm practicing so mine'll be as good as your mother used to make!' "

FRUIT CREAM PIE

Line a 9-inch pie tin with any pastry. Sprinkle the bottom of the shell with **1 tablespoon quick-cooking**

tapioca. Prepare cherries, berries, peaches, etc. Arrange the fruit in the shell and pour over a custard made by adding **¾ cup sugar, ¼ teaspoon salt,** and **2 cups scalded milk** to **3 eggs** which have been beaten slightly. Bake in a hot, 450° F. oven 15 minutes. Reduce the heat to moderately slow, 325° F., and continue baking for 45 minutes.

SETTING HEN FARM GRAHAM CRACKER PIE

Beat **3 egg yolks** slightly in the top of a double boiler. Add **½ cup sugar** mixed with **3 tablespoons cornstarch** and **⅛ teaspoon salt.** Add slowly, beating it in, **2 cups scalded milk.** Cook over hot water, stirring constantly, until the mixture coats the spoon well. Remove from the heat and add **1 teaspoon vanilla.** Cool rapidly and pour into a 9-inch pie tin which has been lined with a **Crumb Crust*** made with graham crackers. Cover with **Meringue Topping*** made with **3 egg whites.** Chill and serve.

JEFF DAVIS PIE

Beat **2 eggs** slightly. Add **1 cup sugar** which has been mixed with **1 teaspoon each of cinnamon, allspice, and nutmeg.** Add **1 cup milk** and **1 tablespoon melted butter** and mix. Pour into an unbaked **8-inch Pastry Shell*** and bake in a hot, 450° F. oven 15 minutes. Reduce the heat to moderately slow, 325° F., and continue baking 45 minutes, or until the tip of a paring knife inserted in the center will come out clean.

JELLY PIE

Cream **¼ cup butter.** Gradually add **1 cup sugar.** Add **2 eggs,** beaten slightly, **1 teaspoon vanilla, ¾ cup tart jelly** (about 1 glass) which has been beaten smooth with a fork, **1 teaspoon lemon juice,** and **½ teaspoon nutmeg.** Stir in **1 cup milk.** Mix and pour into an unbaked **9-inch Pastry Shell*** and bake in a hot, 450° F. oven for 15 minutes. Reduce the heat to moderately slow, 325° F., and bake 45 minutes more or until the tip of a paring knife inserted in the center will come out clean.

If a meringue is desired, use only the yolks of the eggs in the pie and make a **Meringue Topping*** with the 2 whites.

JOHNNY APPLESEED PIE

Peel, core and slice thin **6 medium apples.** Mix together **¾ cup sugar, ⅛ teaspoon salt, 1 teaspoon cinnamon,** and **½ teaspoon cloves.** Mix with the apples. Place in an unbaked **7-inch Pastry Shell.*** Add **1 cup sour cream.** Bake in a hot, 450° F. oven 15 minutes. Reduce the heat to moderately slow, 325° F., and bake 20 to 45 minutes longer.

LAURA WILLEY'S RECEIPT FOR MAPLE CREAM PIE

Measure **1¼ cups shaved maple sugar,** packing it firmly in the cup. Place in the top of a double boiler. Add **2 cups scalded milk** and stir until the sugar is dissolved. Add **⅓ cup cold milk** to **3 tablespoons cornstarch** slowly, and stir until smooth. Add to the scalded milk slowly and cook over hot water, stirring until smooth. Cover and cook 15 to 20 minutes, stirring occasionally, until there is no taste of raw starch. Beat **2 eggs** slightly. Pour the cooked mixture over them slowly, beating it in. Return to the double boiler and cook 1 to 2 minutes more, stirring constantly. Remove from the heat and add **½ teaspoon salt.** Cool rapidly and add **1 teaspoon vanilla.** Pour into a baked, cooled **9-inch Pastry Shell.*** Chill. Just before serving, if desired, top with **1 cup cream,** whipped stiff.

Aunt Sleide says: "Laura Willey is the only girl I know who got a proposal on account of a pie supper. The Ladies' Aid gave the supper to raise money for a new roof for the church. Laura told Sam Willey, her best beau, and Charlie Mack, her second-best beau, which pie was hers. Well, those boys went hog-wild when Laura's pie was being auctioned. Finally Sam bid five dollars more than he could afford, and got the pie. He took it over to Laura's table, slammed it down and said, 'Woman, you're costing me too much money. Let's get married.'"

STARK COUNTY PEACHES AND CREAM PIE

Combine **2 tablespoons flour, 2 tablespoons quick-cooking tapioca, 1/4 teaspoon salt,** and **1/2 cup sugar.** Spread on the bottom and sides of an unbaked **9-inch Pastry Shell.*** Combine **1 cup thick sour cream** and **3/4 cup brown sugar** which has been packed firmly in the cup. Peel **8 peaches** and halve them. Dip each half in the sugar-cream mixture. Arrange the peaches in the pastry shell, cut side down. Pour the remainder of the sugar-cream mixture over the peaches. Sprinkle with nutmeg or cinnamon, if desired. Bake in a hot, 450° F. oven 15 minutes. Reduce the heat to moderate, 350° F., and bake 30 to 45 minutes longer or until the peaches are tender.

PIEPLANT CREAM PIE

Peel pieplant if it is old. Cut in half-inch lengths. Add **1/4 teaspoon salt** and **2 tablespoons flour** to **1 cup sugar.** Add **3 cups pieplant** and beat in **2 eggs.** Mix and turn into an unbaked **9-inch Pastry Shell.*** Dot with **1 tablespoon butter.** Cover with a top crust, glaze it, and bake in a hot, 450° F. oven 15 minutes. Reduce the heat to moderately slow, 325° F., and bake 25 to 40 minutes longer, or until the pieplant is tender and the crust is nicely browned.

CROOKED ELM FARM PUMPKIN PIE

To **1/2 cup brown sugar** which has been packed firmly in the cup add **1/2 teaspoon salt, 2 tablespoons cake flour, 1/4 teaspoon nutmeg, 3/4 teaspoon cinnamon, 1/4 teaspoon ginger, 1 1/2 cups strained pumpkin,** canned or cooked, **1/4 cup light corn syrup,** and **1 cup top milk.** Mix and allow to stand 1 to 2 hours or until the filling is fairly thick, rather than sloppy. Beat in **2 eggs** and turn the filling into an unbaked **9-inch Pastry Shell,*** beating it as it is poured into the shell. Bake in a hot, 450° F. oven 15 minutes. Reduce the heat to moderately slow, 325° F., and bake 45 minutes longer or until the tip of a paring knife inserted in the center will come out clean. Top with **1 cup cream** which has been whipped stiff.

RAISIN SOUR CREAM PIE

Beat **2 eggs** slightly. Add **½ cup sugar, 1 cup thick sour cream, 1 cup seeded raisins, ¼ teaspoon salt, 1 teaspoon cinnamon,** and **¼ teaspoon nutmeg,** and **1 teaspoon lemon juice.** Mix and turn into an unbaked **9-inch Pastry Shell.*** Bake in a hot, 450° F. oven 15 minutes. Reduce the heat to moderately slow, 325° F., and continue baking 45 minutes, or until the tip of a paring knife inserted in the center will come out clean. The raisins may be omitted for plain Sour Cream Pie.

DATE SOUR CREAM PIE

Substitute **1 cup chopped, pitted dates** for the raisins in the above receipt.

PRUNE SOUR CREAM PIE

Make **1 cup prune pulp** as in receipt for **Dried Fruits,*** drain, and substitute for the raisins in **Raisin Sour Cream Pie.***

The drained prune juice may be used as the base for a beverage.

SWEET POTATO PIE

Cream **1 tablespoon butter.** Beat in **¾ cup sugar.** Add **2 eggs, 1 cup milk, 1 cup cooked, mashed sweet potatoes, ⅛ teaspoon salt, ½ teaspoon nutmeg,** and **½ teaspoon cinnamon.** Mix and pour into an unbaked **9-inch Pastry Shell*** and bake in a hot, 450° F. oven 15 minutes. Reduce the heat to moderately slow, 325° F., and continue baking 30 to 45 minutes or until the tip of a paring knife inserted in the center will come out clean.

COUNTY FAIR SQUASH PIE

Cook squash and press through a strainer. Measure **1½ cups squash.** Add **¾ cup sugar, ½ teaspoon salt, ½ teaspoon ginger,** and **¾ teaspoon nutmeg** which have been mixed together. Add **3 eggs,** beaten slightly, **1 cup milk,** and **¼ cup cream.** Mix and fill an unbaked **9-inch Pastry Shell.*** Bake in a hot, 450° F. oven 15 minutes. Reduce the heat to moderately slow, 325° F., and continue baking 45 minutes longer or until the filling does not feel excessively sticky when touched. Serve warm and pass **cream** with the pie.

ODD PIES

ALL-GOOD PIE

Beat **2 egg yolks** well. Beat in gradually **¾ cup sugar.** Add **½ cup raisins, ½ cup nuts, ⅛ teaspoon salt, ½ teaspoon cinnamon, ½ teaspoon allspice,** and **¾ teaspoon vinegar.** Mix well. Fold in **2 egg whites** which have been beaten stiff but not dry. Pour into an unbaked **9-inch Pastry Shell*** and bake in a hot, 450° F. oven 15 minutes. Reduce the heat to moderately slow, 325° F., and bake for 45 minutes more.

BUTTERMILK PIE

Cream **4 tablespoons butter.** Gradually beat in **1 cup sugar.** Add **3 eggs** which have been beaten slightly. Add **3 tablespoons flour, ¼ teaspoon salt,** and **1½ cups buttermilk** which has been scalded. Flavor with **1 teaspoon lemon extract** or **½ teaspoon nutmeg.** Pour into an unbaked **9-inch Pastry Shell.*** Bake in a hot, 450° F. oven 15 minutes. Reduce the heat to moderately slow, 325° F., and continue baking 30 to 45 minutes.

WICOMICO COUNTY CIDER SPICE PIE

Mix **¾ cup sugar, 5 tablespoons cornstarch, ⅛ teaspoon salt, 1 teaspoon cinnamon,** and **½ teaspoon nutmeg** in a saucepan. Add **2½ cups cider** slowly, stirring until smooth. Cover and cook over boiling water about 20 minutes or until there is no taste of raw starch. Stir occasionally. Cool and pour into a baked, cooled **9-inch Pastry Shell.*** Just before serving, whip **1 cup cream** stiff and cover the filling with it. Sprinkle ½ cup toasted salted nuts over the top if desired.

PENNSYLVANIA DUTCH CRUMB PIE

Sift, then measure **¼ cup flour.** Mix with **¾ cup dry cake, cooky, or bread crumbs, ¼ teaspoon salt, 1 teaspoon cinnamon, ½ teaspoon ginger,** and **¼ teaspoon nutmeg.** Cut in **¼ cup butter.** Mix **¾ cup honey** with **¼ cup hot water** and **1 beaten egg.** Pour into an unbaked **7-inch Pastry Shell.*** Sprinkle the crumb mixture over the filling. Bake in a hot, 450° F. oven 15 minutes. Reduce the heat to moderately slow, 325° F., and bake 30 to 45 minutes longer.

LEMON CHIFFON PIE WITH RICH CRUST

Make the crust by cutting **½ cup shortening** into **½ cup flour** which has been sifted, then measured. Chill the mixture. **Cut 4 tablespoons shortening** into **1½ cups flour** which has been sifted, then measured. Beat in **1 egg yolk, 1 tablespoon vinegar,** and enough **water** to make the ingredients hold together. Chill the dough at least 15 minutes. Roll both doughs out together, placing the first mixture on top of the second mixture. Fit into a 9-inch pie tin and crimp the edges. Bake in a hot, 450° F. oven 8 to 15 minutes. Make the filling by beating **5 egg yolks** slightly in the top of a double boiler. Mix in **⅞ cup sugar** (1 cup minus 2 tablespoons) and the juice (about 6 tablespoons)and grated rind of **2 lemons.** Cook over hot water, stirring constantly, until the mixture coats the spoon well. Remove from the heat and add **1 teaspoon unflavored gelatin** which has been soaked for 5 minutes in **1 tablespoon cold water** and stir until the gelatin has dissolved. Cool rapidly. Beat **5 egg whites** with **⅛ teaspoon salt** until they are stiff but not dry. Fold them into the cooled gelatin mixture. Pour into the cooled baked pastry shell and set in the refrigerator or other cold place until firm. The crust makes two 9-inch shells. It may be used with other fillings.

MIZ DAVID PENCE'S RECEIPT FOR STICK-TIGHT PIE

Cream **¼ cup shortening.** Add **½ cup sugar** gradually, and beat the mixture until it is light and fluffy. Add **3 eggs, 1 cup molasses, ⅛ teaspoon salt, 1 tablespoon lemon juice,** and **1 cup broken pecans** and mix well. Pour into an unbaked **9-inch Pastry Shell*** and bake in a moderate, 350° F. oven 40 minutes. Top with **1 cup cream** which has been whipped stiff.

Aunt Sleide says: "When Miz Pence gave me this receipt she told me not to fuss with the rest of the meal when I serve Stick-Tight Pie but just let the family get a glimpse of it before they set down to eat. She said they'd go mighty easy so as to be sure to have enough room for it."

PUMPKIN CHIFFON PIE

Mix together **3 egg yolks, 1 cup sugar, 1¼ cups cooked or canned pumpkin,** strained, **½ cup scalded milk, ½ teaspoon salt, 1 teaspoon cinnamon, ½ teaspoon nutmeg,** and **½ teaspoon ginger.** Cook over hot water, stirring constantly until the mixture coats the spoon well. Remove from the heat, add **1 tablespoon unflavored gelatin** which has been soaked in **¼ cup cold water** for 5 minutes and stir until it is dissolved. Cool the mixture rapidly. Beat

3 egg whites until they are stiff but not dry. Fold them gently into the cooled pumpkin mixture. Pour the filling into a baked, cooled **9-inch Pastry Shell*** and chill until firm. Whip **1 cup cream** for a topping.

SHOOFLY PIE

Fit leftover **pastry** into a pie tin. Cover it thickly with **brown sugar.** Pour **melted butter** over the sugar and bake in a hot, 450° F. oven 15 minutes or until the sugar melts and the crust is browned. Use a proportion of ¼ to ½ cup butter to each cup of brown sugar.

KINSBURY COUNTY VINEGAR PIE

Mix **1 cup sugar** with ¼ **teaspoon nutmeg, 3 tablespoons flour,** and ⅛ **teaspoon salt.** Melt **2 tablespoons butter** in **1 cup water.** Add 3 **tablespoons vinegar.** Add the sugar mixture gradually and stir until smooth. Cook over boiling water until thick, stirring occasionally. Beat **3 egg yolks** slightly and beat in a portion of the hot mixture. Return to the main mixture and cook 1 to 2 minutes longer, stirring constantly. Cool rapidly. Pour into a baked, cooled **9-inch Pastry Shell.*** Make **Meringue Topping*** with 3 **egg whites.**

WARREN COUNTY JELLY TARTS

Prepare any **Pastry.*** Roll out and cut rounds. Press over the backs or inside of muffin tins or patty pans. Bake in a hot, 450° F. oven 8 to 10 minutes. Remove from pans and fill with **jam** or **jelly.**

14

DESSERTS

Unless baked desserts are to be turned out on a serving dish, it is a good idea to bake them in casseroles or other attractive baking dishes. This saves dishes and will help keep the dessert hot.

Most desserts are better when they are served with a sauce. A sauce which complements the dessert in flavor will make it more interesting.

When making a soft custard (a custard cooked over hot water), be sure not to let the water underneath boil. Cook the custard only until it coats the spoon well, as it will thicken on cooling. If boiling water is used, or if the custard is cooked too long, there is danger that the custard will separate. Overheating the custard will cause it to curdle. If the custard is only slightly curdled, it may be beaten smooth with a rotary beater. If badly curdled, beating will not help. As soon as the custard coats the spoon well, it should be poured into a cold container so it will cool rapidly. Or it may be left in the pan in which it was cooked and suspended in cold water.

When a custard is baked, it is placed in a pan of hot water to protect it from overheating. The pan should be filled with the water to a depth of 2 inches. To determine when a baked custard has finished baking, insert the tip of a paring knife in the center. If it comes out clean, the custard is done. Also, the top of the custard will be nicely browned and it will not feel excessively sticky when touched lightly. If a baked custard is overcooked, it will separate and become watery.

Fill baking dishes only two-thirds full of any dessert, as heat will cause the food to rise. Fruit desserts such as **New Farm Apple Crisp*** are the exception, as the fruit will cook down.

Steamed Puddings require special treatment which may seem arduous but which, when once tried, will prove to be very simple. Steamed puddings are so good, being neither doughy nor heavy when correctly made, that they deserve to be served often. Most steamed puddings are very rich, so it is best to serve them when the meal which went before was simple.

A pudding may be steamed in a variety of containers. The containers must not be too large, as then the pudding may not cook through. Pudding molds, a tin container with a tightly fitting cover such as a baking powder tin (the 1 pound size is the best to use), a large cloth, a double boiler with a well-fitting cover, or custard cups, may be used.

Puddings which are steamed in a cloth are called **Bag Puddings,** because the pudding mixture is tied securely in a heavy cloth. It is then set on an inverted saucer in a kettle of boiling water.

All containers except cloth must be greased all over. Fill the containers two-thirds to three-quarters full to allow room for swelling. Put about 1 inch of boiling water in the bottom of a steamer or covered kettle. Place filled pudding molds or tins with tightly fitting covers in the water. The water should be kept at a steady but light boil. To prevent aluminum from darkening, add about 1 tablespoon of vinegar to the boiling water. Replenish the vessel with boiling water when necessary. When using custard cups, cover them loosely with heavy waxed paper and secure the paper with tightly fitting rubber bands. The cups may be steamed in a pan of boiling water either on top of the stove or in a moderate, 350° F. oven. When puddings are steamed in these or other individual containers, cut the time given in the receipts in half.

One of the exciting and traditional holiday rites is to serve a steamed pudding aflame. Pour brandy over the pudding, light it with a match and spoon the flaming brandy over the pudding until the flames die. This distributes the brandy flavor throughout the pudding. Could anything be more gala!

FRUIT DESSERTS, CUSTARDS, AND WHIPS

NEW FARM APPLE CRISP

Grease a baking dish. Arrange in the dish **2 cups apples** which have been peeled, cored and sliced thin. Sprinkle the apples with **1 teaspoon cinnamon** and **½ teaspoon nutmeg.** Pour into a measuring cup the strained juice of **1 orange.** Fill the cup with water to the 1-cup mark. Pour over the apples. Crumb together **¾ cup flour, ½ cup shortening, 1 cup brown sugar** which has been packed firmly in the cup, and **1 teaspoon grated orange rind.** Sprinkle the mixture over the apples. Bake in a moderate, 350° oven 30 to 40 minutes or until the apples can be pierced with a straw. Serve hot or cold. Serves 4.

PEACH CRISP

Sift, then measure **¾ cup flour.** Mix with **¼ teaspoon salt** and **1 cup brown sugar** which has been packed firmly in the cup. Cut in **3 tablespoons shortening.** Peel and slice **8 peaches.** Place the fruit in a greased baking dish. Sprinkle with **¼ cup orange juice.** Strew the shortening mixture over the peaches. Bake in a very moderate, 325° F. oven until the top is nicely browned and bubbling. Serve hot or cold. **Old Farm Heavy Cream*** may be passed with it. Serves 6.

APPLE CUSTARD

Pour **1½ cups milk** over **3 eggs** which have been beaten just enough to blend the whites and the yolks. Stir in **1 cup apple sauce,*** which has been sweetened with **½ cup sugar** and spiced with **⅛ teaspoon cinnamon** and **⅛ teaspoon nutmeg.** Turn the custard into custard cups. Set the cups in a pan containing hot water and bake in a moderate, 350° F. oven 30 to 60 minutes or until the tip of a paring knife inserted in the center will come out clean. Shake nutmeg over the top, if desired. Serves 4.

MAPLE CUSTARD

Beat **4 eggs** just enough to blend the yolks and the whites well. Add **¾ cup maple syrup, 3 cups milk,** and **¼ teaspoon salt.** Fill baking dish or custard cups with the mixture. Place in a pan of hot water and bake in a moderate, 350° F. oven until the tip of a paring knife inserted in the center will come out clean. Individual custards will take about 40 minutes; a large custard about 75 minutes. Serves 4 to 6.

HAMPTON COUNTY GOOSEBERRY FOOL

Place **1 cup water** in a saucepan. Add **⅛ teaspoon salt** and **½ cup sugar.** Boil, stirring until the sugar is dissolved. Cook the syrup 5 to 10 minutes or until thick. Add to the syrup **1 quart gooseberries** (or other fruits) which have been washed and picked over. Cook slowly until the gooseberries are soft, about 10 minutes. Press through a strainer. Cool the mixture. Whip **1 pint cream** stiff. Fold in the fruit mixture. Serve very cold. Serves 4 to 6.

BROOK FARM LEMON SPONGE

Soak **1 tablespoon unflavored gelatin** in **¼ cup cold water** for 5 minutes. Dissolve the gelatin by pouring over it **1 cup boiling water.** Add **1 cup sugar** and the juice of

1 lemon (about 3 tablespoons) and chill until it is thick. Beat with an egg beater until the mixture is frothy. Beat **3 egg whites** foamy. Add **⅛ teaspoon salt** and beat until they are stiff but not dry. Add to the gelatin mixture, and continue beating until the mixture is stiff and will hold its shape. Rinse a mold with cold water. Sprinkle the bottom of the mold with **2 teaspoons grated lemon rind.** Pour in the sponge and chill it until it is firm. Turn out and serve with **Custard Sauce.*** Serves 4 to 6.

FRIED PEARS

Sift, then measure **1 cup flour.** Resift with **1 teaspoon baking powder, ½ teaspoon salt,** and **1 tablespoon sugar.** Beat **3 eggs** well. Beat in **1 cup milk.** Add the liquid ingredients to the flour mixture gradually, and stir until smooth. Peel **6 large, ripe pears.** Halve and core them. Dip each half into the batter. Fry in deep fat hot enough to brown an inch cube of bread in 60 seconds, 360° F., until brown. Drain on unglazed paper. Serve with **Swiftwater Farm Lemon Sauce.*** Serves 6 to 8.

APPLE TAPIOCA

Place in a greased baking dish **3 apples** which have been peeled, cored and sliced thin, and **½ cup seedless raisins.** Add **½ cup brown sugar** which has been packed firmly in the cup, mixed with **⅛ teaspoon salt, ½ teaspoon cinnamon,** and **½ teaspoon nutmeg.** Cook over boiling water for 10 to 12 minutes **⅛ teaspoon salt, ⅓ cup quick-cooking tapioca, ¼ cup brown sugar** which has been packed firmly in the cup, and **2½ cups milk.** Stir frequently. Pour the cooked tapioca over the fruit. Bake in a moderate, 350° F. oven until the apples are soft. Serve hot or cold. Serves 6.

CHERRY WHIP

Place in a saucepan **⅓ cup water.** Add **1 cup sugar** and **⅛ teaspoon salt.** Make a syrup, stirring until the sugar is dissolved. Add **1 quart pitted sour cherries** and cook slowly until they are soft, about 3 minutes. Drain the cherries, reserving the juice. Soak **1 tablespoon unflavored gelatin** in **2 tablespoons cold water** for 5 minutes. Dissolve it in **1 cup hot cherry juice.** Chill the juice until it is thick. Then beat it with an egg beater until it is fluffy and will hold its shape. Beat **3 egg whites** until they are stiff but not dry. Fold in **¼ teaspoon almond extract.** Beat the egg whites into the whipped gelatin and beat until stiff. Rinse a mold with cold water. Pour in a portion of the gelatin mixture. Add part of the cherries. Repeat twice, ending with the gelatin mixture. Chill until firm. Turn out on a serving dish and pass **Custard Sauce,*** flavored with almond extract instead of vanilla. Serves 6.

Aunt Sleide says: "The first time my great-nephew Paul Sleide saw snow, he said, 'Mama! Look at all the milk outside!' "

MINCEMEAT WHIP

Beat **5 egg whites** until they are foamy. Add **¼ teaspoon salt** and beat until they are stiff but not dry. Beat in **½ cup sugar** gradually. Fold in **¾ cup mincemeat** which has been drained well. Add **2½ tablespoons lemon juice.** Pile lightly into a greased baking dish. Bake in a slow, 300° F. oven about 30 minutes or until firm. Serve with **Custard Sauce.*** Serves 4 to 6.

PRUNE WHIP

Substitute **¾ cup prune pulp,** made as in receipt for **Dried Fruits,*** for the mincemeat in the above recipe.

APRICOT WHIP

Substitute **¾ cup apricot pulp,** made as in receipt for **Dried Fruits,*** for the mincemeat in **Mincemeat Whip,** above.

PUDDINGS

GALLATIN COUNTY VANILLA CUP PUDDING

Scald **1½ cups milk** over hot water. Mix in a bowl **3 tablespoons cornstarch, ⅛ teaspoon salt,** and **5 tablespoons sugar.** Add **½ cup cold milk** slowly, stirring until smooth. Stir into the scalded milk. Cook over hot water, stirring constantly until thick and smooth. Cover and cook 15 to 20 minutes more (or until there is no taste of raw starch), stirring occasionally. Cool slightly. Add **1 teaspoon vanilla.** Rinse coffee cups or molds with cold water. Turn the pudding into them. Chill until firm. Unmold. Serve with any sauce. Serves 4.

BUTTERSCOTCH PUDDING

Add **1 cup milk** to **2 cups cooked farina.** Beat **2 eggs** until they are light. Add gradually **1 cup brown sugar** which has been packed firmly in the cup, and beat well. To the egg-sugar mixture add **⅛ teaspoon salt, 2 tablespoons melted butter,** and **½ teaspoon vanilla.** Add the cereal and milk and mix well. Pour the pudding into a greased baking dish and bake in a slow, 325° F. oven 40 to 60 minutes, or until firm. Serve hot or cold with **cream.** Serves 4 to 6.

Aunt Sleide says: "Cassie Blake's little girl told Uncle that three little girls had cried at school. 'Two of them wasn't me,' she said, 'but one of them was.' "

CHERRY BETTY

Pick over and stone **1 quart sour cherries.** Brown **1 cup bread crumbs** in **3 tablespoons melted butter.** Add the juice of **½ lemon** (about 1½ tablespoons). Mix in **⅛ teaspoon cinnamon** and **⅛ teaspoon nutmeg.** Grease a casserole and place a layer of the crumb mixture on the bottom. Cover the crumbs with cherries. Sprinkle the cherries with part of **1 cup sugar.** Alternate layers of crumbs, cherries and sugar, until all are used, ending with crumbs. Dot with **1 tablespoon butter.** Bake in a moderate, 350° F. oven 30 to 40 minutes, or until the cherries are tender. Serve with rich cream or with **Custard Sauce.*** Serves 4 to 6.

CHERRY PUDDING

Cream **2 tablespoons shortening.** Add **1 cup sugar** gradually and beat well. Sift, then measure **2 cups flour.** Resift with **2 teaspoons baking powder** and **⅛ teaspoon salt.** Add the dry ingredients to the batter alternately with **1 cup milk,** beating in the former and stirring in the latter. Pour the batter into an attractive greased baking dish. Mix **2 cups pitted sour cherries** with **1 cup hot water** and **1 cup sugar.** Pour the mixture over the batter. Bake in a moderate, 350° F. oven 30 to 40 minutes. Serves 6.

The result is a cake top with a cherry sauce beneath.

CROOKED ELM FARM CUSTARD RICE PUDDING

Beat **2 egg yolks** well. Beat in **½ cup sugar** gradually. Add **1 tablespoon melted shortening, 1 teaspoon vanilla, ⅛ teaspoon salt,** and **⅓ cup seeded raisins.** Add **1½ cups milk** to **1 cup cooked rice** (⅓ cup raw rice). Add to the yolk mixture. Fold in **2 egg whites** which have been beaten stiff but not dry. Turn into a greased baking dish and bake in a slow, 325° F. oven 40 to 60 minutes. Serve hot or cold with cinnamon and cream or with jelly. Serves 4 to 6.

RACINE COUNTY DATE SPONGE

Beat **3 egg yolks** light. Add **¾ cup sugar** gradually, and beat the mixture thoroughly. Add **½ teaspoon vanilla.** Sift, then measure **½ cup flour.** Resift with **1 teaspoon baking powder** and **⅛ teaspoon salt.** Add to the dry ingredients **½ cup chopped nuts** and **1 cup dates** which have been stoned and cut with a knife or a scissors. Add to the egg yolk mixture gradually, and beat until smooth. Fold in gently **3 egg whites** which have been beaten until they are stiff but not dry. Turn the batter into a greased pan, 8 x 9 x 2 inches, and bake in a slow, 300° F. oven 45 to 60 minutes. Cut in squares when cold and serve with **whipped cream.** Serves 6.

HALF-PAY PUDDING

Cook **1 pound mixed Dried Fruit.*** Put **1 cup dry bread crumbs** in the bottom of an attractive greased baking dish. Cover with half the dried fruit. Mix together **½ cup molasses, ½ cup water, 1½ teaspoons lemon juice,** and **½ teaspoon grated lemon rind.** Pour half of this on the fruit. Cover with an additional **1 cup bread crumbs.** Top with the remainder of the fruit and add the remainder of the molasses mixture. Dot with **2 tablespoons butter.** Bake in a moderate, 350° F. oven 1 hour. Serves 8.

JELLY BREAD PUDDING

Scald **2 cups milk.** Add **1 cup dry bread crumbs** and let cool. Add **2 egg yolks** which have been beaten slightly, **¼ cup sugar, ¼ teaspoon salt, 2 tablespoons melted butter,** and **½ teaspoon vanilla.** Mix and turn into a greased baking dish. Bake in a slow, 325° F. oven 40 to 60 minutes, or until firm. Cool and spread the top with **jelly** which has been beaten with a fork. Make a **Meringue Topping*** with **2 egg whites,** completely cover the top of the pudding with the meringue, and bake in a moderate, 350° F. oven 12 to 18 minutes or until brown.

DELICIOUS FRESH PEACH PUDDING

Peel **2 pounds peaches,** saving the peels. Place the peaches in a casserole and add **2 cups water.** Cover the dish and bake the peaches in a moderate, 350° F. oven 20 to 30 minutes or until tender. Use peels to make **Peachy Sauce.*** When the peaches are tender, remove them from the oven and drain and reserve the juice. When the juice and peaches have cooled, beat **4 eggs** well. Beat in **1 cup sugar** gradually and add **¼ teaspoon almond extract.** Sift, then measure **¾ cup flour.** Resift with **¼ teaspoon salt** and **1 teaspoon baking powder.** Measure the juice which has been drained from the peaches and add **milk** if necessary to make 2 cups liquid. Add to the egg-sugar mixture and stir in the sifted dry ingredients gradually. When smooth, pour the batter over the peaches, filling the baking dish ¾ full. Bake uncovered in a very moderate, 325° F. oven 40 to 75 minutes or until the top is nicely browned and the pudding is firm. If there is too much batter for the casserole, fill custard cups ¾ full with the remainder, first pouring in about **2 tablespoons Peachy Sauce.*** The cups will bake in about 30 minutes. Turn them out into individual serving dishes after baking. Serve the large pudding with Peachy Sauce. Serves 4 to 6.

This is so "Delicious" that even if it were more trouble to make, it would be well worth every minute of the work.

TARRANT COUNTY LEMON PIE CAKE

Cream **3 tablespoons butter.** Add **1 cup sugar** gradually, and beat the mixture until it is light and fluffy. Gradually add **3 egg yolks** which have been beaten until they are very light, the juice of **1 lemon** (3 tablespoons), and **½ teaspoon grated lemon rind.** Sift, then measure **⅓ cup flour.** Mix with **⅛ teaspoon salt.** Add the dry ingredients to the batter. When it is well mixed, add **1 cup milk.** Fold in gently **2 egg whites** which have been beaten stiff but not dry with **⅛ teaspoon salt.** Pour into a greased baking dish. Set the dish in a pan of hot water and bake in a very moderate, 325° F. oven 30 to 40 minutes. Serves 4 to 6.

The result is a cake top with lemon sauce beneath it.

MAPLE PIE CAKE

Combine **1 cup maple sugar** which has been packed firmly in the cup and 3 **tablespoons flour.** Add **3 table-**

spoons maple syrup. Beat **2 egg yolks** with **1 teaspoon lemon juice** until they are light. Add them to the maple mixture and beat smooth. Add **1 tablespoon softened shortening.** Stir in **½ cup milk** and **½ cup cream.** Beat **2 egg whites** with **½ teaspoon salt** until they are stiff but not dry. Fold them gently into the first mixture. Pour into a greased baking dish. Set the dish in a pan of hot water and bake in a very moderate, 325° F. oven 45 to 60 minutes, or until the center is firm. Serves 4 to 6.

WHITLEY COUNTY PERSIMMON PUDDING

Wash persimmons and press the sweet flesh through a strainer to make **2 cups persimmon pulp.** Cream **½ cup shortening.** Add **1 cup sugar** gradually, and beat well. Add **3 eggs,** one at a time, beating after each addition. Add **2 cups milk.** Sift, then measure **2 cups flour.** Resift with **1½ teaspoons baking powder, 1 teaspoon soda, ¼ teaspoon salt, ½ teaspoon allspice,** and **½ teaspoon nutmeg,** and beat it in. Mix in the persimmon pulp. Pour into a large greased baking dish. Bake in a moderate, 350° F. oven 40 to 60 minutes. Serve hot or cold with plain cream or whipped cream. Serves 6.

SWEET POTATO PUDDING

Wash, peel and grate sweet potatoes. To **4 cups potato** add **1 cup brown sugar** which has been packed firmly in the cup, **¼ teaspoon salt, 1 teaspoon allspice, 1 teaspoon cinnamon,** and **4 tablespoons softened butter.** Beat well. Beat **4 eggs.** Beat in **1 cup milk** and **1 cup cream.** Stir into the potato mixture. Turn into a greased baking dish and bake in a very moderate, 325° F. oven 40 to 75 minutes. Serve plain or with any sauce. Serves 6.

STEAMED PUDDINGS

OLD FARM CARROT PUDDING

Cream ½ cup **shortening.** Add **1 cup sugar** gradually and beat until the mixture is light and fluffy. Add **1 cup grated carrot** and **1 cup grated potato.** Sift, then measure **1¼ cups flour.** Resift with **1 teaspoon soda, ¼ teaspoon salt, ½ teaspoon cinnamon, ½ teaspoon nutmeg,** and **½ teaspoon cloves.** Add **1 cup seedless raisins** and **1 cup broken nuts** to the dry ingredients. Beat the dry ingredients into the batter gradually and mix well. Steam for 3 hours. Serve hot or cold with **Red Chimney Farm Pudding Sauce.*** Serves 6 to 8.

BARNSTABLE COUNTY CRANBERRY PUDDING

Sift, then measure **1½ cups flour.** Resift with **¼ teaspoon salt, 1 teaspoon soda,** and **½ teaspoon baking powder.** Add to **2 cups cranberries** which have been picked over and halved. Add **⅓ cup hot water** to **⅔ cup honey.** Add to the cranberry mixture with **1 tablespoon grated orange rind.** Steam for 2 hours. Serves 4 to 6.

FIG PUDDING

Pour **1 cup boiling water** over **1 cup figs** which have been cut with a knife or a scissors. Add **1 tablespoon butter** and let the mixture cool. Beat **1 egg** until it is light. Add **1 cup sugar** gradually and beat well. Stir in the cooled fig mixture. Sift, then measure **1 cup flour.** Resift with **2 teaspoons baking powder, ¼ teaspoon salt, 1 teaspoon soda,** and **½ teaspoon nutmeg.** Add **¾ cup broken nuts** to the dry ingredients. Add the dry ingredients to the batter gradually, mixing them in well. Pour the pudding into a greased mold and steam for 1 hour and 15 minutes. Serves 4 to 6.

JEFF DAVIS PUDDING

Chop **1 cup suet** fine. Add **1 cup molasses** and **1 cup sour milk.** Sift, then measure **3 cups flour.** Resift with **½ teaspoon salt, 1 teaspoon soda, ½ teaspoon allspice, 1 teaspoon cinnamon,** and **½ teaspoon ginger.** Mix the dry ingredients with **1 cup seeded raisins, 1 cup currants,** and **½ cup citron,** cut fine. Add to the first mixture. Steam for 3 hours. Serves 8.

Aunt Sleide says: "Whenever I serve Jeff Davis Pudding, Uncle claims that Jeff Davis was one of his ancestors. And whenever I serve Cherry Pie, I hear the same thing about George Washington. But when I serve Devil's Food Cake, Uncle doesn't say a word."

CROOKED ELM FARM MAPLE PUFF PUDDING

Beat **1 egg** well. Beat in **¼ cup cream** and **¼ cup maple syrup.** Stir in **2 tablespoons butter** which has been melted, then cooled. Sift, then measure **1 cup flour.** Resift with **1 teaspoon baking powder, ¼ teaspoon soda,** and **⅛ teaspoon salt.** Add **1 cup broken nuts** to the dry ingredients. Steam for 1¼ hours. Serve with **La Fourche County Praline Sauce*** if desired, omitting the nuts. Crushed peaches sweetened to taste, or hot maple syrup, are good on the pudding. Serves 4.

HAVEN FARM PLUM PUDDING

Sift, then measure **½ cup flour.** Resift with **2 teaspoons baking powder, 1 teaspoon salt,** and **½ teaspoon each of ginger, cloves, allspice, nutmeg, and cinnamon.** Add to the dry ingredients **1 pound seeded raisins, 1 pound currants, ½ pound citron,** and **1 pound suet,** chopped. Beat **6 eggs** until they are light. Beat in **1 pound brown sugar.** Add **1 cup any fruit juice or ½ cup fruit juice and ½ cup brandy.** (Grape juice is excellent.) Add **1 pound bread crumbs or flour.** Combine the fruit mixture and the egg-flour mixture and mix well. Steam for 5 to 6 hours. Serve flaming, if desired. Serves 12.

SAILOR'S DUFF

Beat **1 egg** until light. Beat in **¾ cup molasses, 3 tablespoons melted butter,** and **1 teaspoon vanilla.** Sift, then measure **1¾ cups flour.** Resift with **½ teaspoon soda, ¼ teaspoon salt,** and **1 teaspoon baking powder.** Add **½ cup seeded raisins** and **½ cup broken nuts** to the dry ingredients. Add the dry ingredients to the batter gradually, beating until smooth. Steam for 1½ hours. Serve hot with any sauce. Serves 6.

BON HOMME COUNTY STEAMED BREAD PUDDING

Mix **2 cups dry bread crumbs** with **1 cup molasses.** Add **½ cup seedless raisins.** Dissolve **½ teaspoon cinnamon, ½ teaspoon cloves, ½ teaspoon allspice, ¼ teaspoon salt,** and **½ teaspoon soda** in **¾ cup hot water.** Mix with the other ingredients. Steam for 2 hours.

THANKSGIVING PUDDING

Cream **¼ cup shortening.** Add **½ cup sugar** gradually, beating well. Beat in **½ cup molasses.** Add **1 cup cooked, sieved pumpkin.** Sift, then measure **2 cups flour.** Resift with **½ teaspoon soda, ½ teaspoon salt, 1 teaspoon cinnamon, ½ teaspoon cloves,** and **¼ teaspoon nutmeg.** Add the dry ingredients to the batter alternately with **½ cup sour milk,** beating in the former and stirring in the latter. Steam for 1 hour. Serve hot or cold with **Red Chimney Farm Pudding Sauce,*** if desired. Serves 6 to 8.

FABULOUS DESSERTS

CROOKED ELM FARM CHEESE CAKE

Line the bottom and sides of a 9-inch spring form with **Crumb Crust*** made with graham crackers. Reserve ½ cup of the mixture to sprinkle over the top of the cake. Pour in the following filling: Cream **1 pound cream cheese.** Gradually add **2 cups cream.** Stir in **½ pound farmer's cheese** (sometimes called "pressed cheese"). Beat **5 eggs** until they are thick and lemon colored. Beat in gradually **½ cup sugar.** Add **1½ tablespoons lemon juice, 2 tablespoons flour, ¼ teaspoon salt, 1 teaspoon vanilla,** and **1 cup white raisins** (raisins may be omitted). Add the cheese mixture to the egg mixture. Pour the filling into the crust. Sprinkle the top with the remainder of the crumb mixture. Bake in a moderate, 350° F. oven 1 hour, or until the center is firm. Turn off the oven and open the oven door, but leave the cake in until it is cold. When cold, remove it from the oven and loosen the crust by running a knife around the edge of the spring form. Remove the sides of the form and place the cake on a serving plate. Serves 12 to 16 lucky people.

CREAM PUFFS

Place in a saucepan **1 cup water** and **½ cup shortening.** Let the mixture come to a boil rapidly. When the boiling point is reached, add all at once **1 cup flour** which has been sifted, then measured and mixed with **¼ teaspoon salt.** Cook the batter, stirring constantly until it is smooth and forms a ball. Remove from the fire. Beat in **3 eggs,** one at a time. The batter has been beaten sufficiently if it breaks when the beater is raised. Grease a cooky sheet or an inverted baking pan. Spoon 12 puffs onto the sheet, allowing 2 inches for spreading. Bake in a hot, 450° F. oven 30 to 35 minutes. If the puffs brown too fast, reduce the temperature to moderately hot, 375° F. oven. Test the puffs for "doneness" by removing one from the oven. If it does not collapse, the puffs have finished baking. Unfortunately, the collapsed puff will have to be thrown away, so try to be sure that the puffs are quite done, but not brittle, before testing them. Remove the puffs and place on a cake rack to cool. When cold, split and fill them with **Vanilla Cream Filling*** or **whipped cream** into which has been beaten **¼ cup sifted confectioners sugar** and **¼ teaspoon vanilla.** Ice with **Chocolate Pour Icing.*** Keep the puffs in a cold place until served.

MAPLE CREAM PUFFS

Fill **Cream Puffs,** above, with unsweetened **whipped cream** and pass hot **maple syrup** instead of icing them.

STRAWBERRY CREAM PUFFS

Mash **½ pint strawberries** which have been washed and hulled. Add to them **½ cup sifted confectioners sugar** and **⅛ teaspoon salt.** Place the sugared berries in the refrigerator or other cold place until the sugar is dissolved. Drain well and add to the pulp **1 cup whipped cream.** Add **¼ teaspoon almond extract.** Fill the puffs with the mixture. Ice them with **Plain Jane Icing,*** using the juice which has been drained from the strawberries as the liquid. Serve immediately. Fills 12 puffs.

JESSIE REIT'S RECEIPT FOR JELLY CAKE

Beat **3 egg yolks** with **2 tablespoons water** until thick and lemon colored. Sift **¾ cup sugar** and add to the beaten yolks gradually, beating the mixture until it is very light. Add **1 teaspoon vanilla.** Sift, then measure **¾ cup cake flour.** Resift with **1 teaspoon baking powder** and **⅛ teaspoon salt.** Add the sifted dry ingredients to the egg-sugar mixture gradually, beating the batter until it is smooth. Beat 3 egg **whites** with **⅛ teaspoon salt** until they are stiff but not dry. Fold the egg whites into the batter gently. Grease a pan 9-x-13-x-2-inches. Put waxed paper in the bottom, and grease the paper lightly. Pour in the batter, and bake the cake in a moderate, 350° F. oven 20 to 30 minutes. When the cake has finished baking, turn it out on a tea towel which has been heavily sprinkled with

confectioners sugar. Working rapidly, remove the waxed paper and cut off the hard edges of the cake. Make a roll with both the towel and the cake. Let the cake cool in the towel. Unroll it and spread it with jelly which has been beaten with a fork to make spreading easier. Traditionally, it is spread 1 inch thick with currant jelly. Re-roll the cake, and serve. Serves 6 to 8.

ABBIE REIT'S RECEIPT FOR REESE ROLL

Beat **4 egg yolks** until thick and lemon colored. Sift **¾ cup sugar** and add to the egg yolks gradually, beating until the mixture is very light. Add **½ teaspoon vanilla** and **2 ounces bitter chocolate,** melted. Sift, then measure **6 tablespoons cake flour.** Resift the flour with **¾ teaspoon baking powder** and **⅛ teaspoon salt.** Add the sifted dry ingredients to the egg-sugar mixture gradually, beating the batter until it is smooth. Beat **4 egg whites** with **⅛ teaspoon salt** until they are stiff but not dry. Fold them into the batter gently. Grease a pan, 9 x 13 x 2 inches. Put waxed paper in the bottom and grease the paper lightly. Pour in the batter, and bake the cake in a moderate, 350° F. oven 20 to 30 minutes. Turn the cake out, remove the paper, cut off the edges, and roll, as above, omitting the confectioners sugar. When the cake is cold, unroll it and spread it with **1 cup rich cream,** whipped stiff. Ice with **Chocolate Pour Icing.*** Serves 6 to 8.

Aunt Sleide says: "None of the Reit boys ever proposed to a girl. They just asked her if she could cook."

SAUCES

CHERRY SAUCE

Measure the juice from canned cherries. Allow **1 tablespoon cornstarch** for each cup of juice. Dissolve the cornstarch in a little of the cold liquid and make a smooth paste. Add to the remainder of the liquid, stirring it in until smooth. Cover and cook, until the mixture is of the desired consistency and no taste of raw starch remains, about 15 minutes. Stir occasionally. Add ¼ **teaspoon almond extract** for each cup of juice.

The juice from other canned fruits may be made into a sauce the same way. Use any desired flavoring.

RED CHIMNEY FARM PUDDING SAUCE

Mix **1 cup sugar** with ¼ **teaspoon salt** and **1 tablespoon flour.** Add to ½ **cup boiling water** slowly to avoid lumps. Add ⅓ **cup butter.** Cook 5 minutes or until thick, stirring constantly. Cool and add **1 teaspoon vanilla.** Serve cold. One-half fresh nutmeg, grated (or ¾ teaspoon ground nutmeg) may be added when the sauce has cooled slightly. Makes about ¾ cup sauce.

BROWN SUGAR SAUCE

Place ½ **cup water** and ¼ **teaspoon salt** in a saucepan. Add **1 cup brown sugar** which has been packed firmly in the cup. Boil until thick, about 10 minutes, stirring until the sugar is dissolved. Remove from the fire and add **1 tablespoon butter.** Serve hot on baking powder biscuits, waffles, griddlecakes, or desserts.

HI-HILL FARM BUTTERSCOTCH SAUCE

Place in a saucepan **1¼ cups brown sugar** which has been packed firmly in the cup, ⅛ **teaspoon salt,** ⅔ **cup corn syrup,** and **4 tablespoons butter.** Stir until the sugar is dissolved. Let the mixture boil until a little of it will form a soft ball, 236° F., when tested in cold water. Remove from the heat immediately and stir in ¾ **cup top milk.** Serve hot or cold. The sauce may be reheated in a double boiler. Makes about 1½ cups sauce.

DORCHESTER COUNTY CHRISTMAS SAUCE

Cream **1 tablespoon butter.** Gradually add **1 cup confectioners sugar** which has been sifted with ⅛ **teaspoon salt.**

Add **1 egg** and **½ teaspoon vanilla** and beat well. Beat **¾ cup cream** until it is stiff. Fold into the egg mixture.

CIDER SAUCE

Melt **1 tablespoon butter.** Blend in **1 tablespoon flour.** Gradually add **1½ cups cider,** stirring constantly to prevent lumps. When the sauce comes to a boil, cook for a minute or two longer. Serve hot or cold. Makes about 1½ cups sauce.

CHOCOLATE SAUCE FOR A DIP

Melt **2 ounces bitter chocolate** in **6 tablespoons water.** Add **½ cup sugar** and **⅛ teaspoon salt** and cook, stirring until the sugar is dissolved. Continue cooking until the sauce is slightly thickened. Remove from the fire and add **3 tablespoons butter** and **¼ teaspoon vanilla.** Makes about 1 cup sauce. Serve on ice cream.

CUSTARD SAUCE

Beat **2 egg yolks** slightly in the top of a double boiler. Stir in **1 cup milk, ⅛ teaspoon salt,** and **2 tablespoons sugar.** Cook the mixture over hot, not boiling, water, stirring constantly until the mixture coats the spoon well. Pour the custard into a cold dish immediately. When the custard is cool, stir in **¼ teaspoon vanilla** or other flavoring.

OLD FARM HEAVY CREAM

Sweeten **1 pint rich cream** by stirring **2 to 4 tablespoons confectioners** sugar into it until dissolved. Flavor with **¼ teaspoon cinnamon, nutmeg, or vanilla.** Pass with desserts in place of plain cream.

HARD SAUCE

Cream **½ cup butter.** Gradually add **1 cup confectioners sugar** which has been sifted with **⅛ teaspoon salt** and cream the mixture until it is light and fluffy. Flavor the sauce with **1 teaspoon flavoring,** beating it in. For flavoring, use vanilla, almond, orange, lemon, etc. Orange or lemon juice may be used in place of extract. When the sauce is smooth, pack it into a small serving dish and chill it until it is firm. Makes about 1 cup sauce.

FRUITED HARD SAUCE

Cream **6 tablespoons butter.** Add **1 cup sifted confectioners sugar** gradually, beating it in well. Press through a strainer and beat in **¾ cup crushed strawberries, ¾ cup crushed raspberries, or ½ cup banana pulp.** Add **1 teaspoon vanilla** or other flavoring. Pack into a serving dish and chill until firm. Makes about 1½ cups sauce.

LOTTIE HERBEL'S RECEIPT FOR ALL-PURPOSE LEMON BUTTER

Beat **3 eggs** slightly in the top of a double boiler. Add **1 cup sugar, ⅛ teaspoon salt, ¼ cup butter,** and the juice of **1 lemon** (3 tablespoons). Cook over hot water, stirring constantly until the mixture coats the spoon well. Remove from the fire and stir in the grated lemon rind. This may be used as a filling for cakes and tarts or as a spread for bread or hot rolls.

Aunt Sleide says: "Lottie Herbel is noted for being extra clean. One day after she'd had company, she saw that her bureau was a little out of place, and she wondered what had happened to it. The explanation came a day or two later. The guests wrote a note saying that they'd wanted to see if her house was really as clean as folks said it was, so they'd moved her bureau and run their fingers over the woodwork behind it. It was clean back there, they said, clean as a whistle."

SWIFTWATER FARM LEMON SAUCE

Mix **1 tablespoon cornstarch** with ½ **cup sugar** and ⅛ **teaspoon salt** in a saucepan. Slowly stir in **1 cup boiling water.** Cook the sauce until it boils, stirring constantly. Remove from the fire and add **1½ tablespoons butter,** the juice of **1 lemon** (about 3 tablespoons), and ½ **teaspoon grated lemon rind.**

MAPLE WHIP CREAM SAUCE

Fold **2 tablespoons maple syrup** into ½ **cup cream** which has been whipped stiff with ⅛ **teaspoon salt.** If not sweet enough, add confectioners sugar to taste.

SETTING HEN FARM MOLASSES SAUCE

Mix in a saucepan **1 cup molasses, 2 tablespoons lemon juice,** and **1 tablespoon butter.** Bring to the boiling point slowly. Cook over very low heat for 10 minutes, stirring constantly to prevent burning. Serve hot.

PEACHY SAUCE

Cook the skins from **2 pounds peaches** in **2 cups water** 15 to 20 minutes or until soft. Strain and measure the juice. Add half as much **sugar** as juice and boil 3 to 5 minutes, stirring until the sugar is dissolved. Add ⅛ **teaspoon salt** and **1 teaspoon lemon or lime juice** to the syrup. Use the sauce hot or cold, on peach pudding, custard, ice cream, etc. Makes about 1 cup sauce.

LA FOURCHE COUNTY PRALINE SAUCE

Place ¾ **cup maple syrup, 2 tablespoons butter,** and ⅛ **teaspoon salt** in a large pan. Boil until a little of the liquid tested in a cup of cold water will form a very soft ball, 234° F. Remove from the heat and gradually add ¼ **cup heavy cream,** ½ **teaspoon lemon extract,** and **1 cup broken pecans.** Serve hot or cold.

MONONA COUNTY SOFT SAUCE

Melt ½ **cup butter** in the top of a double boiler. Blend in **2 tablespoons flour** mixed with **1 cup sugar.** Add **2 cups boiling water** slowly, stirring constantly to avoid lumps. Cook the sauce over boiling water, stirring until it thickens. Add the juice of **2 lemons** and **1 orange.** Makes about 2½ cups sauce.

15

FROZEN DESSERTS

Before making ice cream or other frozen desserts, test the freezer to make sure that it is in good working order. Clean the freezer can, the can cover, and the dasher by scalding them with hot water. Then chill by running cold water over them. Dry thoroughly. Set the can in the freezer and adjust the dasher. Fill the freezer can only two-thirds full of the mixture to be frozen to allow room for swelling. Chop ice fine. Fill the freezer about one-half full of ice before beginning to add salt. Then add rock salt and ice in alternate layers. Use 1 part salt to 6 or 8 parts ice by weight. A proportion of 1 part salt to 6 parts ice by weight is equal to 1 part salt to 12 parts ice by measure.

It is better not to mix the salt and ice outside the freezer. Start turning the freezer crank slowly. As soon as the crank begins to drag, turn it more rapidly. The cranking should be stopped as soon as the crank turns with difficulty. The mixture should not be cranked solid. Do not drain off the brine formed by the ice and salt while cranking.

As soon as the crank turns with difficulty, wipe off the top of the freezer can and remove the cover. Take out the dasher and scrape back into the can any ice cream which is clinging to it. Press the ice cream down solidly in the can. Place waxed paper over the can and replace the cover. Cork the hole in the cover. Now drain off the excess brine. If the ice cream is to be used soon, the freezer may be packed with a freezing mixture containing a higher percentage of salt than that which was used for freezing. If the ice cream is allowed to stand for a length of time before serving, the freezer may be packed with the same mixture used for freezing or a mixture containing less salt (about 1 part salt to 12 parts ice by weight).

Cover the freezer with a clean old rug or a burlap bag to hold in the cold and set it aside until ready to use the dessert.

Twenty or 25 per cent cream is specified in the receipts but heavier cream may be used for a richer product.

Homemade ice cream with real cream and real eggs may be part of what keeps 'em "down on the farm"!

MIZ JUD LENFESTY'S RECEIPT FOR CUSTARD ICE CREAM

Beat **4 eggs** in a double boiler just enough to blend the whites and yolks. Add **1 cup sugar** and mix well. Add **2 cups 20% cream** which has been scalded, stirring it in. Cook over hot water, stirring constantly, until the mixture coats the spoon well. Cool the custard rapidly. Add **2 cups 20% cream, 2 teaspoons vanilla,** and **⅛ teaspoon salt** and freeze. Makes about 1½ quarts.

Aunt Sleide says: "Uncle never misses a chance to get over to Miz Jud Lenfesty's after she's made ice cream. She serves it in soup plates."

CHOCOLATE ICE CREAM

Add **¼ cup boiling water** to **¼ cup cocoa** gradually, making a smooth paste. Add **1 cup sugar** gradually. Cool the mixture. Add **1 quart 25% cream, 1 tablespoon vanilla,** and **⅛ teaspoon salt.** Freeze. Makes about 1½ quarts.

Aunt Sleide says: "Uncle says he wants to get his fill of this while he's here, because where he's going it'll be too hot to freeze it!"

TWO HILLS PLANTATION ICE CREAM

Add **2 cups sugar** to the juice of **2 lemons** and **2 oranges** and stir until the sugar is dissolved. Add **3 mashed bananas.** Add the mixture to **4 cups 25% cream** and freeze. Makes about 1½ quarts.

QUICK VANILLA ICE CREAM

Scald **1 cup 25% cream.** Add **1 cup sugar.** Cool the mixture. Add **3 cups 25% cream, ⅛ teaspoon salt,** and **1 teaspoon vanilla.** Freeze. Makes about 1½ quarts.

Aunt Sleide says: "When we make ice cream for the church socials, we figure out how much each young un can hold and then we multiply by three."

FRUIT ICE CREAMS

Strawberry. Crush **1 quart hulled strawberries** and add **1 cup sugar** and **1 teaspoon lemon juice.** Chill the berries until the sugar dissolves. Then add **1 quart 25% cream** and **1 teaspoon almond extract.** Freeze.

Peach. Peel and mash **4 pounds ripe sweet peaches.** Stir in **½ cup granulated sugar, 2 tablespoons red sugar,** and **1 teaspoon lemon juice.** Chill until the sugar dissolves. Add **1 teaspoon almond extract** and **½ cup sugar** to **1 quart 25% cream.** Add the peaches and freeze.

Apricot. Substitute **apricots** for peaches in the above receipt.

Raspberry. Press **1 quart red or black raspberries** through a colander, then through a strainer. Add **1 teaspoon lemon juice, ¾ cup sugar,** and **1 quart 25% cream** and freeze.

Each of these recipes makes about 1½ quarts ice cream.

CRANBERRY ICE

Pick over **4 cups cranberries.** Add **1½ cups boiling water** and simmer until the skins burst. Press through a strainer.

Add **2¼ cups sugar, ⅛ teaspoon salt,** and the juice of **1 orange.** Cool and freeze. Serves 6 to 8.

OLD FARM LILAC SHERBET

Heat **2 cups grape juice.** Dissolve in it **1 cup sugar** and **⅛ teaspoon salt.** Cool and add **4 cups milk.** Freeze. Makes about 1½ quarts.

TIFT COUNTY WATERMELON ICE

Make a syrup by boiling **½ cup sugar** and **½ cup water.** (Stir until the sugar is dissolved.) Add **3 cups watermelon juice,** the juice of **1 lemon** (3 tablespoons), and **⅛ teaspoon salt.** Cool and freeze. The ice may be made in a refrigerator tray. Soak **1 tablespoon unflavored gelatin** in **¼ cup cold water** for 5 minutes. Dissolve over hot water and add to the syrup mixture. Then pour it into the refrigerator tray. Beat the ice when it begins to freeze, return to the tray and freeze firm. Makes about 1 quart.

16

CONFECTIONS

When cooking candy, it is important to remember to stir the mixture only until the sugar dissolves. Some candies must also be stirred toward the end of the cooking period in order to prevent burning. This will be specified when necessary.

As candy cooks, sugar crystals form on the sides of the container. They should be wiped down with a dampened pastry brush or with a dampened cloth which has been wrapped around the tines of a fork. If these crystals fall into the solution, it will crystallize. Be sure that the spoon used for testing the candy is cleaned each time after it is dipped into the mixture so that it cannot introduce sugar crystals into the candy.

When testing candy for "doneness," very cold water should be used. The candy should be removed from the fire, tested, then returned to the fire if it has not cooked long enough.

Here's to that sweet tooth!

ELM TREE FARM BUTTERSCOTCH

Place in a large pan **1 cup brown sugar** which has been packed firmly in the cup, **2 tablespoons light corn syrup, ½ cup water,** and **⅛ teaspoon salt.** Cook, stirring only until the sugar is dissolved. Continue cooking until a portion of the mixture will form a hard ball, 250° F., when tested in cold water. Add **¼ cup butter** and stir to keep the candy from scorching. Cook until a portion of the mixture will separate into hard but not brittle threads, 270° F., when tested in cold water. Add 3 **drops vanilla.** Pour in a thin sheet on the greased back of a baking pan or on a greased slab. Mark into squares while still warm, creasing deeply. Break the candy into pieces as soon as it is cold.

MAPLE STIR CANDY

Boil **4 cups maple syrup** until a portion of it will form a soft ball, 236° F., when tested in cold water. Let it cool to lukewarm. Then stir until it is light-colored and very creamy, or pour portions into saucers, give each person a spoon, and let him stir his own candy. After the first few luscious mouthfuls, a bite of dill pickle, the traditional accompaniment, will be extremely welcome to cut the sweetness of the candy.

MAHASKA COUNTY CANDY FRUIT LOAF

Chop coarsely **1 cup seeded raisins, 1 cup nuts, ½ cup figs,** and **½ cup dates** which have been pitted. Add **⅛ teaspoon salt** to **2 tablespoons honey or corn syrup.** Mix with the fruit. Add more honey or syrup, about 2 tablespoons, to form a stiff roll. Wrap the roll in waxed paper. Chill until firm. Cut in slices and roll in **confectioners sugar.**

OLD FARM PEANUT BRITTLE

Place **1 cup sugar** in a skillet. Melt it over a very low flame, stirring constantly. When light brown, stir in **1½ cups peanuts** which have been blanched and roasted. Other nuts may be substituted. Break them if desired. Pour the candy onto a greased slab or on the greased back of a large baking sheet. Smooth it with a spatula. After about 30 seconds, grasp the edges of the candy, lift it from the pan slightly, and pull it very thin. Break into pieces.

MOLASSES PEANUT BRITTLE

Place ½ **cup molasses,** 1½ **cups sugar,** and **1 teaspoon vinegar** in a saucepan and cook over a low flame, stirring until the sugar is dissolved. Continue cooking slowly until a portion of the mixture will form threads which are hard and brittle, 300° F., when tested in cold water. Remove from the fire and stir in ½ **teaspoon soda,** ¼ **teaspoon salt,** and 1½ **cups peanuts,** which have been blanched and roasted. Pour onto the greased back of a baking sheet and proceed as above.

POPCORN

Pop **corn** in a popper or in any covered pan or skillet. Do not try to pop too much corn at once or the kernels that open last will not have room to pop. A single layer of corn on the bottom of the skillet is the best amount to use. Melt **1 tablespoon shortening, oil, or lard** and **1 tablespoon butter** in a large pan. Let heat, then add ½ **cup unpopped corn.** Cover the pan and cook over a medium flame, shaking the pan occasionally. When the corn has finished popping (don't wait for the very last kernel to pop, or the others may burn), turn it into a bowl and stir in ¼ **teaspoon salt** and additional melted butter if desired. If the corn will not pop well, cover it with water for about 3 minutes. Drain and dry thoroughly, and pop again. Makes about 4 cups corn.

GOOCHLAND COUNTY CRACKER JACK

Pop **2 cups corn** as above and discard the unpopped kernels. Mix the corn with **1 cup unsalted roasted peanuts** and ¼ **teaspoon salt.** Melt ¼ **cup butter** and ¼ **cup lard** in a saucepan. Add **3 cups brown sugar** which has been packed firmly in the cup, **6 tablespoons light corn syrup,** ⅛ **teaspoon salt,** and ⅛ **teaspoon cream of tartar.** Cook, stirring until the sugar is dissolved. Wipe down any sugar crystals. When a portion of the mixture will form a firm ball, 250° F., when tested in cold water, add **1 teaspoon soda** and stir just enough to mix well. Pour over the corn and nuts. Mix well. Form into balls if desired, using as little pressure as possible so as not to crush the corn. Wrap the balls in waxed paper to keep.

HONEYED POPCORN BALLS

Pop **3 cups corn** as in receipt for **Popcorn.** Discard the unpopped kernels. Place the corn in a large bowl and mix it with **½ teaspoon salt.** Place in a large saucepan **1¼ cups light corn syrup, ¾ cup honey, ¼ teaspoon salt,** and **1½ teaspoons lemon juice.** Cook until a portion of the mixture, when tested in cold water, will separate into hard and slightly brittle threads (275° F.). To prevent burning, stir almost constantly at the end of the cooking period. Add **2 tablespoons butter** and stir just enough to mix well. Pour slowly over the corn and mix thoroughly. Shape rapidly into balls, using as little pressure as possible so as not to crush the corn. Makes about 12 balls 4 inches in diameter.

POPCORN BALLS

Pop **3½ cups corn** as in receipt for **Popcorn.** Discard the unpopped kernels. Place the corn in a large bowl and mix it with **¾ teaspoon salt.** Place in a saucepan **1 cup water, 3 cups sugar, ¼ teaspoon salt,** and **1¼ cups light corn syrup.** Cook, stirring constantly, until the sugar is dissolved. Continue cooking, wiping down the sugar crystals. Test in cold water and remove from the fire when a small portion of the mixture will separate into threads which are slightly brittle, 270° F. Stir constantly toward the end of the cooking period to prevent burning. Add **4 tablespoons butter.** Pour the syrup slowly onto the corn and proceed as above. Makes about 15 balls 4 inches in diameter.

Aunt Sleide says: "Ralph Kingman brought the makings

for popcorn balls over to Nettie Raymond's house when he was courting her. Her mother was so put out that Nettie almost didn't marry Ralph. Mrs. Raymond said, 'Ralph, I don't mind your bringing popcorn. And I don't mind your bringing syrup. But what kind of a house do you think I run when you bring *salt*!' "

MAGNOLIA PLANTATION PRALINES

Place **1 cup maple syrup, ½ cup cream, 2 cups confectioners sugar,** and **⅛ teaspoon salt** in the top of a double boiler. Cook until a portion of the mixture will form a soft ball when tested in cold water, 236° F. Beat the mixture until it starts to thicken and begins to sugar. Place it over hot water. Stir in **½ pound pecans** which have been heated and crisped in a slow, 250° F. oven. Drop from a spoon onto waxed paper, making patties 2 inches in diameter.

'LASSES TAFFY

Place in a large saucepan **3 cups sugar, 1 cup molasses, 1 cup water,** and **3 tablespoons vinegar.** Cook slowly, stirring until the sugar is dissolved and wiping down the sugar crystals. Stir the candy toward the end of the cooking period to keep it from burning. Cook until a portion of the mixture will form a hard, yet plastic ball, 265° F., when tested in cold water. Add **¼ cup butter, ¼ teaspoon soda,** and **⅛ teaspoon salt** and stir just enough to mix well. Turn the mixture into a greased bowl and let it cool until the edges begin to stiffen and it may be handled. Be careful not to let it get too cool. It is not necessary to grease the hands for taffy pulling. Use just the thumb and fingers, and pull the candy until it is cold, rather firm, and light yellow in color. Stretch it into a long rope. Cut it into pieces with a scissors, wrapping the pieces in waxed paper if they are to be stored. Place the pieces on a buttered plate, well separated, if they are to be served immediately.

CAVALIER COUNTY ICE CREAM TAFFY

Place in a large saucepan **1 cup water, 2 cups sugar, 3 tablespoons vinegar,** and **1/8 teaspoon salt.** Cook, stirring until the sugar is dissolved. Continue cooking, wiping down the sugar crystals, until a portion of the mixture will form a hard ball, 265° F., which is still plastic when tested in cold water. Pour the mixture into a greased bowl. When the edges begin to stiffen and it is cool enough to handle, add **1 teaspoon vanilla,** pouring it into the middle of the candy. Gather the candy up to the vanilla so as not to lose any of it. Pull as above until the candy is white and rather firm. Continue as above.

OPEN GATE FARM SPICED NUTS

Mix together **1 tablespoon cinnamon, 1/8 teaspoon salt,** and **1/4 cup sugar.** Beat 1 egg white slightly and place **1 tablespoon egg white** in a bowl with **1 cup walnuts, pecans, or cashew nuts.** Mix with the fingertips until the nuts are well coated. Add the sugar and cinnamon and mix well. Lift the nuts with two forks and shake off the excess sugar. Spread them out on a baking sheet. Bake the nuts in a slow, 300° F. oven 20 to 30 minutes, or until delicately browned.

17

BEVERAGES

CIDER HOT

Fill mugs with piping hot **apple cider.** A stick of **cinnamon** or a few **cloves,** or both, may be placed in each mug. Offer warmth and hospitality by greeting a guest with this on a very cold night. Traditionally, it is stirred with a red hot poker just before serving. Doughnuts make a good accompaniment.

TOLLAND COUNTY CRANBERRY DRINK

Pick over **1 pint cranberries.** Place in a saucepan with **1 pint water, 3 cloves,** and **½ stick cinnamon** and cook until the fruit is very soft. Strain. Add **1 cup sugar** to the juice and simmer, stirring until the sugar is dissolved. Cool and add **¼ cup orange juice** and **1 tablespoon lemon juice.** Serves 4.

HI-HILL FARM SPICED GRAPE JUICE

Place in a saucepan **4 cups grape juice, ¼ cup sugar, 2 cups water,** and **¼ cup lemon juice.** Tie loosely in a cheesecloth **1 teaspoon whole cloves** and **1 piece cinnamon** 1 inch square. Place the spices in the pan and simmer 10 minutes, stirring until the sugar is dissolved. Strain and serve hot. Serves 4 to 6.

LEMONADE

Place in a saucepan **4 cups water.** Add **1 cup sugar.** Bring to a boil, stirring until the sugar is dissolved, and boil 2 minutes. Remove from the fire immediately and chill. Add the juice of **2 lemons** (about 6 tablespoons) and **⅛ teaspoon salt.** Additional sugar, water, or lemon juice may be added to taste. Serve very cold, or over cracked ice. Serves 4 to 6.

The lemonade may be made without any cooking, but the flavor is not as good. The juice of other fruits may be combined with the lemonade in any desired proportion.

JESSIE DE VRIES' RECEIPT FOR LEMON CORDIAL

Place in a saucepan **2 cups water, ⅛ teaspoon salt,** and **1 cup sugar.** Boil for 12 minutes, stirring until the sugar is dissolved. Add **⅓ cup lemon juice.** Cool and store in the refrigerator or other cold place. To serve, dilute with ice water to taste and serve in glasses with ice.

Aunt Sleide says: "Jessie de Vries is a leading WCTU worker, but she'll never live down her past. When she was a little girl, she drank up her papa's Rock and Rye, trying to get the rock candy."

LAMOILLE COUNTY MAPLE-ALE

Add **4 cups milk** to **6 tablespoons maple syrup** and mix well. Pour into 6 tall glasses. Fill the glasses with **ginger-ale.** Serves 6.

PIEPLANT PUNCH

Add **6 tablespoons lemon juice** (about 2 lemons) to **1 cup tea.** Stir in **½ cup honey.** Add **8 sprigs of mint, 1 stick of cinnamon, ⅛ teaspoon salt,** and **2 cups pieplant juice,** strained from cooked, sweetened pieplant. Chill. Remove the cinnamon stick before serving, and add **1 quart cold water.** Serve an **orange slice,** a **sprig of mint** and ice in each glass. Serves 12 to 14.

OLD FARM SORGHUM PUNCH

Stir **6 cups milk** into **¼ cup sorghum.** Add **⅛ teaspoon salt.** Flavor with **½ teaspoon ginger.** Serves 6.

Molasses may be substituted for sorghum.

YOUR OWN FRUIT JUICE DRINK

The juice of any fruit which has been drained, may be used as the base of a refreshing beverage. Canned fruit juice or the juice from dried fruit may be used, or any fruit which is too ripe for eating may be cooked to a pulp with a little water, then strained. If the juice is heavy, it may be diluted with water. Sugar or honey may be used to sweeten the beverage. The juice from different kinds of fruit may be combined and diluted and sweetened if necessary. The fruit juice may be added to gingerale when that combination would be pleasing. Serve very cold or over cracked ice. A sprig of mint in the glass, a few pieces of fruit, or both, will make the drink look very special.

PAPA'S WINE

Mash **20 pounds berries or grapes** in a large stone jar or crock. Add **5 quarts boiling water.** Cover the jar and let stand 3 days. Then strain the contents through a cheesecloth. Return the strained juice to the jar and add **10 cups sugar.** Place the jar in a pan to catch any juice which may overflow. Cover the jar and let stand until fermentation has ceased. Remove the scum. Strain the juice again and bottle it, making sure that the seal is tight.

Aunt Sleide says: "This is a genuine receipt written down by my mother in 1889. Papa made it, but she dispensed it, and I can still hear him growling, 'Why in tunket does she have to serve it in glasses no bigger than a chicken's wrist!' "

FRUIT BRANDY

Before bottling berry or grape wine, measure it and add ½ **pint rye whiskey** to each gallon of wine.

BLACKBERRY CORDIAL

Extract 1 quart juice from **blackberries.** Place in a saucepan with **1 pound sugar.** Tie loosely in a cheesecloth **1 whole nutmeg, 1 piece cinnamon** 1 inch square, and **1 teaspoon whole cloves.** Add the spices and bring to a boil, stirring until the sugar is dissolved. Boil for 15 minutes. Skim and add **1 pint brandy.** Put in a closely covered container to cool. When perfectly cold, strain through cheesecloth and bottle tightly, sealing the cork with paraffin.

AUNT ADORA'S RECEIPT FOR CHERRY BOUNCE

Pick over and stem **6 pounds cherries.** Place in a large stone jar or crock with **5 pounds sugar,** alternating layers of sugar and cherries. Less sugar may be used if the cherries are not acid. Pour in **1 pint pure alcohol.** Cover the crock. Stir the cherries twice a day until the sugar is dissolved. It will take about 3 days. Cover the crock tightly. After 5 months add **1 pint distilled water.** Strain the liquid and bottle it. The cherries which are strained out are shriveled little nuggets of brandied goodness. Serve them with meat.

Aunt Sleide says: "This is a genuine receipt of my Great-Aunt Adora's, written in 1885. She didn't have my mother's scruples about serving liquor, though she used it mainly in case of sickness. Whenever one of my cousins came reeling up to our gate, we'd know he'd had a stomach ache and was still under the influence of Aunt Adora's cure."

DELAWARE COUNTY DANDELION WINE

Pick only fresh blossoms and remove every bit of the stem. Measure **1 quart dandelion blossoms,** packing them tightly, but being careful not to crush them. Place in a pan with **2 lemons,** sliced, **2 oranges,** sliced, and **1 quart boiling water.** Let stand 24 hours. Strain and add **1 cup sugar** to each quart of juice. Stir until the sugar dissolves. Pour the juice into jars and set them into a large pan, or pans, as fermentation will cause the liquid to run over. Use the juice from one jar to refill the other jars each morning. Continue this until fermentation ceases. Then empty the wine, wash the jars, put jar rubbers on, refill the jars to overflowing, and seal.

18

CANNING

In order to obtain fine quality canned goods, it is necessary to use only good, sound foods which are in prime condition. For a uniform product, use fruits and vegetables of the same size which have reached the same degree of ripeness.

Before canning, wash all foods thoroughly and remove any traces of soil. If foods have been sprayed, the stem and blossom ends of the fruit must be discarded, as spray collects there. Spots of spray residue on the skins of fruit should be peeled away, since soap and water will not remove poison spray.

For optimum results, can fruits and vegetables as soon as possible after gathering them. It is best to can them within 2 hours. If this is impossible, keep fruits or vegetables in small lots in a cool, well-ventilated place. Refrigerate meats at 30° to 32° F. if they are to be held for several days.

To be sure that glass jars and caps are in good condition, examine them carefully before use, and discard any with chips, cracks, or dents. Any of these defects would prevent an airtight seal. Jars larger than pint or quart size require longer processing periods than are given in this book.

If necessary, tighten the wire clamps on lightning-type jars by removing the top wire, bending it down in the middle, and bending the sides inward to fit the jar.

Jar rubbers may be used again if they show no impressions from contact with the jar and top, if they do not crack when they are doubled over and the fold is pressed with the fingers, and if the rubber will stretch to twice its length, then return without changing shape.

To prepare jars and tops for use, wash them in hot, soapy water, then rinse them. Place a rack or cloth in the bottom of a pan of warm water. Place jars and tops in the pan and heat the water to boiling. Keep the jars and tops hot until they are needed. Merely dip rubber rings in boiling water and place them on jars just before they are filled. Pour boiling water over jar caps that have a sealing composition. To sterilize jars, see **Open Kettle Canning.***

While the jars are heating, prepare syrups if they are to be used, and precook foods if indicated in the receipt.

Pack jars quickly, removing from the hot water only the jar which is being packed. Liquids and solids are packed in proportion so the pack will not be too dense or too thin. Use a spatula and press the food down into the cans firmly in order to work out the air bubbles. Be careful not to exert too much pressure on fruit.

At least ½ inch head space should be left when filling jars, for every method except open kettle canning, in which case they are filled to the top. Starchy foods such as corn, peas, and beans are the exception. They expand, so an inch of head space is required when they are packed. Be sure that the liquid covers the solid material in the jars. If there is not enough juice to cover fruits, add syrup. If there is not enough water left to cover vegetables after they are cooked, add boiling water.

Wipe off each jar carefully after it is packed, to be sure that no food particles adhere to the sealing edge of the jar or the rubber ring. Process foods immediately after packing.

For all processes except open kettle canning, jars should be sealed almost, but not quite, tight during cooking. If using a mason jar, screw the cap on until it is tight, then turn it back ¼ inch. If the lightning type jars are being used, place only the top clamp in position. If using the vacuum or self-sealing jars, put the screwbands on tightly or adjust the clamps.

When the canning process is over, screw the tops on mason jars as tightly as possible. Snap the side clamp down on lightning-type jars. If the screw band is loose on vacuum jars, hold the lid in place so it will not turn and screw the band tightly. Remove screw bands when the jar has completely cooled, and keep them to use again.

Cool all jars in an upright position. They should not be covered with blankets or cloths during cooling and they should be kept out of drafts. If food has been processed in a pressure canner, the danger of breakage will be reduced if the jars are left in the canner 3 to 4 minutes after it has been opened.

When the jars have cooled completely, test to be sure the seal is perfect. Invert those with rubber rings to see if any leakage has occurred. If the jars have been sealed with lacquered metal tops, rap the top of the jar with a spoon. If the sound is clear and ringing, the seal is good. If the sound is dull, examine to determine the cause. If the gasket was defective, reprocess the food, using a new gasket if necessary.

Label containers with the name, the date, and the lot number, if more than one lot was canned during the day. (Then if any show signs of spoilage, carefully examine all in that lot.) It is best not to store foods for a week or ten days after canning. During that time, keep them at room temperature in a convenient place so they may be observed for any signs of spoilage.

For best results, store canned foods in a dry, cool place. Foods in glass jars require protection from light. The quality of canned food is best the first year after canning.

For methods of canning in tin, write to the U. S. Department of Agriculture for "Home Canning," Farmers Bulletin 1762.

OPEN KETTLE CANNING

Only fruits and tomatoes may be canned by this method. Caps and jars must be sterilized before they are used. To sterilize them, wash in hot, soapy water, then rinse. Place on a cloth or rack in the bottom of a pan of warm water. Heat the water to boiling, and boil 15 to 20 minutes. Do not boil rubber rings, merely dip them in the boiling water. then place on the jars before filling.

If necessary, add water or syrup to the food which is to be canned, then cook until tender. Fill the jars to the top with the boiling hot food. Seal each jar tightly immediately after filling.

OVEN CANNING

Oven canning is most successful for small fruits. If used for larger fruits such as apricots, peaches, quartered apples, or pears, the fruits must be precooked or they are likely to develop a brownish discoloration.

Pack fruits into clean containers to within an inch of the top of the jar and cover with liquid to within ½ inch of the top. Partly seal the jars and place them 2 inches apart. (To keep the oven clean, set the jars in a pan to catch the liquid which bubbles out.) Process in a slow, 250° to 275° F. oven. Remove from the oven and complete the seal immediately. The time given in the recipes will vary slightly, depending upon whether the fruits are unusually hard or soft. For altitudes 4,000 feet or more above sea level, additional time will be required. The bulletin mentioned above gives exact information on canning at these altitudes.

WATER BATH METHOD

The best method for canning acid foods (fruits and tomatoes) is the water bath method. A wash boiler, bucket, or any large vessel with a tightly fitting cover may be used. The vessel should have a rack for holding the jars, as this will keep them from breaking. A wire mesh rack is the best to use, because it allows the water to circulate under the jars. The jars are placed in the container far enough apart to allow the water to circulate around them.

Either preheat the jars in water and leave them there until used, or fill them with hot foods to keep them from breaking when they are placed in the water bath. Fill jars to within 1 inch of the top, then cover with liquid to within ½ inch of the top. If the liquid is poured into the jars boiling hot, seal them completely before processing. If it is not boiling hot, only partially seal the jars. The water in the bath should be boiling hot before the jars are added, and it should come over the tops of the jars by 1 to 2 inches. As the water boils away, add more boiling water to keep it at this level. Begin to count time as soon as the water returns to a vigorous boil. Keep the water boiling rapidly throughout the entire processing period. Remove jars from the water one at a time and seal tightly if necessary. The processing periods given are for pressure-temperatures at sea level.

STEAMER

A steamer may be used instead of the water bath for canning acid foods. If a steamer is used, the processing periods are the same as they are in the water bath. The steamer method is only efficient if a good circulation of steam is maintained.

STEAM PRESSURE CANNING

All types of food except fruits and tomatoes must be canned in a pressure canner. Any other method is dangerous to health as the temperatures reached in other methods are not high enough to kill harmful organisms. Follow the manufacturer's directions for using the steam pressure canner. Non-acid foods should be preserved by drying, storing, quick freezing, or pickling if a pressure canner is not available.

When glass jars are used for pressure canning, there is often a loss of liquid. Never, after processing, open jars in order to add more liquid.

FRUIT

CANNED FRUIT AND JUICES

Fruit may be precooked or packed raw. The advantages to precooking fruit are many. Juice is extracted from juicy fruits as they cook and may be used to cover the fruit in the jars. Precooking shrinks the fruit, so a fuller pack is obtained. Precooking shortens the period for processing the fruit in the hot water bath. Precooked fruit has more flavor and food value than fruit which is packed raw.

PRECOOKING FRUIT

To precook fruits such as berries, cherries, ripe peaches, pears, or plums, sweeten them to taste. Let stand with the sugar for a moment to start the flow of juice. Then bring slowly to boil, stirring occasionally to prevent scorching. The fruit may be placed over hot water to cook, or cooked covered in a moderate, 350° F. oven. When precooked, juicy fruits if cut or sliced will probably form sufficient juice for canning liquid.

Additional liquid may be needed if juicy fruits are to be canned whole or in halves. Fruit juice rather than syrup may be used for this. Set aside the small or dead-ripe fruit to use for making juice. Crush it and heat to the boiling point. Strain and sweeten to taste. Heat the fruit in this juice, then pack rapidly into hot containers. Bring the juice to the boiling point and pour it over the fruit, filling the containers to within ½ inch of the top. Seal and process.

Apples, firm peaches and pears will probably not give enough juice for use as canning liquid. To obtain the most possible juice, slice or cut them and add sugar before heating. If necessary, add a little water to prevent sticking. If sufficient juice has not been extracted, add boiling hot syrup to cover the fruit, filling the jars to within ½ inch of the top. Seal and process.

SUGAR SYRUPS

The amount of syrup necessary to cover fruit is ½ cup for pint jars and 1 to 1½ cups for quart jars. For a richer product, use fruit juice for all or part of the water in the syrup.

To make syrup, combine liquid and sugar and boil approximately 5 minutes, stirring until the sugar is dissolved. Remove any scum which may have formed.

For a **very thin syrup,** use 1 cup sugar plus 4 cups water or juice.

For a **thin syrup,** use 1 cup sugar plus 3 cups water or juice.

For a **medium syrup,** use 1 cup sugar plus 2 cups water or juice.

For a **thick syrup,** use 1 cup sugar plus 1 cup water or juice.

For a **less sweet syrup,** use corn syrup for part of the sugar. It may be used to replace up to one-third of the sugar called for. For example, use 1 cup water or fruit juice and ⅔ cup sugar plus ⅓ cup corn syrup if preparing a thick syrup.

Part of the sugar in a syrup may be replaced with honey. Use honey to replace up to one-half the sugar called for. For example, if making a thin syrup, use 3 cups water or juice and ½ cup sugar plus ½ cup honey. Use a large kettle when preparing a syrup with honey so it will have plenty of room to boil up. The syrup may need to be cooked a little longer than it would be if sugar alone were used.

APPLES

Select sound, tart apples which are slightly underripe. Peel, and slice or dice them. If preparing a large quantity, to prevent discoloration, drop the prepared pieces into water which contains 2 tablespoons salt and 2 tablespoons vinegar in each gallon. Do not allow the apples to stand in the brine for any length of time. Drain on dish towels or cheesecloth. Precook by boiling 5 minutes (adding a little sugar to draw out the juice), or boil 5 minutes in a very thin syrup. Pack hot into containers. Cover to within ½ inch of the top with boiling juice or syrup. If there is not enough juice, cover the apples with boiling syrup and process pint and quart jars 15 minutes in the boiling water bath.

If oven canning, process at 250° F. quarts 75 minutes, pints 50 minutes.

Two and one-half pounds apples (7 or 8), will fill 1 quart jar.

APPLE SAUCE

Wash apples. Quarter them and discard soft or decayed portions. Cook tender in a covered pan, adding just enough water to prevent burning. Press through a strainer. Season with sugar to taste, approximately ½ to 1 cup sugar for each quart of sauce. Bring sauce to the boiling point and pack immediately into jars, packing to within ½ inch of the top. Process in the boiling water bath 5 minutes.

BERRIES

Any of the following methods may be used for canning loganberries, blueberries, dewberries, elderberries, huckleberries, gooseberries, mulberries, raspberries, or blackberries. For best results, work with 1 to 3 quarts of berries at a time. One and one-half quarts fresh berries (5 cups), will make 1 quart jar of canned fruit. Remove caps and stems after washing berries.

Method 1. Pack the fruit into the jars raw, shaking it down gently to insure a full pack. Cover with boiling hot medium syrup and fill jars to within ½ inch of the top. Process quart and pint jars 20 minutes in the boiling water bath. For a richer product, use part or all fruit juice for the syrup.

Gooseberries must be canned in heavy syrup.

Method 2. This method prevents the berries from shrinking and floating. Prepare medium syrup and lower the berries into the simmering syrup a quart at a time. Hold them in the syrup 15 to 30 seconds. Remove and pack into hot jars immediately and cover with the boiling syrup to within ½ inch of the top. Process pint jars in the hot water bath 6 minutes. Process quart jars 8 minutes.

Method 3. Prepare any syrup, using part or all fruit juice. Heat until the sugar is dissolved. Cook the berries in the syrup, pack boiling hot into containers, and cover with hot juice to within ½ inch of the top. Process quarts and pints 5 minutes in the boiling water bath. If oven canning, process at 250° F., quarts 70 minutes, pints 45 minutes.

CHERRIES

Select ripe cherries and can them pitted or unpitted. If pitting the cherries, work over a bowl and save all the juice. Shrink the cherries by cooking over low heat in the juice for 5 minutes. Add sugar to taste. Pack into hot containers and cover the fruit to within ½ inch of the top with the boiling juice in which they were cooked. Process pints or quarts 5 minutes in the boiling water bath.

If the cherries are canned unpitted, prick them over a

bowl and save the juice for part of the liquid in the syrup. Pack raw into hot containers and cover to within ½ inch of the top, sour cherries with thick syrup and sweet cherries with medium syrup. The syrup should be boiling hot. Process pints and quarts 25 minutes in the boiling water bath. The cherries may be covered with juice instead of syrup. To obtain juice, heat small or dead ripe cherries slowly with sugar to taste. Strain and heat the juice to boiling before pouring over the cherries. Cover the cherries to within ½ inch of the top.

If oven-canning, process at 250° F., quarts 70 minutes, pints 45 minutes.

One and one-half quarts unpitted cherries will fill 1 quart jar. Six quarts unpitted cherries will make 1 quart jar of pitted cherries.

CURRANTS

Can currants as for **Berries.***

GRAPES

Can as for **Berries.***

PEACHES

Prepare peaches for canning by immersing in boiling water 30 seconds or until the skins loosen. Plunge into cold water and slip the skins off. To prevent darkening, if preparing the peaches in large quantities, drop peeled peaches into a weak brine of 2 teaspoons salt to each quart of cold water. Drain on dish towels or cheesecloth. Crack 1 or 2 peach pits and place in each jar to give the peaches additional flavor, if liked.

The peaches may be precooked in their own juice. If the peaches are sliced before precooking, more juice will be extracted. Sweeten sliced or halved peaches to taste and bring to the boiling point slowly, stirring from time to time to prevent scorching. The peaches may be cooked over hot water or they may be covered and cooked in a moderate, 350° F. oven. Do not cook the peaches until they are soft. If the peaches are not juicy, it may be necessary to precook them in a thin or medium syrup. Pack quickly, packing halved peaches with the cups downward. Fill the jars to within ½ inch of the top with boiling juice or syrup to cover the fruit. Process quarts and pints 15 minutes in the boiling water bath.

If the peaches are to be packed raw, prepare thin or medium syrup, halve the peeled peaches and pack into hot containers, cups downward. Cover the fruit with boiling syrup to within ½ inch of the top. Process pints and quarts in the boiling water bath 30 minutes.

If oven canning, process at 250° F., quarts 70 minutes, pints 45 minutes.

Two to 3 pounds peaches (8 to 10) will fill 1 quart jar.

PEARS

Select pears which are not quite ripe. Peel, halve, and core them. If desired, they may be sliced. To prevent discoloration, if preparing a large quantity, drop the peeled fruit into a weak brine made by adding 2 tablespoons salt and 2 tablespoons vinegar to each gallon water. Do not allow the pears to stand in the brine for any length of time. Drain on dishtowels or cheesecloth.

Cook in a thin or medium syrup 4 to 8 minutes, adjusting the time to the size and ripeness of the fruit. Pack tightly into hot containers, cups downward, packing to within ¾ inch of the top. Cover to within ½ inch of the top with the hot syrup in which they were cooked. Process pints and quarts in the boiling water bath 20 minutes.

If oven canning, process at 250° F., quarts 75 minutes, pints 50 minutes.

Two to 2½ pounds pears (5 or 6), will fill 1 quart jar.

PIEPLANT

Do not peel pieplant. Wash young tender stalks and cut into ½- to 1-inch pieces. Pack into jars tightly and cover with boiling syrup, medium or thick, to within ½ inch of the top. Process pints and quarts 20 minutes in the boiling water bath.

The pieplant may be precooked, then canned. Wash and dice as above. Measure, and to each cup of pieplant add ¼ cup sugar. Mix well and turn into a baking dish. Cover and bake in a hot, 400° F. oven until tender. Turn into hot containers, covering with the juice to within ½ inch of the top. The pieplant may be precooked by simmering on top of the stove 5 minutes. Process precooked pieplant in the boiling water bath 5 minutes.

If oven canning, process at 250° F., quarts 30 minutes, pints 5 minutes.

PLUMS

Plums are canned just as they are beginning to ripen and soften. They are usually canned whole. One and one-half to 2 pounds plums (24 to 32) will fill 1 quart jar.

Prick each plum with a fork to keep the skins from bursting. Precook as for **Peaches*** in a small amount of medium to thick syrup. Pack into hot containers and cover the fruit to within ½ inch of the top with boiling syrup. Process pints or quarts 5 minutes in the boiling water bath.

The plums may be packed raw. Prick and pack into hot jars. Cover with boiling hot medium syrup to within ½ inch of the top. Process pints and quarts 20 minutes in the boiling water bath.

If oven canning, process at 250° F., quarts 70 minutes. pints 45 minutes.

QUINCES

Can as for **Apples.***

STRAWBERRIES

Hull berries. Add sugar to taste. Place in a kettle and bring to the boiling point slowly. Let cool in the kettle overnight. In the morning, bring to the boiling point rapidly, pack into containers, and cover with hot syrup to within ½ inch of the top. Process quarts and pints in the boiling water bath 5 minutes.

Strawberries may be precooked in the oven. Place single layers of berries in shallow pans. Sweeten to taste. Cook in a slow, 250° F. oven 1 hour. Pack hot in sterile jars, and cover to within ½ inch of the top with the juice they have formed. Process quarts and pints 5 minutes in the hot water bath.

If oven canning, process at 250° F., quarts 50 minutes, pints 25 minutes.

Three to 4 quarts of strawberries will fill 1 quart jar.

TOMATOES

Can only firm, ripe tomatoes of medium size and uniform shape. Place shallow layers in a wire basket. Dip into vigorously boiling water for 1 minute or until the skins will loosen. Plunge into cold water. Drain tomatoes. Cut out the cores and remove the blossom ends. Slip off the skins and pack the tomatoes into the containers as closely as possible. Fill the jars with tomato juice to within ½ inch of the top and add 1 teaspoon salt to each quart of tomatoes. Process quarts and pints in the boiling water bath 45 minutes.

If oven canning, process at 250° to 275° F., quarts 75 minutes, pints 50 minutes.

Two and one-half to 3½ pounds tomatoes (8 to 10) will fill 1 quart jar.

FRUIT JUICES

A thermometer is almost a necessity when canning fruit juices. Its use will assure retention of as much of the original fruit flavor and color as possible. Berries, cherries, plums, currants, or grapes may be used for making juice. Wash and drain the fruit. Crush it in a saucepan. (Cherries must be pitted before crushing.) Add about ½ cup water (depending upon the juiciness of the fruit) to each pound of fruit, if desired. Berries do not require water. Heat to 170° to 180° F. and hold at that temperature several minutes, or until the juice can be separated from the pulp. Extract the juice, using a fruit press, or strain through several layers of cheesecloth. If using a press, avoid crushing berry seeds as they will spoil the flavor of the juice. Straining a second time, without pressure, will make the product more clear. If desired, add sugar at this time. It may be omitted, but it will preserve color and flavor. Use ½ to 1 cup sugar for each gallon of juice. Heat the juice to 160° to 170° F. and pour into hot sterile jars or bottles to within ⅛ inch of the top. (If using bottles, crown caps and a capping device must be used. Sterilize the bottles as for jars but merely dip the caps into the boiling water.) Process in a hot water bath (180° F.) at once, processing pints and quarts 20 minutes. Glass bottles must be laid on their sides in the water bath.

GRAPE JUICE

Because of the cream of tartar crystals which form in grape juice, special care must be taken when making it. Wash ripe grapes (Concord or other slip-skin grapes may be used), and remove from the stems. Add 1 cup water to each 4 quarts grapes. Heat slowly to simmering, 165° to 175° F., and hold at this temperature 10 to 12 minutes, or until the grapes are soft. Remove from the heat and let stand 5 minutes. Clarify the juice by straining it through

4 thicknesses of cheesecloth. Add 2 to 4 tablespoons sugar to each quart of juice, if desired. Pour into sterile jars and partially seal. Place in a hot water bath at simmering temperature, 170° F. Hold at that temperature and process quarts 25 minutes. Remove and complete the seal. Let stand a few weeks before using and decant carefully, as the crystals will have settled on the bottom of the jar.

FRUIT PUREE

Fruit puree may be made from almost any soft fruit. Cook the fruit, press it through a fine sieve and heat to 160° to 170° F. Pack and process quarts and pints 20 minutes in the boiling water bath.

TOMATO JUICE

Use fully ripe tomatoes which are firm and bright-red in color. Discard green, moldy, or decayed tomatoes. Work with only 1 to 2 gallons of tomatoes at a time. Quarter the tomatoes and press slightly in order to start the flow of juice. Simmer until softened. Press through a fine bowl- or cone-shaped sieve, using a wooden masher or a glass jar or bottle for forcing the pulp through. Place the juice in a pan. Add ½ to 1 teaspoon salt to each quart juice. Heat the juice just to boiling. Fill sterile jars or bottles to the top and seal. Invert the jars and let cool.

Season the tomato juice to taste before serving. To each quart of tomato juice, add any or all: ¼ teaspoon sugar, ⅛ teaspoon pepper, ¼ teaspoon salt, 2 teaspoons lemon juice, and 1 teaspoon onion juice.

VEGETABLES

BABY RED BEETS

Wash tender young beets. Cut off the tops, leaving on about 1 inch of stem. Do not remove the roots. Two and one-half to 3 pounds trimmed beets will fill 1 quart jar.

Scald in boiling water or steam for about 15 minutes, or until the skins will slip off easily. Skin the beets, remove the roots, and pack loosely into jars to within 1 inch of the top. Add 1 teaspoon salt to each quart. Add hot water to within ½ inch of the top. Process in a steam pressure canner, processing pints 30 minutes and quarts 35 minutes at 240° F. or 10 pounds of pressure.

BABY CARROTS

Can as for **Baby Red Beets,** above.

SNAP BEANS

Wash young tender snap beans. One and one-half pounds raw beans will fill 1 quart jar. Break into pieces of desired size and string. Wash again. Add boiling water to cover, and simmer until the beans are wilted and will bend without breaking, about 5 minutes. Pack hot into containers, filling jars to within 1 inch of the top. Cover with the hot water in which they were cooked, adding it to within ½ inch of the top. Add 1 teaspoon salt to each quart jar. Process in a steam pressure canner, pint jars 30 minutes, and quart jars 35 minutes at 240° F., or 10 pounds of pressure.

BABY LIMA BEANS

Gather young, tender lima beans. Wash, shell, wash again, and bring to a boil in cold water to cover. Pack hot into containers to within 1¼ inches of the top. Cover to within 1 inch of the top with the hot water in which they were cooked, and add 1 teaspoon salt to each quart. Process immediately in a steam pressure canner at 240° F., or 10 pounds pressure, 50 minutes for pint jars, and 55 minutes for quart jars.

Two pounds shelled lima beans will fill 1 quart jar.

BLACK-EYE PEAS

Can as for **Baby Lima Beans**, above.

KERNEL CORN

Only tender young sweet corn which is freshly gathered should be used for canning corn in the kernel. Shuck the corn and remove all the silk. Clean well. Remove the kernels from the cob as in **Sweet Corn.*** Add 1 teaspoon salt to each 4 cups corn. Weigh the corn and add half as much boiling water by weight. Heat rapidly to boiling. Pack into pint jars to within 1¼ inches of the top. Cover with the hot water in which it was cooked, to within 1 inch of the top. Process pint jars in a steam pressure canner 60 minutes at 240° F., or 10 pounds of pressure. Process quart jars 70 minutes at 240° F., or 10 pounds pressure.

Four to 6 ears of corn will yield 1¼ pints.

CREAM SWEET CORN

Corn gathered for cream-style sweet corn may be more mature by 3 or 4 days than corn canned in the whole kernel. Clean as for **Kernel Corn**, above. Cut off only the tips of the kernels and scrape to remove the milk, as for **Sweet Corn.*** Add ½ teaspoon salt to each pint of corn. Weigh the corn and add half as much boiling water by weight. Heat quickly to boiling. Pack hot into pint containers, filling them to within 1 inch of the top. Process 75 minutes at 250° F., or 15 pounds of pressure. It is not advisable for the home canner to can cream sweet corn in jars larger than pint size.

Four to 6 ears of corn will yield 1¼ pints.

NEW GREEN PEAS

Gather young tender peas, and wash. Shell and add hot water to cover. Simmer 3 to 5 minutes. Pack hot into pint jars, filling them to within 1 inch of the top. Cover with the hot water in which they were cooked. Add ½ teaspoon salt to each pint jar. Process in a steam pressure canner 45 minutes at 240° F., or 10 pounds of pressure. It is not advisable for the home canner to can peas in jars larger than pint size.

Two and one-half to 3 pounds peas in the pod will yield 1¼ pints. One pound shelled peas will yield 1¼ pints.

CANNED MEAT, CHICKEN, AND SOUP

Pork, beef, veal, lamb, mutton, and chicken may be home-canned under steam pressure. Any other method of canning them is dangerous to health, and even to life.

Only meats and poultry which are slaughtered and handled in a strictly sanitary manner should be canned. Allow them to cool after slaughtering until they are completely free from animal heat. If not to be canned immediately, they must be chilled until ready for use. Raw meat is easier to handle after chilling and it may be kept cold for 2 or 3 days. Frozen meat does not make a good grade canned product. If it has become frozen, saw or cut it into strips of uniform length, 1 to 2 inches thick, but do not thaw it out. Immerse in boiling water at once. Simmer until the raw meat color has almost disappeared, then pack and process immediately.

The best utensils to use for cooking meat for canning are aluminum, retinned metal, enamel, or stainless steel. Copper and iron utensils may discolor meat to be canned. If galvanized iron is used, the meat must not remain in contact with it for longer than 30 minutes or zinc may be taken up in harmful quantities.

Meat is best when canned in pint jars. It should never be canned in containers larger than quart size.

Head space is most important in the canning of meat. Meat which is not covered by liquid will turn color and lose flavor. There must be ½ inch head space in glass jars.

If there is not sufficient broth to cover the meat, add boiling water.

It is possible to can meat with other products added, such as vegetables for making stews, but it is better to can meat alone, then cook it in a variety of ways when it is removed from the jars.

Use seasonings lightly. White pepper is superior to black pepper for canning.

Meats should be precooked in water or in the oven before being packed into containers. This makes a more attractive pack with a shorter processing time. It is undesirable to precook meat by frying, as the resulting canned product is hard and dry, with poor flavor.

MEAT COOKED IN WATER

To precook meat in water, cut the meat into pieces of uniform size, weighing about 1 pound each. Place in boiling water. Partially cover the pan and simmer 12 to 20 minutes, or until the raw meat color has almost disappeared from the center of the meat. Cut the meat into smaller pieces immediately and pack into jars. Use a spatula to press the meat down tightly. Add broth to cover the meat, and process immediately.

MEAT PRECOOKED IN THE OVEN

To precook meat in the oven, cut the meat into approximately 1-pound pieces of uniform size. Cook in a moderate, 350° F. oven 30 to 40 minutes, or until the red or pink color of raw meat disappears from the center. Cut the meat into small pieces for packing, allowing at least two pieces for each container. Pack tightly. Cover with pan drippings, and process immediately.

PRECOOKING POULTRY

Two-year-old hens and spring roosters are the best poultry for canning, therefore the time to can poultry is from August to November. When precooking poultry in water, simmer only 8 to 10 minutes because the pieces are smaller than those of meat. Poultry precooked in the oven requires only 20 to 30 minutes.

The following directions are for meat and chicken canned in glass only.

After opening canned meats or poultry, it is safest to boil them uncovered for 10 minutes before eating them.

CHUCK ROAST

Wipe meat with a damp cloth. Remove bone and gristle. Leave on only enough fat to give a flavor. Precook in water or in the oven. Add ½ teaspoon salt to pints, 1 teaspoon salt to quarts. Cover to within ½ inch of the top with liquid from the meat, adding boiling water if not enough broth is available. Process quarts 120 minutes, pints 85 minutes at 250° F. or 15 pounds pressure in a steam pressure canner.

ROUND STEAK

Follow directions for **Chuck Roast**, above.

BEEF RUMP

Follow directions for **Chuck Roast.***

LOIN OF BEEF

Follow directions for **Chuck Roast.***

BEEF RIBS

Follow directions for **Chuck Roast.***

GROUND BEEF

Select tougher cuts of meat which have a good deal of bone, for ground beef. Wipe with a damp cloth, cut the meat from the bone, and trim off excess fat. Run the meat through the ⅛-inch plate of the food chopper. Add ½ cup salt for every 12½ pounds meat, and mix thoroughly. Form into patties which will fit into the jars nicely. Precook in the oven. Pack hot and cover with pan drippings to which boiling water has been added, if necessary. Leave ½ inch head space. Process at once at 250° F. or 15 pounds of pressure, pints 90 minutes, quarts 120 minutes.

CORNED BEEF

Wash the corned beef. Cut into 1 pound pieces of uniform size. Cover with cold water, bring to boil, and drain. Repeat. When the second addition of water comes to a boil, reduce the heat to simmer and cook very slowly until the meat is heated throughout. Remove from the broth a piece at a time. Cut into smaller pieces and pack into containers immediately. The broth may be seasoned with nutmeg, bay leaves, or cloves if desired. Bring to the boiling point and cover the meat with broth, leaving ½ inch head space. Process in a steam pressure canner, pints 85 minutes and quarts 120 minutes at 250° F. or 15 pounds pressure.

MUTTON OR LAMB

Use the fleshy parts and proceed as for **Chuck Roast.***

VEAL

Use the fleshy parts and proceed as for **Chuck Roast.***

PORK

Ham and shoulder pork may be canned, but curing is the usual method for preserving them. Precook meat from the spareribs and loin as for **Chuck Roast*** and proceed, using the same methods of packing and the same time and pressure.

The pork loin and lean trimmings may be canned as sausage.

PORK SAUSAGE

Grind lean meat (pork loin and trimmings) twice. For approximately 6 pints, mix thoroughly 6 pounds pork, 3 tablespoons salt, 1 teaspoon white pepper and, if desired, ½ teaspoon cayenne pepper. One tablespoon any herb except sage may be used. Shape into cakes which will go into the jars easily. Brown in a moderate, 350° F. oven until the color of raw meat has almost disappeared from the center. Pack and cover with pan drippings or boiling water. Process at 250° F. or 15 pounds pressure, quarts 120 minutes, pints 90 minutes.

POULTRY

Only healthy poultry should be canned. A dressed chicken weighing from 3½ to 4 pounds will fill 1 quart jar. Kill it and allow it to bleed and cool thoroughly before canning. Dress for cooking. The meat is unfit for canning if the gall bladder is broken, so be careful to remove it whole. Remove eggs, kidneys, and lungs. Disjoint the chicken and separate the meaty parts (legs, thighs, upper-wing joints, and breasts) from the bony parts (necks, wings, backs, and skinned feet) and the giblets. If desired, the skin may be removed. Trim off lumps of fat as very fat chicken is difficult to process. Make broth with the bony pieces by covering them with lightly salted cold water and simmering until tender. Use the drained broth as liquid for canning the meaty pieces. If broth is liked jellied, for each quart of broth soak 5 tablespoons unflavored gelatin in ¼ cup cold broth or cold water for 5 minutes. Dissolve in the boiling broth. The flavor of canned chicken is better if the bones are not removed. However the chicken may be boned to save room in jars. Precook the meaty pieces in water or in the oven. Add ½ teaspoon salt to pints, 1 teaspoon salt to quarts. Allow the skin rather than the flesh to touch the jar. Place a piece of dark meat with skin on top of the jar. Cover with broth or pan gravy to within ½ inch of the top.

Process boned poultry at 250° F., or 15 pounds pressure, pints 85 minutes, quarts 120 minutes. Process poultry with bone at 250° F., or 15 pounds pressure, pints 65 minutes, quarts 75 minutes.

Giblets should not be canned with the other meat, as they will flavor and discolor it. If giblets are to be canned, pack hot into pint jars, cover with broth to within ½ inch of the top and process at 250° F., or 15 pounds pressure for 85 minutes.

MEAT OR CHICKEN SOUP

Crack the bones and place them in a pan with the meat scraps cut small. Cover with cold water. Bring to a boil and simmer covered until the meat falls from the bones. Add boiling water from time to time if necessary to keep the bones covered with liquid. Strain and chill. Remove fat. If the broth has not jellied, simmer in an open kettle to reduce it. The broth should be fairly concentrated, but not at the expense of flavor, which is lost with prolonged cooking.

Rice or barley may be added to the soup. Measure 1 cup uncooked cereal for each gallon of clear soup. Wash the cereal and boil in a quantity of salted water 15 minutes. Drain. Rinse with cold water and add to soup which has been brought to the boiling point. Season to taste.

Turn soup into jars to within ½ inch of the top. Process at 250° F., or 15 pounds pressure. Process clear soup in pints 25 minutes, in quarts 30 minutes. Process soup with added cereal in pints 35 minutes, in quarts 40 minutes.

Soup may be canned with meat and bones. Do not overcook during the precooking process. Remove all the fat from the fairly concentrated soup. Pack and process as above, pints 40 minutes, quarts 45 minutes.

19

SWEET SPREADS

Be sure that fruit is clean before it is made into jelly, jam, preserves, etc. Remove any damaged parts of fruit. Discard the caps and stems of berries, but leave the skins on currants. Scrub hard fruits with a brush. The skins should be left on grapes and hard fruits, but dried spray spots must be peeled off. Remove the blossom ends of apples, quinces, and crab apples, as the poisonous spray residue collects there. Cut fruits into small, uniform pieces.

JELLY

Fruit must have pectin and acid in proper proportions or it cannot be converted into jelly. Pectin and acid decrease as the fruit ripens, so it is best to use a combination of ripe and slightly underripe fruits for making jelly. If fruit contains sufficient acid to jell, but is poor in pectin, pectin powders and extracts may be used to convert the fruit into jelly.

Prepare fruits for jelly in small quantities, using only 6 quarts of berries at a time and 8 pounds of fruits, such as apples or grapes.

A pint of juice is obtained from 2 pounds of prepared fruit. A pint of juice made into jelly with an equal quantity of sugar will yield 4 average-sized jelly glasses or 1½ pints of jelly.

The fruit is boiled to extract the juice. Water is added to fruits to soften them. Soft fruits require the addition of little or no water. The best utensil for boiling the fruit is a flat broad-bottomed kettle. Crush soft fruits in the kettle to start the flow of juice. Boil rapidly and count time after the fruit reaches the boiling point. Stir during cooking to prevent scorching.

Pour the entire contents of the kettle into a jelly bag immediately and let the juice drip into a bowl. Press the jelly bag to obtain the maximum amount of juice after the dripping has almost stopped. Wring a fresh jelly bag out in hot water and strain the juice through this bag to insure a clear jelly.

Wash the jelly glasses and covers. Then sterilize the glasses by placing them on a rack in a pan, covering with cold water, and boiling 15 to 20 minutes. Keep them hot until used. As each glass is removed and filled with jelly, another may be put in its place to sterilize. Put it into the water with a scooping motion to prevent breakage.

Measure juice and sugar accurately for optimum results. It is best to work with 8, or less, cups of juice at a time. Use ¾ to 1 cup sugar for each cup of juice. If the fruit seems to be low in acid, 1 tablespoon strained lemon juice may be added to each cup of fruit juice. If the juice and sugar have not jelled because of insufficient acid, they may be recooked with lemon juice.

Place juice and sugar in a large flat-bottomed pan and use a high flame to bring the syrup to a boil quickly. Stir only until the sugar is dissolved. Keep at a rapid boil until the jelly stage is reached. The sheet test is used to determine the jelly stage. Dip a large spoon into the syrup, tilt the spoon, and allow the syrup to run off the side. The jelly has finished cooking when the syrup runs off in two distinct lines of drops which "sheet" from the spoon.

The syrup may be left in the kettle until the glasses are drained. If scum has formed on the syrup, remove it by skimming. Pour the syrup into the glasses carefully to avoid splashing or dripping. If the kettle in which the syrup was made is unwieldy, pour the syrup into a pitcher or other container, then fill the glasses. Fill jelly glasses to within ¼ inch of the top. Place the covers on immediately and let the syrup set undisturbed.

The jelly is ready to seal as soon as it is firm and well set. In order to obtain a good seal, the inside and rim of the jelly glass must be perfectly clean and dry. If jelly has dripped on the glasses it is easiest to remove it by wiping it off with a cloth dipped in alcohol.

PARAFFIN

For best results, melt paraffin just before ready to use it. Melt it in an old container of some kind to be kept solely for that purpose. A tin can is ideal. If the paraffin is not heated slowly, or if it is not heated just before use, it may shrink from the sides of the glasses, breaking the seal. To be sure that it is heated slowly enough, melt it over hot water, over very low heat, or in a container placed on an asbestos pad. Pour on enough paraffin to cover the jelly well. Tilt the glass and rotate it to be sure that the paraffin will form a perfect seal at the edges. To be doubly sure that the paraffin will completely exclude air, pour a thin film of it on the syrup while the jelly is still hot. When the film hardens, add a second coating of paraffin.

Label the jelly, and store it in a cool dry place. If the storage room is warm or damp, the jelly will have to be stored in a jar which is equipped with a composition gasket, or sealed in a jar which has a rubber ring.

It is not necessary to make fruit juice into jelly immediately. It may be stored for as long as 6 months before being made up, although the color and flavor, especially in red fruits, will not be so good as if it had been made up fresh. There are several advantages to not making the fruit juice into jelly immediately. Fruits are ready to be made into jelly during the hottest part of the summer and it is more convenient to cook the jelly in cooler weather. Fruits which mature at different times may be combined if the juice is bottled and made up at a future date. To can the juice, pour it into hot sterile jars after it has dripped. Partially seal the jars and place them in a hot water bath at 185° F., or simmering temperature. Bring the water back to simmering and hold pints or quarts in it 20 minutes. Remove and complete the seal at once. Store in a cool dry place and protect from light.

JELLIES

CURRANT JELLY

Wash currants and place in a preserving kettle with any water which adheres to them in washing. If the currants are not juicy, drain them, then add ¼ cup water to each pound of fruit. Crush to start the flow of juice. Count time as soon as the boiling point is reached, and boil 5 to 10 minutes or until the currants are soft, stirring to prevent scorching. Pour into a jelly bag immediately and allow to drip. Squeeze to extract all the juice. Strain through cheesecloth. Allow 1 cup sugar for each cup of juice. Use a large, flat-bottomed kettle and rapidly heat fruit juice and sugar to boiling, stirring only until the sugar is dissolved. Keep at a vigorous boil until the jelly stage is reached. Skim, turn into sterile jelly glasses, and seal with paraffin.

RED RASPBERRY JELLY

Proceed as for **Currant Jelly,** above, using no water when cooking the fruit. Use 1 cup sugar for each cup of fruit juice.

PEPPERMINT APPLE JELLY

Do not peel or core apples except to remove spray residue. Cut into small pieces of uniform size and place in a broad, flat-bottomed kettle with 1 cup water for each pound of fruit. Count time when the boiling point is reached and boil 20 to 25 minutes or until the fruit is soft, stirring to prevent scorching. Turn into a jelly bag immediately, and let drip. Measure the strained juice and allow ¾ cup sugar for each cup of juice. Return the fruit and sugar to the kettle and rapidly heat to boiling, stirring only until the sugar is dissolved. Boil vigorously until the jelly stage is reached. Remove scum. Use green food color sparingly and tint the syrup. Add a few drops essence of peppermint. Turn into sterile jelly glasses, and seal with paraffin.

SPICY CRAB APPLE JELLY

Prepare and cook the fruit as above. Let drip. Use 1 cup sugar to each pound of fruit, then cook to the jelly stage with one 3-inch stick of cinnamon and 7 whole cloves for 4 pounds fruit. The spices should be tied loosely in cheesecloth. At the end of the cooking period, remove spices, skim the syrup, turn into sterile jelly glasses, and seal with paraffin.

QUINCE JELLY

Prepare and cook quinces as for apples in **Peppermint Apple Jelly,** above, using 2 cups water for each pound of fruit and ¾ cup sugar for each cup of quince juice. Omit color and flavoring.

BLACK RASPBERRY OR BLACKBERRY JELLY

If the fruit is very firm, add ¼ cup water to each cup of fruit. Soft fruit requires no water. Cook as for **Currant Jelly,*** using 1 cup sugar for each cup of juice extracted from black raspberries. Use ¾ to 1 cup sugar for each cup of juice extracted from blackberries.

SLIP-SKIN GRAPE JELLY

Pick slip-skin grapes (such as Concord) from the stems and place in a broad, flat-bottomed kettle. Mash. Heat to simmering and simmer slowly until soft, about 10 minutes, being careful not to overcook the fruit. Turn into a jelly bag immediately and let drip undisturbed. Let the juice stand in a cold place overnight. The next morning dip the juice out of the container and strain through a jelly bag again. This precaution is taken to avoid gritty cream of tartar crystals which form in grape jelly. Place the grape juice in a large, flat-bottomed kettle, adding ¾ to 1 cup sugar for each cup of juice. Proceed as for **Currant Jelly.***

The pulp left in the jelly bag may be made into **Haven Farm Grape Butter.***

SPICY CONCORD GRAPE JELLY

Place 3 **pounds grapes** in a preserving kettle with ½ **cup vinegar, 1½ whole cloves,** and **one 3-inch stick cinnamon.** Cook 5 to 10 minutes or until soft. Strain and proceed as above.

WILD GOOSE PLUM JELLY

Wash plums and add ½ cup water to each pound of plums. Proceed as for **Currant Jelly,*** cooking 15 to 20 minutes. Add ¾ cup sugar to each cup of juice and continue as for **Currant Jelly.**

Aunt Sleide says: "The other day at the Ladies' Aid we got to talking about the letters we used to get from our beaus. Sarah Proctor was the only one who hadn't saved hers. She couldn't because they were too sticky. Sarah's mother steamed the letters open and censored them before she gave them to Sarah. To seal them again, she used jelly."

ELDERBERRY JELLY

Gather berries on a sunny day. Remove stems and extract juice as for **Currant Jelly.*** Combine 2 cups elderberry juice with each cup of juice extracted from apples in **Peppermint Apple Jelly.*** Do not add color or flavoring. Add 1 pound sugar to each 2 cups of combined juices. Proceed as for **Currant Jelly.**

JAM

For making jam, use well-ripened, sound berries, and fruits with soft flesh such as plums, apricots, and peaches. Measure the sugar by weight, using three-quarters to 1 part of sugar by weight to 1 part of prepared fruit by weight. The fruit is crushed, combined with the sugar, allowed to stand until the juices flow, then heated slowly and stirred until the sugar is dissolved. Then bring the mixture to boil and cook, stirring constantly, until the fruit is transparent and the jam somewhat thick.

BERRY JAM

Remove hulls from berries. Weigh the fruit and measure an equal weight of sugar. Crush the berries and bring to the boiling point slowly, stirring constantly. Add the sugar and boil until the mass is jellylike in consistency, stirring constantly. Turn into hot, sterile containers and seal.

If jam without seeds is desired (black raspberry and blackberry), boil the crushed fruit a few minutes, then force through a fine sieve. Weigh the pulp, add the sugar. and continue as above.

LA FOURCHE COUNTY HEAVENLY JAM

Use sound, mature strawberries. Remove hulls. Prepare pineapple by slicing it into rings, holding the top. Peel the rings, removing the eyes. Slice the rings into ½-inch cubes. Weigh the pineapple, and prepare 2 pounds strawberries for each pound of pineapple. For each 2 pounds strawberries allow 1½ pounds sugar. Allow 1 pound sugar for each pound of pineapple. Place pineapple and equal its weight in sugar into a preserving kettle. Heat, stirring until the sugar is dissolved. Bring to a vigorous boil and cook 10 minutes, stirring constantly. Add the strawberries and the remainder of the sugar. Add the juice of 1 lime (about 2 tablespoons) to each 3 pounds of fruit and boil, stirring, 15 to 20 minutes or until the jam is fairly thick. Turn into hot sterile containers and seal.

PEACH JAM

Scald peaches to remove skins as for **Peaches.*** Halve the fruit and discard the pits. Weigh, and allow ¾ to 1 pound sugar for each pound of fruit. Place fruit in a preserving kettle, crushing each layer and sprinkling with sugar until all is used. Let stand until the juices begin to flow, 3 to 4 hours. Then heat slowly, stirring until the sugar is dissolved. As soon as the boiling point is reached, stir constantly until the fruit is transparent and the syrup is somewhat thick. Turn into hot sterile containers and seal.

APRICOT JAM

Prepare as for **Peach Jam,** above, removing skins and pits. For each pound of prepared apricots use ¾ pound sugar and 2 tablespoons lime juice (about 1 lime). Proceed as for **Peach Jam.**

PLUM JAM

Wash and drain tart plums. For each pound of fruit allow 1 cup water and ¾ pound sugar. Place plums and water in a preserving kettle and boil until the skins are tender, 10 to 15 minutes. Add the sugar and boil, stirring, until the jelly stage is reached. Turn into hot sterile containers and seal.

MARMALADE

HILL 'N' DALE FARM HONEY CARROT MARMALADE

Place in a preserving kettle **2 cups tart apples,** diced, **2 cups carrots,** diced, **1 cup peaches,** diced, **3 tablespoons lime juice** (1 to 2 limes), and **2 tablespoons grated rind** of the lime, **2 cups sugar,** and **1 cup honey.** Heat to boiling slowly. Boil until thick and clear, about 1 hour, stirring the mixture as it cooks down, to prevent scorching. Turn into hot sterile containers and seal. The marmalade may be turned into sterile jelly glasses and sealed with paraffin.

NYE COUNTY GREEN TOMATO MARMALADE

Core and slice green tomatoes. Place **4 pounds tomatoes** in a preserving kettle. Add **2 pounds sugar** and **¼ teaspoon salt.** Peel **5 lemons.** Cut the peel into thin strips and boil in **1 cup water** 5 minutes. Repeat, using fresh water, if the bitter flavor in the rind is objectionable. Add the drained peel to the tomatoes with the sliced, seeded pulp of the lemons. Heat slowly, and stir until the sugar is dissolved. Boil, stirring, until the marmalade is rather thick and the fruit is transparent, about 1 hour. Turn into hot sterile containers immediately, and seal.

OLD FARM PIEPLANT MARMALADE

Place in a preserving kettle **9 cups pieplant** which has been cut into small pieces. Do not peel. Add **3½ cups sugar** and let stand overnight. Run **2 small oranges** (seeded, but not peeled), through the medium blade of the food chopper and add to the pieplant with **⅛ teaspoon salt.** Boil about 30 minutes, or until the jelly stage is reached, stirring to prevent scorching as the mixture cooks down. Turn into hot, sterile containers and seal.

PRESERVES AND HONEYS

Preserves can only be made from fruits which will retain their shape and color, such as cherries, quinces, peaches, etc. The fruits should be made into preserves when they are in the firm-ripe stage. Sugar is measured for preserves by weight. Three-quarters to 1 part sugar by weight is used for 1 part fruit by weight. For best results, work with only 6 to 8 pounds of fruit at a time.

Preserves are boiled until the fruit is fairly transparent and the syrup is quite thick. It is best to use glass fruit jars for storing preserves. Fill the jars three-quarters full with fruit, then add syrup to completely fill the jars. Seal while hot.

SEDGWICK COUNTY CHERRY PRESERVES

Wash and drain sour red cherries. Discard the imperfect cherries. Remove stems and stone, being careful to keep the fruit as nicely shaped as possible. Use ¾ to 1 pound sugar for each pound of pitted cherries. Place fruit and sugar in layers in a preserving kettle. Let stand overnight to start the flow of juices. Heat slowly to boiling, stirring carefully until the boiling point is reached. Boil rapidly and stir occasionally to prevent scorching. Cook until the syrup has thickened somewhat, about 20 minutes. Skim, turn into hot sterile containers, filling them three-fourths full with the fruit, then adding enough syrup completely to fill the containers. Seal immediately.

PEACH PRESERVES

Select firm, ripe, white or yellow peaches. Scald to remove peels as for **Peaches.*** The peaches may be left whole, halved, quartered or sliced. Proceed as above.

STRAWBERRY PRESERVES

Remove the caps from large, tart, firm berries. Allow 1 pound sugar for each pound of fruit. Proceed as for **Cherry Preserves** (two receipts above), allowing about 5 minutes less time for boiling the fruit.

BIG BAY FARM TOMATO PRESERVES

Peel **2 pounds firm, ripe tomatoes,** as for **Tomatoes.*** Quarter and place in a preserving kettle. Wash **2 medium lemons.** Slice and seed, but do not peel them. Place in the kettle with the tomatoes. Add **2 pieces ginger root** cut in small pieces. Stir in **4 cups sugar.** Stir carefully, and bring slowly to the boiling point. Boil rapidly, about 15 minutes, or until the syrup is rather thick, stirring constantly to prevent burning. Skim, turn into hot sterile containers and seal.

Red or yellow tomatoes may be used.

QUICK PRESERVES

Core, dice, and peel **1 large apple.** Seed and dice **1 medium orange.** Do not peel it. Place in a saucepan. Add **¼ cup sugar,** stir and bring to the boiling point. Boil rapidly until the syrup is thick and the fruit transparent, stirring constantly to prevent burning. Skim, turn into hot sterile containers and seal.

QUINCE PRESERVES

Select firm, yellow quinces. Wash, peel and quarter the fruit. Remove the cores. Allow 1¾ cups water and ¾ pound sugar for each pound of fruit. Make a syrup by boiling the sugar and water for 5 minutes in a preserving kettle, stirring until the sugar is dissolved. Add the fruit and boil slowly 1½ to 2 hours, stirring occasionally to prevent burning. The preserves have finished cooking when the fruit becomes clear and reddish in color and is tender, and when the syrup reaches the jelly stage. Turn into hot, sterile containers and seal.

DAMSON PLUM PRESERVES

Prick each plum in three or four places. Allow ½ cup water and ¾ to 1 pound sugar for each pound of plums. Place sugar and water in a preserving kettle and bring to the boiling point, stirring until the sugar is dissolved. Boil the plums in the syrup gently, cooking until the fruit is tender. Skim off the pits, which will rise to the top as soon as the plums are soft. Some of the pits will not rise to the surface. The only way to be perfectly sure that there are no pits in the preserves is to remove them before cooking the plums. To do this, halve the plums, discarding the pits. Do not prick the fruit. Cook until the jelly stage is reached. Pour into sterile containers and seal.

FRUIT SUNSHINE

Sun preserves may be made from sweet cherries, strawberries, raspberries, or blueberries. There must be sufficient hot sunshine to cause rapid evaporation. Use ⅞ cup sugar for each cup of fruit. In the morning, place fruit and sugar in layers in a preserving kettle. Let stand 1 hour or until juice has formed. Add ¼ teaspoon lemon juice to each cup of fruit. Cook over low heat, stirring until the sugar has dissolved. Then boil rapidly 5 minutes. Skim. Pour on clean platters and let stand in a closed sunny window until thick. Protect the fruit from dust by covering with waxed paper. It may stand as long as 3 days. When thick, turn into sterile containers and seal with paraffin.

The fruit may be left in the kettle. Cover with window glass propped up about ¼ inch from the kettle, and place outdoors in the sun.

HI-HILL FARM PEAR HONEY WITH GINGER

Stem, peel, and core **3 pounds pears.** Run them through the coarse blade of the food chopper and directly into the preserving kettle, if possible, so as not to lose any of the juice. Add **3¼ cups sugar, ½ teaspoon ginger, ¼ cup lemon juice,** and **¼ teaspoon grated lemon rind.** Cook, stirring until the sugar dissolves. Boil rapidly until the syrup is somewhat thick, about 20 minutes. Turn into sterile containers and seal with paraffin.

GRANT COUNTY HONEYED GOOSEBERRIES

Stem perfect gooseberries. Drain well and weigh. Weigh an equal amount of strained honey. Heat the honey in a large kettle with ¼ teaspoon lemon juice for each cup of fruit and simmer the gooseberries in it 3 to 4 minutes. Remove the fruit with a slotted spoon and turn into sterile jars. Continue boiling the honey until it thickens. Pour over the gooseberries, filling the containers completely, and seal with paraffin.

CONSERVES

NEOSHO COUNTY CANTALOUPE-PEACH CONSERVE

Peel and dice **1 quart peaches.** Dice **1 quart cantaloupe.** Place in a preserving kettle with **6 cups sugar,** the grated rind and juice of **4 lemons** and **⅛ teaspoon salt.** Cook slowly until a syrup forms, stirring carefully until the boiling point is reached. Boil rapidly about 30 minutes or until the fruit is transparent and the mixture is somewhat thick. Add **1 cup chopped nuts.** Turn into sterile containers and seal with paraffin.

NOVEMBER CONSERVE

Pick over cranberries and discard any that are soft or specked. Peel, core, and chop quinces. Discard the cores, then chop apples. Place **2 cups quinces, 2 cups apples,** and **3 cups cranberries** in a preserving kettle with the juice and diced rind of **1 orange.** Add **4 cups sugar** and **⅛ teaspoon salt.** Cook, stirring constantly until the boiling point is reached. Then boil rapidly about 30 minutes or until the jelly stage is reached. Add **1 cup chopped nuts.** Turn into sterile containers and seal with paraffin.

GRAPE CONSERVE

Wash and drain **6 to 7 pounds slip-skin grapes,** such as Concords. Place in a preserving kettle and mash slightly. Heat until the seeds will separate from the pulp easily, about 10 minutes. Press through a strainer. To each 4 cups of pulp, add **3 cups sugar, 2 pounds seedless white grapes,** and **3 oranges** which have been sliced thin and seeded but not peeled. Cook, stirring until the boiling point is reached. Then boil rapidly, stirring to prevent scorching. Cook about 30 minutes or until the jelly stage is reached. Stir in **1 cup broken nuts.** Turn into sterile containers and seal with paraffin.

BREVARD COUNTY SIMPLE CONSERVE

After making **Spicy Crab Apple Jelly,*** press the pulp which is left in the jelly bag through a colander, then through a strainer. Add **2 cups sugar** and **1 orange,** sliced thin and seeded but not peeled, to each 2 cups of pulp. Stir until the boiling point is reached, then boil rapidly until clear and thick, about 30 minutes. Add **½ cup chopped nuts.** Turn into sterile jars and seal, or turn into sterile jelly glasses and seal with paraffin.

SETTING HEN FARM SUMMER CONSERVE

Prepare **1 quart currants, 1 quart gooseberries,** and **1 quart raspberries.** Stem the currants and gooseberries. Wash and pit **1 quart sour cherries** which are firm and ripe. Weigh the fruits. Use ¾ as much **sugar** by weight as there is fruit. Place fruits and sugar in layers in a preserving kettle. Add ⅛ **teaspoon salt.** Let stand until the juices begin to flow, 1 to 2 hours. Cook, stirring until the boiling point is reached. Then boil rapidly 10 to 12 minutes, or until somewhat thick. Add **1 cup nuts, chopped.** Turn into sterile containers and seal with paraffin.

FRUIT BUTTER

To make fruit butter, cook the fruit until it is soft, stirring constantly. Press through a strainer or colander and add sugar to taste, adding about half as much sugar as there is fruit pulp. One-quarter to ½ teaspoon salt is added to each gallon of butter. Then the butter is boiled rapidly and stirred constantly to prevent burning.

As the butter cooks down and thickens, reduce the heat to prevent spattering. When the butter is thick, test it for "doneness" by pouring a small portion of it on a cold plate. No rim of liquid should separate around the edge of the butter. Use only fresh spices for fruit butters and do not use so much spice that the flavor of the fruit is obscured. A good proportion is 1 to 2 teaspoons mixed ground spices for each gallon of butter. Whole spices may be tied loosely in a cheesecloth and removed after the butter has finished cooking if a light-colored butter is desired. Pour the boiling hot butter into sterile containers and seal.

SWEETWATER COUNTY CIDER APPLE BUTTER

Quarter, core and peel **1 peck apples.** Add **2 quarts boiled cider** and **½ teaspoon whole allspice, ½ teaspoon whole cloves,** and **¼ ounce stick cinnamon** which have been tied in a cheesecloth. Bring to the boiling point. Turn into a roaster or a large flat baking pan and bake in a moderate, 350° F. oven, stirring occasionally until the fruit has absorbed most of the cider, 3 to 5 hours. Remove from the oven and add **1½ pounds sugar** and **1 teaspoon salt.** Stir until they are dissolved. Bring to the boiling point, turn into sterile containers and seal.

CHERRY BUTTER

Wash and stem sour cherries. Cook until soft, about 10 minutes. Press through a colander, then through a strainer. Add 1 cup sugar for each cup of pulp. Place in a pan with 1 stick cinnamon and ¼ teaspoon salt for each 3 cups pulp. Boil rapidly, and stir constantly to prevent burning. To prevent spattering, reduce the heat as the butter cooks down. The butter will finish cooking in 3 to 5 hours. Test for "doneness" (p. 287). Remove the cinnamon and pour the boiling hot butter into hot sterile containers and seal.

HAVEN FARM GRAPE BUTTER

Grape butter may be made with the pulp left from **Slip-Skin Grape Jelly.*** Press the pulp through a colander, then through a strainer. Measure it and use ⅔ cup sugar for each cup of pulp. Place sugar and pulp in a preserving kettle and to each 4 cups pulp add 3 thin slices of orange, seeded but not peeled, and a 2-inch stick of cinnamon, 3 whole allspice, and 2 whole cloves which have been tied in a cheesecloth. Boil rapidly and stir constantly to prevent burning. As the butter cooks down, reduce the heat to prevent spattering. The butter will finish cooking in 3 to 5 hours. Test for "doneness" (p. 287). Remove the spices and pour the boiling hot butter into hot sterile containers and seal.

PEACH BUTTER

Wash peaches and dry with a towel, rubbing off the fuzz. Chop and place them in a preserving kettle with a few cracked peach pits. If the peaches are not juicy, add a small quantity of water. Cover and cook until soft.

Press through a colander, then through a strainer. Add 1/3 to 1/2 cup sugar to each cup of pulp. Place in a kettle, adding to each gallon of butter 1/4 teaspoon salt and 12 whole cloves which have been tied in cheesecloth. Boil rapidly and stir constantly to prevent burning. To prevent spattering, reduce the heat as the butter cooks down. The butter will finish cooking in 3 to 5 hours. Test for "doneness" (p. 287). Remove the spices and pour the boiling hot butter into hot sterile containers. Seal.

EMMONS COUNTY HONEYED PLUM BUTTER

Wash plums and drain. Crush them in a preserving kettle. Add a small amount of water, if necessary, to keep them from scorching. Cook until tender, stirring constantly to prevent burning. Press pulp through a colander, then through a strainer. Add 1/2 cup honey to each cup of plum pulp. Add 1/2 teaspoon lemon juice to each gallon of pulp. Proceed as for **Cherry Butter.***

20

PICKLES

Produce used for pickling must be crisp and fresh. It is best if it is not quite ripe, and it should be used as soon as possible after gathering. The salt used in preparing the products should be pure, with nothing added to it, to prevent caking. Light-colored vegetables such as onions and cauliflower will remain white if a clear, colorless distilled vinegar is used for pickling them. For other than light colored products, use a good grade of cider vinegar. Granulated sugar is best for making pickles. Whole, rather than powdered spices should be used. Employ them in moderation. Prepare whole spices for use by tying them loosely in cheesecloth, then pound them lightly. Soft water is best for making pickles. If only hard water is available, boil the water and strain it through several thicknesses of cheesecloth, or allow the boiled water to settle, then pour off the clear water for use. One-half to 1 cup vinegar may be added to each gallon of hard water.

The best containers for fermenting and storing pickles are gallon and half-gallon all-glass fruit jars. Mason jars and similar containers covered with zinc screw caps, even if porcelain lined, are undesirable because the caps are corroded by the acids in the brine, and the zinc salts formed are poisonous. Crocks may be used, but they are not as convenient as the all-glass jars which are very easy to adjust. All-glass jars with covers do not require a weight. If using an all-glass jar, put the rubber and top clamp in place, but leave the side bale up.

If using a crock or other container, have a piece of wood cut to fit each crock, or use a plate. A sheet of rubber cut larger than the opening of the crock, or several thicknesses of cheesecloth or muslin, may be used to cover the plate or wood. For a weight, a sandbag is excellent. It may be made by filling a large cloth or cloth sack with enough sand to make it heavy. Allow room for tying, and secure the bag so no sand will fall out. A heavy stone may be used instead of a sandbag. The amount of brine which it will take to fill a container is equal to half the volume of the container. For instance, 2 quarts is the amount of brine to prepare for a 4-quart (gallon) crock.

To freshen the vegetables after brining, drain off the brine and place them in clear water which feels fairly hot to the hands. Let them remain at this temperature 10 to 12 hours or more, depending upon the flavor desired. Stir occasionally and change the water from time to time. The vegetables should not be soaked until all the salt is removed, as some is necessary for flavor. When freshened, the vegetables are ready to be made into sweet, spiced, salt, or sour pickles, piccalilli, etc.

To freshen vegetables which have been brined overnight only, soak in clear cold water the next day for about an hour, changing the water twice.

Store pickles in a cool, dry place after they have been sealed.

BRINE FOR CUCUMBERS

For One 4-Gallon Crock or Four 1-Gallon Lightning-Type Glass Jars or One 4-Gallon Paraffined Wooden Container

Wash well and place in containers 12 pounds (approximately ¼ bushel) cucumbers which have been picked very recently and on which ⅛ inch of stem has been left. Do not use bruised cucumbers. Pack into glass jars to within 1 inch of the top. Pack crocks to within 2 inches of the top. Fill to overflowing with a brine which will just float a fresh egg; that is, **2 pounds salt** (about 3¼ cups) dissolved in **9 quarts soft water** (2¼ gallons). If rapid fermentation is desired, add **¼ cup sugar.** The second day place **19 ounces salt** (about 1⅞ cups) on the plate, board, or cover so it will dissolve before sinking to the bottom. The seventh day place **5 ounces salt** (about ½ cup) on the plate, board, or cover, and continue, adding **5 ounces salt** once a week for 5 weeks. Place rubber rings on glass jars and put the top clamp in place. But leave the bale up while fermentation is proceeding. Cover and weight the crock, if one is used.

Place the containers in a pan or in a place where the overflowing brine will cause no damage. If possible, keep the containers in a room of even temperature, 70° to 80° F. Every few days, renew with fresh brine, any brine which has been lost through overflowing. If an open crock is used, or if the crocks or jars are not filled to overflowing, scum will form on top of the brine. Skim it off the surface carefully as it forms, being careful not to stir the brine.

When the fermentation ceases (the bubbles disappear), the curing is complete. The cucumbers will be crisp and firm, throughout, free from whitish spots, and extremely salty. Freshen, then use.

If the cucumbers are not to be made up immediately, place a lid on the crock and seal around it with paraffin.

SNAP BEANS IN BRINE

Wash beans but leave intact. Place in **Brine for Cucumbers,** above, and freshen to use.

GREEN PEPPERS IN BRINE

Remove stems and seeds from peppers and pack them blossom end down. Proceed as for **Brine for Cucumbers.***

CAULIFLOWER IN BRINE

Divide cauliflower into flowerets or leave the heads whole. Proceed as for **Brine for Cucumbers.***

FAYETTE COUNTY CUCUMBER PICKLES

Remove 2 quarts cucumbers from **Brine for Cucumbers*** and freshen. Cover with good cider **vinegar** and store for a week or 10 days. Prepare spiced vinegar by mixing together **1 quart good cider vinegar** and **½ cup sugar.** Tie loosely in a cheesecloth **1 tablespoon celery seed, 3 tablespoons grated horseradish, 1½ teaspoon whole cloves, 1 teaspoon mustard seed, 3 dried red peppers, 1½ teaspoon whole cloves,** and **1 tablespoon whole black peppers.** Pound spices lightly and simmer with vinegar and sugar 5 minutes, stirring until the sugar is dissolved. Leave the spices in the vinegar overnight. Pack the cucumbers into sterile containers, discarding the vinegar in which they were stored. Fill to overflowing with the syrup. Seal and store. Makes 2 quarts.

DILL PICKLES

Wash **40 to 50 cucumbers.** Set in crocks or all-glass jars, placing a layer of fresh or dried **dill** in the bottom of each container. Tuck in additional sprigs of dill. Fill containers to overflowing with a brine made by mixing together **2 cups vinegar, 1 pound salt, ¼ cup sugar,** and **2 gallons soft water.** Top with a thick layer of clean grape leaves or a layer of dill. Cover and weight. Remove scum daily if in open containers. After 2 weeks the pickles should be ready to use. They will be pleasantly flavored and dark green in color. Pack the pickles into sterile jars, adding **½ cup fresh vinegar** to each jar. Place a sprig of dill in each jar and **1 tablespoon mixed pickle spices.** Bring to a boil the brine in which the pickles were soaked. Cool it and fill the jars to overflowing. Seal and store.

WHITE PINE COUNTY SWEET PICKLES

Remove **very small cucumbers** from **Brine for Cucumbers*** and freshen them. To prevent shriveling, prick the cucumbers through several times with a silver fork. Place in a container and add vinegar to cover. Let stand 1 week. Drain and discard all but 1 quart of the drained vinegar. Make a syrup by simmering the following ingredients 5 minutes, stirring until the sugar is dissolved: **1 quart vinegar drained from the pickles, 1 quart fresh vinegar, 2 cups sugar,** and spices tied loosely in a cheesecloth: **1 teaspoon whole cloves, 2 tablespoons mustard seed, 2 tablespoons broken stick cinnamon,** and **1 teaspoon ginger root.** Let stand overnight. Pack the pickles in sterile jars. Remove the spices and pour the syrup over the pickles, filling the jars to overflowing. Seal and store. One quart pickles will fill 1 quart jar.

BREAD AND BUTTER AND JAM PICKLES

Wash **15 medium cucumbers** and slice ⅛ to ¼ inch thick. Place in a crock or other container and cover with a brine made by dissolving **½ pound salt** in each gallon of water. Let stand overnight. Drain thoroughly. Scald the cucumbers for about 5 minutes (until tender, but not soft) in **2½ quarts vinegar** and **2½ quarts water** in which **4 teaspoons ginger** have been dissolved. Discard the liquid. Make a syrup with the following, stirring until the sugar is dissolved and tying the spices in a cheesecloth: **4 cups vinegar, 2 cups water, 3 pounds sugar, 12 cassia buds, 3 sticks cinnamon,** and **12 whole cloves.** Boil about 5 minutes or until well flavored. Pack the cucumbers into sterile jars and fill them to overflowing with the hot syrup. Seal and store. Makes 4 to 6 quarts.

Aunt Sleide says: "It's Uncle's idea to call these Bread and Butter AND JAM Pickles. He says if bread and butter pickles are called bread and butter pickles because bread and butter's so good, then these should be called Bread And Butter AND JAM Pickles!"

QUICK OIL PICKLES

Wash **50 small cucumbers** and slice them 1/8 to 1/4 inch thick. Peel and slice thin **1 cup small white onions.** Sprinkle cucumbers and onions with 1/2 **cup salt** and let stand overnight. The next day, drain in a cheesecloth bag, pressing out as much juice as possible. Add **5 tablespoons celery seed, 3 tablespoons mustard seed, 1½ teaspoons whole black peppers,** and 1/2 **cup salad oil** to the vegetables. Pack into sterile jars and fill the jars to overflowing with cold **vinegar.** Seal. Makes about 4 quarts.

These pickles will remain firm for only a few months so use them as soon as possible.

SACCHARINE PICKLES

Pack **cucumbers** into clean jars. If the cucumbers are not of uniform size, pack the largest ones together, cutting them in quarters. Halve the medium cucumbers and pack them together. Pack the small cucumbers together whole. Combine enough of the following to cover about 4 quarts cucumbers: **4 quarts cider vinegar, 1 tablespoon saccharine, 1 tablespoon powdered alum,** 1/2 **cup salt,** and **3 tablespoons dry mustard.** Add to the cucumbers in the jars, filling them to overflowing, and seal.

GLASS JAR SAUERKRAUT

Hold sound heads of cabbage at room temperature 24 hours to make shredding easier. Remove all bruised or decayed leaves. Wash and quarter the cabbage. Cut the core very fine. Shred the cabbage, making shreds about as thin as a dime. Cut only 5 pounds cabbage at a time. Mix 2 ounces salt with each 5 pounds cabbage, mixing lightly but thoroughly until the juices begin to flow freely. When the salt has dissolved, pack the cabbage gently but firmly into clean jars. A large wooden masher may be used to press out the air, but care must be taken not to pound the cabbage. Pack jars to within an inch of the top to leave space for the juice which overflows. Put rubbers in place. Seal screw-top jars tightly. Leave the side bale up on all-glass jars. Place jars in a pan to catch any overflow juice. Keep at a temperature of 70° to 75° F. When the fermentation has stopped (the liquid settles and bubbles cease rising to the surface), in about 10 days or two weeks, and the cabbage is light yellow, tighten the screw-top jars or clamp down the side bale on all-glass jars. Store and use in about 6 weeks. Can the sauerkraut, if desired. See below.

CROCK SAUERKRAUT

Prepare and salt cabbage as above and pack gently but firmly into a crock, filling the crock almost full. Cover with a clean cloth and weight the crock. Place in a temperature of 70° to 75° F., setting it in a pan to catch any overflow juices. Remove scum as it forms and wash and scald the covering cloth frequently. Fermentation will cease in 10 days to 2 weeks (see above). Store in a cool room and use as needed. To insure a good supply throughout the year, can the sauerkraut after fermentation is complete. Heat it to simmering, about 180° F., then pack it firmly into sterile jars. Fill the jars to within ⅛ to ¼ inch of the top with brine from the kraut. If there is not enough, prepare additional brine by dissolving 2 tablespoons salt in each quart of hot water. Adjust rubbers and covers and partially seal the jars. Place in a boiling water bath and process pints 25 minutes, quarts 30 minutes.

CHESTERFIELD COUNTY RUMMAGE PICKLES

Soak the following overnight in salt water (½ cup salt to each 2 quarts water) to cover: **1 cup green tomatoes,** chopped, **1 cup cabbage,** chopped, **½ cup sweet red peppers,** chopped, **½ cup green peppers,** chopped, **1 cup cucumbers,** sliced, and **1 cup onions, sliced.** The next day, cook the following until tender, in boiling salted water (1 teaspoon salt to each quart water) to cover: **1 cup snap beans,** cut in 1-inch pieces, and **1 cup carrots,** chopped. Drain. Drain the vegetables which have been soaking in salt brine by squeezing in a cheesecloth. Combine all the vegetables and add **1 cup celery,** diced, **2 tablespons celery seed, 1 tablespoon turmeric, 2 tablespoons mustard seed, 2 cups cider vinegar,** and **2 cups sugar.** Boil 10 minutes, stirring until the sugar is dissolved. Turn into sterile jars, filling them to overflowing. Seal and store. Makes about 2 quarts.

PICCALILLI

Wash **1 gallon green tomatoes.** Peel **6 large onions.** Slice both ⅛ to ¼ inch thick. Sprinkle with **½ cup salt** and let stand overnight in a crock or in an enamel container. Drain in a cheesecloth, pressing to extract all the liquid. Mix the vegetables with **½ medium lemon,** sliced thin, **3 green peppers,** chopped, **2 tablespoons mustard seed, 2 tablespoons celery seed,** and **3 cups brown sugar.** Tie in a cheesecloth and add the following spices to **3 cups vinegar: 1 tablespoon whole cloves, 1 tablespoon whole allspice,** and **1 tablespoon whole black peppers.** Add to the vegetable mixture and cook slowly until tender, about ½ hour, stirring until the sugar is dissolved. Stir occasionally to prevent burning. Remove the spice bag. Turn into sterile jars, fill to overflowing, seal, and store. Fills 4 or 5 quart jars.

CRISP PICCALILLI

Follow the receipt above. Heat the vinegar. Mix all the ingredients together. Pack into sterile jars, and seal. Do not cook.

WATERMELON PRESERVES (PICKLED WATERMELON RIND)

Use only the greenish-white portion of thick watermelon rind. Remove the green outer skin. Trim off the pink flesh, but leave a faint dappling of color. Cut the rind into ¾-inch cubes and weigh it. Soak in salt water (1 tablespoon salt to each quart of water) overnight. Drain and rinse. For each **4 pounds rind**, weighed before soaking, measure **8 cups sugar, 4 cups water,** and **4 cups vinegar.** Boil 5 minutes (stirring until the sugar is dissolved) with **1½ tablespoons whole cloves, 2 sticks cinnamon, 1 tablespoon whole allspice,** and **1 small piece ginger root** which have been tied in a cheesecloth. Add the watermelon rind and **2 lemons,** sliced thin and seeded, but not peeled. Boil 1 to 2 hours, or until the rind is clear and the syrup is fairly thick. Stir constantly to prevent burning, as soon as the syrup begins to thicken. Pack into sterile jars immediately, and seal.

OLIVE KAYSON'S RECEIPT FOR CHOW CHOW (MUSTARD PICKLES)

Slice **1 quart cucumbers** ⅛ to ¼ inch thick. Peel **2 cups pickling onions,** or slice large onions. Cut into small pieces **2 cups green tomatoes.** Divide into flowerets **2 cups cauliflower.** Slice diagonally into inch pieces **½ cup snap beans.** Dice **½ cup celery.** Slice into strips lengthwise **1 cup carrots.** Seed, and cut into strips **2 sweet red peppers** and **4 green peppers.** Soak all the ingredients overnight in a brine to cover, made by dissolving **1 cup salt** in each **2 quarts water.** Drain by pressing in a cheesecloth, then freshen (p. 291). Pour over the vegetables **3 cups vinegar** mixed with **3 cups water.** Let stand 24 hours. Heat the mixture to boiling and discard the liquid. Mix together in the top of a double boiler **1¼ cups sugar, 4 tablespoons flour, 1½ teaspoons turmeric, 2 teaspoons celery salt,** and

6 tablespoons dry mustard. Add **1½ quarts hot vinegar** slowly, stirring constantly to prevent lumps. Cook over hot water, stirring constantly until the boiling point is reached. Add **1 tablespoon celery seed.** Pour over the hot, drained vegetables. Mix well. Pack into sterile jars, fill to overflowing, and seal. Fills 2 or 3 quart jars.

Aunt Sleide says: "Olive Kayson entered a jar of her famous Chow Chow at the county fair last year and almost took first prize with it. In fact, the Chow Chow was so good that one of the judges couldn't resist another taste. She bit into an onion and for a minute she looked as if she was about to die. Then she spit the mouthful out. Olive had somehow mixed a camphor ball in with the pickling onions!"

OLD FARM PICKLED BEETS

Trim **6 bunches small beets** of uniform size (6 or 7 beets to a bunch), leaving on 2 inches of stem and the entire root. Cook until tender. Drain, saving 2 cups of the water in which the beets were cooked. Plunge the beets into cold water and slip off the skins. Remove roots and stems. If only large beets were obtainable, slice them. Make a syrup by cooking **2 cups cider vinegar, 2 cups sugar,** and **2 cups water** in which the beets were cooked and the following spices tied loosely in a cheesecloth: **½ teaspoon whole cloves, 1½ teaspoons allspice,** and **1 teaspoon whole black peppers.** Stir until the sugar is dissolved. Pour over the beets and simmer 15 minutes. Remove the spices. Pack the beets into sterile jars, and fill to overflowing with the syrup. Seal and store. Fills 5 to 7 quart jars.

CORN RELISH

Cut the kernels from **12 large ears of corn** (about 8 cups cut corn) as for **Sweet Corn.*** Grind **2 sweet red peppers** and **4 medium onions.** Chop **1 small head cabbage.** Mix the vegetables together. Make a paste by moistening **2**

cups brown sugar packed firmly in the cup, **2 tablespoons salt, 1 tablespoon dry mustard, 1 tablespoon turmeric,** and **1 cup flour** with **1½ quarts vinegar,** adding the vinegar to the dry ingredients gradually. Add to the vegetables and bring to a boil. Cook 20 minutes after the boiling point is reached, stirring frequently. Turn into sterile jars, fill to overflowing, and seal. Makes about 1½ quarts.

FLATHEAD COUNTY PEPPER HASH

Grind **12 large sweet red peppers, 12 large sweet green peppers,** and **15 small onions.** Add boiling water to cover and let stand 5 minutes. Drain. Mix together and bring to a boil **1 cup vinegar** and **2 cups water.** Pour over the drained vegetables and let stand 10 minutes. Drain. Add to the vegetables **1 pint vinegar, 3 cups sugar, 2 tablespoons salt,** and **2 tablespoons whole mustard seed.** Boil 2 minutes. Turn into sterile jars, filling them to overflowing, and seal while hot. Fills 3 or 4 quart jars.

TOMATO HOT

Peel **1 peck ripe tomatoes** as for **Tomatoes.*** Chop them and drain well. Chop fine **2 red peppers, 1 sweet green pepper, 2 cups celery,** and **2 cups onions.** Grate **2 cups horseradish.** Heat **4 cups vinegar** with **2 cups sugar, ½ cup white mustard seed, 1 tablespoon mixed pickle spices,** and **⅓ cup salt** and stir until the sugar is dissolved. Add the vegetables. When the mixture comes to a boil, boil vigorously for 5 minutes. Fill sterile jars to overflowing, and seal. Fills about 6 quart jars.

CLATSOP COUNTY CHILI SAUCE

Peel **12 medium tomatoes,** as for **Tomatoes.*** Peel **4 medium onions.** Run the onions through the food chopper with **3 medium sweet red peppers** and **1 hot red pepper.** (Protect the hands when handling the hot pepper as it may burn them.) Place in a saucepan with **2 cups sugar, 3 cups**

vinegar, and **2 tablespoons salt.** Boil 2 to 3 hours (stirring until the sugar is dissolved), or until thick and reduced to about half. Stir constantly when the sauce begins to thicken, to prevent scorching. Add **2 tablespoons cornstarch** dissolved in **¼ cup cold water** and boil about 10 minutes, or until the starch is thoroughly cooked. Fill sterile jars to overflowing, seal, and store. Makes 1½ quarts.

TOMATO KETCHUP

Cut up **1 peck ripe tomatoes.** Chop **4 large onions** and **3 sweet red peppers.** Add to the tomatoes. Tie in cheesecloth **2 teaspoons celery seed, 2 tablespoons mixed pickle spices,** and **2 sticks cinnamon.** Add to the vegetables with **1 cup sugar, 2½ cups vinegar, 1 tablespoon pepper, 2 teaspoons salt,** and **¼ teaspoon red pepper.** Boil the mixture 2 or 3 hours (stirring until the sugar is dissolved), or until it is thick and reduced to about half. Strain. Reheat and turn into sterile jars, filling them to overflowing. Seal immediately. (Sterile bottles may be used. Use crown caps and a capping device. The bottles should be boiled as are jars, but the caps are only dipped into boiling water just before sealing. Fill bottles to overflowing.) Makes about 3 quarts.

RED CHIMNEY FARM CUCUMBER KETCHUP

Peel **18 medium cucumbers.** Chop them fine with **7 large onions.** Turn into a sieve. Cover with **¾ cup salt** and let drain overnight. Place in a saucepan with **½ cup white mustard seed, 1 teaspoon celery seed, 3 tablespoons pepper,** and **10 cups cider vinegar.** Cook until the vegetables are soft. Press through a strainer which is fine enough to keep out the seeds. Reheat and fill sterile jars to overflowing. Seal immediately. See receipt above, if using bottles. Makes 2 or 3 quarts.

PICKLED AND SPICED FRUIT

SPICED KUMQUATS

Scrub **1 quart bright orange kumquats** thoroughly with a stiff brush. Cut two slight gashes at right angles across the blossom ends of each. Make a syrup by boiling **1½ cups water** with **1½ cups sugar,** stirring until the sugar is dissolved. Cool. Add the kumquats and the following spices which have been tied in a cheesecloth: **1 stick cinnamon,** broken, **1 tablespoon whole cloves,** and **2 teaspoons whole allspice.** Cover the pan and cook about 1 hour or until the fruit is transparent. Turn off the flame, but leave the cover on the pan, and let the kumquats stand in the syrup until cold. Turn into sterile jars, fill to overflowing with the syrup, seal, and store. Will fill about 1 quart jar.

BRANDIED PEACHES

Peel large, high-quality clingstones as for **Peaches.*** Weigh the fruit and measure 1 pound sugar for each pound of fruit. Allow 1 pint brandy for each 4 pounds fruit. Place peaches and sugar alternately in a crock. Add brandy. Cover with a piece of heavy cloth, then with a cover. Make sure that the crock is covered closely. Let ripen several months, then use.

SYRUP FOR SPICY FRUIT PICKLES

Select fresh, high-quality fruits and grade for uniformity of size and degree of ripeness. Tie loosely in a cheesecloth and pound slightly **12 whole cloves, 12 whole allspice,** and **3 sticks of cinnamon.** Place the spices in a kettle with **4 pounds sugar, 2 cups cider vinegar,** and **2 cups water.** Cook, stirring until the sugar is dissolved, then boil about 5 minutes or until well flavored. This amount of syrup is for 8 pounds of fruit. If not enough syrup is left after the fruit is cooked to fill the jars to overflowing, prepare fresh syrup.

PICKLED PEARS

Wash **pears.** Remove blossom ends, but leave stems on. Peel or not, as desired. If peeling the pears, drop them into salt water (1 tablespoon salt to each quart of water) to prevent discoloration. Cover the pears with water and boil 10 minutes. Drain, saving the water. Stick a whole **clove** into the blossom end of each pear, if desired. Prick the skins in several places with a silver fork if the pears have not been peeled. Place in boiling **Syrup for Spicy Fruit Pickles,** above, using the water in which the pears were cooked for all or part (if the amount is insufficient) of the water called for in the syrup receipt. Cook gently until tender, but not soft, and fairly transparent, about 20 minutes. Cover the kettle and let stand overnight. Sterilize jars, and place a piece of **preserved ginger** in the bottom of each jar. Pack the pears into the jars. Bring the syrup to boiling, remove the spices, and fill the jars to overflowing. Seal and store. Fills 6 quart jars.

PICKLED PEACHES

Peel **peaches,** as for **Peaches.*** Drop into a solution of salt water (1 tablespoon salt to each quart of water) to prevent discoloration. If peaches are very hard, precook as for **Pickled Pears,** above. Stick each peach with **2 or 3 cloves.** Proceed as for **Pickled Pears.** Fills 6 quart jars.

PICKLED CRAB APPLES

Do not precook **crab apples.** Remove blossom ends and stick each with a **clove.** Do not peel or remove stems. Prick several times with a silver fork to prevent bursting. Proceed as for **Pickled Pears,*** omitting the preserved ginger. Fills about 6 quart jars.

PICKLED APRICOTS

Do not peel **apricots.** If very hard, precook and prick with a silver fork in several places, as for **Pickled Pears.*** Proceed as for **Pickled Pears.** Fills 6 quart jars.

PICKLED PLUMS

Do not peel **plums.** Continue as for **Pickled Apricots,** above. Fills 6 quart jars.

Aunt Sleide says: "There are hardships aplenty on a farm, and slackers had better go elsewhere. But there's a sight of beauty if you've got the eyes to see it, and manifold satisfaction in a barn full of hay, a cellar full of preservings and a smokehouse full of meat. And every spring, the good Lord says, 'Here's more. Here's lots more!'"

INDEX

[NOTE: Throughout the preceding pages, a star (*) indicates a receipt or directions to be found in this book. For exact page number, the reader should consult the Index.]

Q

Y

About the Author

Helen Worth's work always adds up to kitchen tantalization of the highest order. She has been a leader in culinary education since 1940—first in Cleveland, Ohio, then in New York City, and now in Charlottesville, Virginia.

She always knew she wanted to be a writer—her college major was English literature and composition—but did not anticipate wedding words with food. However, a beloved grandmother of legendary culinary expertise conferred on her an avid interest in cooking. This combination assures that the reader can depend on finding practical recipes, written with clarity and providing delicious results. Thanks to intensive research, fascinating background information frequently precedes them.

Writing for national publications, as both newspaper and magazine food editor, earned Mrs. Worth an Outstanding Journalism Award. She has five cook books to her credit. Those published since inception of the book clubs all have been selections. Those published since initiation of the Tastemaker Awards have been winners. These include: *The Down-on-the-Farm Cook Book* (1943), housed in Cornell University's Herndon Collection of rare books, reissued by Gramercy Publishing Company; *Shrimp Cookery* (hard- and soft-cover); and award-winners *Hostess Without Help* and the historically fascinating *Damnyankee in a Southern Kitchen*.

Her classic book, *Cooking Without Recipes,* expounds her cooking principles. It has been in print since the original 1965 publication and also has been made into both Talking Books and Educational Tapes for the blind.

Worth has lectured on food and wine and has appeared on radio and television. She originated a course in Food and Drink Appreciation at Columbia University and has lectured at California State University as a participant in their Distinguished Visiting Professor program.

Her New York City school has been hailed as "the Radcliffe of cooking schools," and she has been called the doyenne of cooking schools. Worth developed an epicurean yet practical approach to teaching: once you learn the basic principles, you can apply them to down-home cooking or to classic international specialties. Her Helen Worth Original recipes are famous, as are her culinary methods for modernizing the classics.

Graduates of her schooling range from people on a slim budget who realize that a culinary education is cheaper in the long run, to men and women famous in the professions and arts.

Brown-Quick, a quick-browning aid she created, is nationally distributed. She is vice-president of Good Taste Products, Inc., and works as food consultant to other major associations and corporations. Worth has judged international professional cooking competitions, was a guest at the Restaurateurs Program at Oxford University's prestigious Centre for Management Studies, and creates menu concepts and recipes for restaurants.

Recently remarried to novelist Arthur M. Gladstone, she currently works and teaches in her handsome kitchen on an estate called Bending Oaks in Ivy, Virginia, a Charlottesville suburb.

Her home reflects her pleasure in the beautiful. She considers food and wine beautiful as well as fascinating because "there always is something new to learn." And she adds, "Their study has a happy ending—it means you can offer enjoyment to others."

Worth is listed in many biographical references, including *Who's Who in The East; World's Who's Who of Women; World's Who's Who of Authors; International Authors and Writers Who's Who; Who's Who in Consulting*.